Middle-Class African American English

African American English (AAE) is a major area of research in linguistics, but until now, work has primarily been focused on AAE as it is spoken amongst the working classes. From its historical development to its contemporary context, this is the first full-length overview of the use and evaluation of AAE by middle-class speakers, giving voice to this relatively neglected segment of the African American speech community. Weldon offers a unique first-person account of middle-class AAE, and highlights distinguishing elements such as codeswitching, camouflaged feature usage, Standard AAE, and talking/sounding "Black" versus "Proper." Readers can hear authentic excerpts and audio prompts of the language described through a wide range of audio files, which can be accessed directly from the book's pages using QR technology or through the book's online Resource Tab. Engaging and accessible, it will help students and researchers gain a broader understanding of both the African American speech community and the AAE continuum.

TRACEY L. WELDON is a sociolinguist, specializing in African American Language varieties at the University of South Carolina. She is an Associate Dean in the College of Arts and Sciences, Associate Producer of the documentary *Talking Black in America*, and chair of the LSA Committee on Ethnic Diversity in Linguistics.

T0384577

Middle-Class African American English

Tracey L. Weldon

University of South Carolina

Shaftesbury Road, Cambridge CB2 8EA, United Kingdom

One Liberty Plaza, 20th Floor, New York, NY 10006, USA

477 Williamstown Road, Port Melbourne, VIC 3207, Australia

314–321, 3rd Floor, Plot 3, Splendor Forum, Jasola District Centre, New Delhi – 110025, India

103 Penang Road, #05–06/07, Visioncrest Commercial, Singapore 238467

Cambridge University Press is part of Cambridge University Press & Assessment,
a department of the University of Cambridge.

We share the University's mission to contribute to society through the pursuit of
education, learning and research at the highest international levels of excellence.

www.cambridge.org
Information on this title: www.cambridge.org/9780521719667

DOI: 10.1017/9781139021531

First published 2021
First paperback edition 2023

A catalogue record for this publication is available from the British Library

Library of Congress Cataloging-in-Publication data
Names: Weldon, Tracey L., author.
Title: Middle-class African American English / Tracey L. Weldon.
Description: New York : Cambridge University Press, 2021. | Includes
    bibliographical references and index.
Identifiers: LCCN 2020027585 (print) | LCCN 2020027586 (ebook) |
    ISBN 9780521895316 (hardback) | ISBN 9780521719667 (paperback) |
    ISBN 9781139021531 (epub)
Subjects: LCSH: Black English–Phonology. | African Americans–Languages. |
    Middle class African Americans. | English language–Dialects–United States. |
    Sociolinguistics–United States.
Classification: LCC PE3102.N42 W45 2021 (print) | LCC PE3102.N42 (ebook) |
    DDC 427/.97308996073–dc23
LC record available at https://lccn.loc.gov/2020027585
LC ebook record available at https://lccn.loc.gov/2020027586

ISBN   978-0-521-89531-6   Hardback
ISBN   978-0-521-71966-7   Paperback

For my children
Christian and Rupert
And in memory of my dad
Paul Isaiah Weldon
1933–2019

Love takes off the masks that we fear we cannot live without and know we
cannot live within

—James Baldwin, *The Fire Next Time*

Contents

x   Contents

Figures

Tables

Acknowledgments

The process of writing this book has been a journey. However, it is a journey that I would never have started or finished had it not been for the persistence and patience of the commissioning editor, Helen Barton. I thank you! Thanks also to the anonymous readers who provided valuable feedback on the manuscript, to the Cambridge team for supporting the project, and to Isabel Collins, Bob Ellis, Niranjana Harikrishnan, and Penny Harper for guiding me through the final stages of the publication process.

As with any long journey, there are countless others who provided support along the way. I would like to thank the many administrators at the University of South Carolina (UofSC) who generously contributed the financial support and release time needed to do this work – Provosts Michael Amiridis and Joan Gabel; Deans Maryanne Fitzpatrick and Lacy Ford; English Department Chairs Nina Levine, Steve Lynn, and Bill Rivers; and Linguistics Program Directors Anne Bezuidenhout, Robin Morris, and Mila Tasseva-Kurktchieva.

This project was also generously supported by several UofSC fellowships, awards, and grants, including the English Department's Morrison Fellowship, sponsored by Gail and Stephen Morrison; the Institute for African American Research's Research and Creative Projects Award; the Institute for Southern Studies' Travel Grant; the College of Arts and Sciences' Associate Professor Development Award; and the Provost's Humanities Grant.

I am eternally grateful to the many dedicated students who assisted over the years with various aspects of the project, including transcriptions, coding, digitizing, census research, formatting, and copyediting – Anusha Anand, Tracy Bealer, Brandon Cooper, Brianna Cornelius, Anyssa "AJ" Murphy Dillon, Stephen Mann, Bianca Robinson, Angelina Rubina, and Francis Scott.

A very special thanks to Wilma Sims and Paul Reed for consulting on various aspects of the statistical analysis and to Paul Reed and Al Montgomery for advice on the acoustic analysis.

To the speakers who generously contributed their voices to the project and the survey respondents who generously participated, I thank you! Thanks also to the many colleagues who helped to recruit and encourage responses to the surveys, including Jessica R. Berry, Millicent Brown, Elaine Chun, Bobby

Donaldson, Janice Jake, Regina Lemmon, Alison McCletchie, Katherine Wyly Mille, Christine Ofulue, Iyabo Osiapem, Melissa Pearson, Monika Shehi, Scott Trafton, and Patti Walker. And thanks to those who offered advice, resources, and contacts along the way, including David Crockett, Jason Cummings, Rachel Davis, Stanley Dubinsky, Janet Fuller, Michael Geis, Lea Harper, Michael Montgomery, Jennifer Nguyen, Erik Thomas, Rudolph Troike, and Rose Wilkerson.

I am indebted to the many friends, family members, and colleagues, both inside and outside of the academy, who encouraged and inspired me, especially when the journey got long – Michelle Bryan, Reese Carleton, Elaine Chun, Melissa Cooper, Vennie Deas-Moore, John Dozier, Victoria Dozier, Dianne Johnson-Feelings, Lucy Annang Ingram, Daisy James, Greta Little, Monique McDowell, Bettina Migge, Johnnie McFadden, Cecelia Richardson, Tarsha Robinson, Asad Ruffin, Boh Ruffin, Gyasi Ruffin, Zuri Ruffin, Todd Shaw, Kimberly Simmons, Tiana Stewart, Rheeda Walker, Delo Washington, Qiana Whitted, and Tanya James Wilson.

Though it is impossible to name them all, I would like to take this opportunity to acknowledge some of the African American English scholars on whose shoulders this project stands, many of whom inspired this book not only through their own incredible bodies of work, but also through their guidance, support, and encouragement – Samy Alim, John Baugh, Renee Blake, Erica Britt, Mary Bucholtz, Elizabeth Dayton, Charles DeBose, Walter Edwards, Shelome Gooden, Lisa Green, Jessica Grieser, Nicole Holliday, Mary Rhodes Hoover, Anne Charity Hudley, Jamila Jones, William Labov, Sonja Lanehart, Claudia Mitchell-Kernan, Simanique Moody, Marcyliena Morgan, Salikoko Mufwene, Iyabo Osiapem, Dennis Preston, Jacqueline Rahman, John Rickford, Edgar Schneider, John Singler, Geneva Smitherman, Arthur Spears, Marsha Houston Stanback, Orlando Taylor, Alicia Beckford Wassink, Walt Wolfram, and Donald Winford. And a special "shout out" to my writing partner, Jennifer Bloomquist, who helped keep me on the path during the final stretches of the journey as we held each other accountable for completing our respective manuscripts.

Of course, I could never have completed this journey without the steadfast love and support of my parents, Paul and Frances, who anchored me; my husband, Cuthbert, whose optimism helped keep me afloat; my sister, Millicent, who offered direction whenever I felt lost; and my children, Rupert and Christian, who always kept my eyes set on the horizon.

Finally, to all speakers of African American English, from all walks of life, I offer the faithful words of author and activist James Weldon Johnson ...

> Lift ev'ry voice and sing
> Till earth and heaven ring
> Ring with the harmonies of liberty

Let our rejoicing rise
High as the list'ning skies,
Let it resound loud as the rolling sea
Sing a song full of faith that the dark past has taught us
Sing a song full of the hope that the present has brought us
Facing the rising sun of our new day begun
Let us march on till victory is won

1 Introduction

> Definitions of "Black English" are in need of serious re-thinking and refinement. Scholars have obviously erred in defining Black English as a nonstandard variety of English exclusively, and in implying that vernacular forms of language are spoken primarily, if not exclusively, by lower-class, nonstandard speakers.
>
> —Orlando Taylor (1983)

African American English (AAE)[1] is a systematic, rule-governed variety deeply rooted in the history and culture of its speakers. While its origins may date back to the earliest days of language contact brought about by the Atlantic slave trade, it remains today a vibrant symbol of African American kinship, creativity, and survival. It also remains one of the most disparaged varieties spoken in the United States – a linguistic testament to the racial discrimination and stereotyping that African Americans[2] have endured. Linguists first began studying AAE in an effort to improve the success of

---

[1] "African American English" has been called by many different names in the linguistic literature, including (but not limited to) "Negro Dialect," "Negro English," "Black English," "African American English," and "African American Language," as well as more creative, but less commonly used labels such as "Black Street Speech" (Baugh 1983) and "Spoken Soul" (Rickford and Rickford 2000; originally coined by Claude Brown 1968). The term "Ebonics" was first introduced in the 1970s by psychologist Robert Williams, as a label to describe "the linguistic and paralinguistic features which on a concentric continuum represent the communicative competence of the West African, Caribbean, and United States slave descendent of African origin" (Williams 1975: vi). "Ebonics" was introduced to the general public in 1996–97 when the Oakland School Board made a resolution to recognize the variety in their public schools. It was during this time that the label came to be used in reference to a US language variety, similar to the other terms listed above (Baugh 2000a). Unless citing literature that uses other labels, I will use "African American English" as the default label for the variety described in this book, as this remains one of the most commonly used terms among linguists today, although "African American Language" has also gained currency (see, e.g., Lanehart 2015). Further discussion regarding my use of "African American English," particularly vis-à-vis "African American Vernacular English," will be reserved for later in this chapter.

[2] I will use the term "African American" for most contemporary references, although "African American" and "Black" will sometimes be used interchangeably, as they are among members of the general public. Where relevant, I will take a similar approach with the labels "European American" and "White."

vernacular speakers in schools (see, e.g., Labov et al. 1968; Wolfram 1969). For more than half a century now, sociolinguists have scrutinized its origins, development, structure, usage, relationship to other varieties, and role in education, yielding a larger body of research on AAE than on any other variety of American English (Schneider 1996: 3). However, the bulk of this research has been drawn from working-class speech communities, while the use of AAE by middle-class speakers has remained relatively unexamined. This bias in the linguistic literature has been guided by a tendency for researchers to define AAE in terms of a fairly narrow set of vernacular (i.e., nonstandard) structural features, coupled by the assumption that such features are used primarily, if not exclusively, by working-class speakers.

In his seminal book *Language in the Inner City*, William Labov directed attention to the "Black English Vernacular" (BEV) as "that relatively uniform grammar found in its most consistent form in the speech of black youth from 8 to 19 years old who participate fully in the street culture of the inner cities" (1972a: xiii).[3] Those who fell outside the limits of this "street" (or "vernacular") culture were subsequently dismissed as "lames" (1972: 285ff.). As a result, little consideration was given to the linguistic dexterity of middle-class speakers and the extent to which they might also employ the vernacular. And little consideration was given to the ways in which more standard varieties might also be used to index African American identity and culture (cf. Irvine's 2001 concept of "erasure"). As observed by Marcyliena Morgan,

> because vernacular AAE has been defined as hip, male, adolescent, street, or gang-related speech, nonvernacular speech is described as weak, lame, or white (Labov 1972a). Those who do not fit the model of the vernacular-idealized speaker ... are therefore, according to this sociolinguistic paradigm, not African American or, to put it in modern terms, not the "authentic Other." (Morgan 1994: 135)

Mary Bucholtz (2003) described such tendencies in terms of a type of "sociolinguistic nostalgia," by which researchers deemed the most "exotic" linguistic practices to be the most authentic. (See also Wolfram 2001b.) However, she also described this practice as one of "strategic essentialism," by which linguists focused on the most marginalized and stigmatized members of the African American speech community in an effort to highlight the systematic, rule-governed nature of the variety and to debunk circulating myths about the vernacular.

> A strategic use of essentialized and hence authentic identity is similarly evident in sociolinguists' validation of African American Vernacular English (AAVE) as a legitimate linguistic variety, a revolutionary viewpoint that challenged generations of racism, linguistic and otherwise. Indeed, what made this challenge so powerful was

---

[3] In this same text, Labov later described the age range as that of nine to eighteen (1972a: 257).

Table 1.1 *Language levels grid (adapted from Hoover 1978: 72, table 3)*

	Phonology	Grammar	Vocabulary	Tone, intonation
VBE [Vernacular Black English]	+	+	+	+
SBE [Standard Black English]	=	−	=	=
SE [Standard English]	−	−	−	−

Notes: + Contains vernacular features; − Contains very few vernacular features;
= Contains vernacular features in varying degrees according to the situation

precisely the sociolinguistic commitment to describing the speech of inner-city youth, who had been – and continue to be – maligned and misrepresented in public discourse. In such a context, a demonstration of, say, the linguistic flexibility of bidialectal middle-class African Americans would have failed to persuade skeptical teachers, policy-makers, and researchers in other disciplines of the value of AAVE. (Bucholtz 2003: 402)

Despite these fairly myopic sociolinguistic tendencies, broader definitions of AAE have actually been in circulation since the earliest days of research on the variety. While Labov's early attention to the vernacular set the agenda for decades of research to follow, he proposed from the outset that a distinction be made between the terms "Black English Vernacular" and "Black English" (BE), with the latter being used as a more general cover term for "the whole range of language forms used by black people in the United States: a very large range indeed, extending from the Creole grammar of Gullah spoken in the Sea Islands of South Carolina to the most formal and accomplished literary style" (Labov 1972a: xiii).[4] In an essay entitled "Black English: An agenda for the 1980's," Orlando Taylor (1983) urged researchers to look beyond working-class communities for vernacular usage and to broaden definitions of the variety to allow for consideration of more standard uses (see also Taylor 1975). Taylor used the label "Standard Black English" (SBE) to describe the speech of African Americans who use primarily standard grammatical constructions in combination with "Black rhetorical style, prosodic features, and idioms" (1983: 135). Relatedly, Hoover (1978: 72) offered the grid shown in Table 1.1 as an illustration of the distinction between Standard English, as traditionally defined, and standard and vernacular varieties of Black English.

Arthur Spears proposed that AAE be used as a cover term for "Standard African American English" (SAAE) and "African American Vernacular English" (AAVE), both of which would serve as cover terms for collections

---

[4] As discussed later in this chapter, the question of whether Gullah exists on a continuum with other African American language varieties has been a topic of debate among linguists (see Mufwene 2001 and Weldon and Moody 2015 for fuller discussion).

of varieties themselves (Spears 1998). It is from this perspective that Spears (1988) estimated that roughly 85 percent of African Americans speak some form of AAE (cf. Dillard 1972). As observed by Salikoko Mufwene, broader definitions such as these are not only more inclusive, but more consistent with community notions of "talking Black."

> There are very large proportions of African Americans whose day-to-day speech does not include the kinds of styles used in ritual insults or Hip-Hop lyrics. There are many who are often constrained by their professions from using some of the non-standard features associated with AAVE, even in their more relaxed modes of communication such as in the privacy of their homes or in the intimate settings of their friends' company. Yet all such individuals would be recognized as "talking Black" among African Americans. (Mufwene 2001: 35)

Given these acknowledgments of the breadth and diversity of the African American speech community, it is perhaps surprising that there have been so few sociolinguistic examinations of middle-class AAE. Indeed, the only early study to provide a thorough quantitative analysis of the use of AAE by middle-class speakers was Wolfram (1969), which looked at the social stratification of phonological and grammatical variables among African American speakers in Detroit, Michigan. In his 2001 article, "Reconsidering the sociolinguistic agenda for African American English: The next generation of research and application" Wolfram essentially reissued the call made decades earlier by Orlando Taylor:

> As one who must bear partial responsibility for the current structural biases (Wolfram 1969; Fasold and Wolfram 1970; Wolfram and Fasold 1974), I can only say that we need to reconsider the basis of definition [of AAE] from a broader, more inclusive perspective; we also need to arrive at a definition that is sensitive to the identification and labeling of speakers by the speech community itself. (Wolfram 2001b: 334)

In recent years, researchers have begun to address some of these gaps in the sociolinguistic literature, with studies of *social stratification* (Nguyen 2006; Jones and Preston 2011), *intraspeaker variation* (Debose 1992; Rickford and McNair-Knox 1994; Linnes 1998; Hay et al. 1999; Kendall and Wolfram 2009; Scanlon and Wassink 2010; Rickford and Price 2013; Grieser 2014; Holliday 2016; Wolfram et al. 2016), *performative language practices* (Weldon 2004; Kendall and Wolfram 2009; Britt 2011a, 2011b; Alim and Smitherman 2012; Wolfram et al. 2016), and *attitudes and perceptions* (Garner and Rubin 1986; Koch et al. 2001; Rahman 2008). Some of these studies are discussed in more detail in the next chapter and, where relevant, in the chapters to follow.[5] The goal of this book, however, is to offer a broader look at the use and perception of African American English by

---

[5] See Britt and Weldon (2015) for an overview of this burgeoning line of research.

middle-class speakers, and, in so doing, to extend our understanding of the range of varieties and perspectives that comprise the AAE continuum. As a first step in this effort, I discuss below the emergence of the African American Middle Class and linguistic debate over the origins of African American English. I also offer working definitions for these concepts as they apply to the goals and interests of this book.

The Emergence of the African American Middle Class

Scholars studying the emergence of the African American middle class have identified three key phases in its development. The first phase (roughly 1865 to 1915), described by Landry (1987) as the period of the "old mulatto elite," was ushered in by practices that began during the plantation era when mixed-race individuals (aka "mulattos"), who were primarily the offspring of Black enslaved women who had been raped by their White masters, were afforded certain "privileges" by virtue of their kinship to their owners.[6] Many were freed prior to emancipation and allowed to learn to read, develop a trade, and in some instances even receive a formal education, all of which led to greater wage-earning opportunities during the post–Civil War Reconstruction era. It was during this period, when federal laws were put in place to protect the civil rights of Black Americans, that this group began to reap the benefits of economic and political power. Serving the needs of wealthy White clients as skilled artisans, entrepreneurs, and domestic ser-vants, this group of mixed-race elites established a separate community unto themselves (Landry 1987).

Feeling superior to the unmixed Negroes around them, they held themselves apart and developed their own social and community life – often patterned after the life style of whites whom they were able to observe closely because of their frequent contacts in service capacities. The clearly defined status group of mulattoes that had appeared by the time of the Civil War rose to the top of the social pyramid in black communities and continued to grow during the fifty years after emancipation. (Landry 1987: 25)

The status of this group, however, was grounded more in subjective evaluation and behavioral patterns than in material capital (cf. Bourdieu's 1986 theory of symbolic capital). It was for this reason that Landry, drawing on the work of German sociologist Max Weber ([1920] 1968),

---

[6] Vestiges of the color discrimination (or "colorism") that grew out of this color hierarchy still exist today, both within and outside the African American community (see, e.g., Russell et al. 1993; Hunter 2007; Norwood 2014). Circulating labels such as "light-skinned," "redbone," or "high-yellow" vs. "dark-skinned" or "chocolate" illustrate the continued salience of these distinctions within the African American speech community.

referred to these early elites as a "status group," rather than a social class.[7] Citing seminal studies of Black social structure at the turn of the twentieth century in Philadelphia (Du Bois 1967) and Boston (Daniels 1914), Bowser (2007) also acknowledged the strong "social psychological" component of the Black status hierarchy, including the importance of language as a symbol of social status.[8] In a comparison of Du Bois's middle and lower classes in late nineteenth-century Philadelphia, for example, Bowser noted that the Black middle class "dressed, *talked*, and acted (in public) like the white middle class" in contrast to the "bright and gaudy dress of common blacks, *black dialectic speech*, unladylike and ungentlemanly behavior, and the dirty chaotic households of commoners" (Bowser 2007: 56–57; emphasis added). Unlike the emerging White middle class, however, which was largely comprised of European immigrants who came to the United States to take part in the growing industrial economy, members of the Black elite, regardless of their mixed-race status, still had to endure the brunt of racial oppression and discrimination.

The ascending black middle class could not become white; only European immigrants were granted that privilege ... For many blacks the presumption of white superiority and black inferiority became a psychological mark of inferiority that was internalized. They may have felt superior to other blacks because of their higher class standing, and if they were mulatto, they may have felt superior because of their lighter skin color. But whites considered them all to be inferior. Whereas aspiring Europeans were accepted into the middle class, claims of Anglo conformity, bourgeois morality, and occupational and educational status by blacks were not just roundly rejected; they were mocked. (Bowser 2007: 40–41)

In 1877, federal troops that had been sent to the South to enforce the Civil Rights Act of 1866 were withdrawn, bringing an end to Reconstruction and to the rise of this early elite group. In 1896, the US Supreme Court handed down the *Plessy* v. *Ferguson* decision, legalizing racial segregation and allowing states to enforce "separate but equal" policies in public facilities. In the South, the "Black Codes" – a set of post–Civil War policies aimed at maintaining White supremacy and suppressing the upward mobility of Blacks who had benefited from the federal protections and opportunities of the Reconstruction

---

[7] While there is no consensus among sociologists about how to define class, two German theorists – Karl Marx and Max Weber – have been particularly influential in shaping the way that Western scholars approach it. Marxian approaches to class emphasize the conflict between capitalists (or the "bourgeoisie"), who control the "means of production," and members of the working class (or "proletariat"), who are paid for their labor. Weberian approaches, on the other hand, emphasize the importance of status, culture, and lifestyle as representative of economic power.

[8] Unlike Landry, however, Bowser (2007) contended that the "mulatto elite" did, in fact, constitute a social class (58).

era – became the law of the land. And thus began a new period of violence, oppression, and discrimination, known as the Jim Crow era.[9]

Ironically, it was in the context of these systematic efforts to disenfranchise Black Americans and restrict their upward mobility that the Black middle class ultimately crystallized. According to Landry (1987), the period from 1915 to 1960 marked the second phase in the development of the Black middle class. The strict segregationist policies and brutal violence of the Jim Crow era forced Blacks to retreat to their own communities for survival. Members of the "old mulatto elite" who had depended on White patronage for employment found themselves losing access to jobs that had once been their mainstay, often being passed over in favor of White immigrants. Then, in 1924, an immigration bill restricting the number of European immigrants to the United States opened up opportunities in the factories and steel mills of the industrial North for jobs that Blacks had previously been denied. Millions of Blacks fled the South in search of employment, forming isolated communities in the urban North, where they often faced discrimination by Whites who refused to provide them personal and professional services (Landry 1987). It was in these segregated communities that the potential for a diverse Black workforce was realized. "The burgeoning black urban communities provided an opportunity for the emergence of a black middle class of teachers, doctors, dentists, undertakers, realtors, insurance agents, ministers, newspaper editors, and small businessmen who attempted to meet the needs of a black community that whites were often unwilling to serve" (Landry 1987: 21). College education was, of course, a key component to accessing these middle-class jobs. According to Bowser (2007), "more than ninety black colleges, universities, and technical schools were started to supplement the dozen black colleges started after the Civil War and during Black Reconstruction" (55). Black illiteracy rates dropped significantly. And the number of Blacks receiving four or more years of college rose from 1 percent to 3 percent in the period from 1940 to 1960 (Landry 1987: 64).

Regardless of talent or ambition, however, the status and earning potential of the Black middle class was confined to Black communities. Bowser (2007) compared the findings of two seminal studies on social class structure during this period – Warner and Lunt's 1941 study of White residents in 1930s Newberryport, Massachusetts (aka "Yankee City") and Drake and Cayton's 1945 description of Black residents in the 1930s Bronzeville District of

---

[9] Many attribute the name "Jim Crow" to a stereotypical Black character performed by actor Thomas D. Rice in minstrel shows in the early nineteenth century. The song "Jump Jim Crow" was first performed by "Daddy Rice" in 1828 (Lewis and Lewis 2009).

Chicago. Noteworthy in this comparison was the absence of a Black upper class and a White underclass, highlighting the lack of class comparability across races during this time. As observed by Bowser (2007), the commitment to a Protestant work ethic failed to translate into mainstream economic success for members of the Black middle class.

In the absence of opportunities to compete in the mainstream economy, where the "means of production" were controlled by Whites, members of the Black middle class made their status known through various forms of "conspicuous consumption" (Veblen 1899 [1994]). They purchased homes, formed exclusive clubs, and participated in lavish social events that symbolized their status (Drake and Cayton 1945; Frazier 1957). It was in this segregated context that Arthur Spears (2015) identified the social locus for African American Standard English (AASE), which he defined as a variety of AAE that is devoid of vernacular features, but contains "Distinctively Black Grammatical Features" (DBGFs), such as remote stressed BIN[10] (shown in example 1), whose distinctiveness vis-à-vis Mainstream Standard English (MSE) is linguistically camouflaged.[11]

1. *They've BIN living in Chicago* (Spears 2015: 794)
   "They've been living in Chicago a long time and still are living there"

Similar to the various forms of conspicuous consumption described above, Spears identified AASE as a form of "cultural capital" (cf. Bourdieu 1986, 1991) used as a status symbol by members of the Black elite.

In the absence of wealth or affluence, which was usually the case with individuals and families in the Black community, AASE and what it indexed became all the more important in securing social status ... AASE was a form of cultural capital unhinged from financial capital and thus almost served as a substitute for it, in a zone where capital accumulation was systematically repressed by community-external forces. (Spears 2015: 796–97)

During World War II, employment opportunities for Blacks peaked again, as European immigration was curtailed and young White men were drafted into

---

[10] Remote stressed BIN is often spelled with an "i" rather than "ee" in the linguistic literature as a means of orthographically representing the [ɪ]/[ɛ] merger characteristic of the African American speech community. The capitalization represents the primary stress that it receives when used as a remote past marker. (For more on this feature, see Rickford and Rickford 1976 [1999]).

[11] Spears (2015) makes a distinction between SAAE, which is more or less indistinguishable from mainstream varieties in terms of its grammatical features (cf. Hoover 1978), and AASE, which is defined by the presence of significantly more DBGFs, which "are found in the lexicon, phonology, and other parts of grammar" (792). The latter, he argues, is an endangered variety spoken primarily by those aged sixty and above who were raised in all-Black communities under segregation. For the purposes of this book, all such varieties will be referred to under the label SAAE.

the military. These changes led to another mass migration in the 1940s, when Blacks moved out of the Jim Crow South and into the industrial North for jobs. The growth of Black working-class communities in the urban North subsequently fed the growth of the Black middle class, which provided professional services to these communities. As African Americans enlisted in the military and entered the war, parallels between Jim Crow and the fascism that the United States and its allies were fighting against abroad became increasingly apparent, giving traction to the Black Civil Rights movement, under the leadership of Dr. Martin Luther King Jr. and other civil right activists. Following the end of WWII, several key pieces of legislation were passed that ultimately brought an end to the Jim Crow era. The 1954 *Brown* v. *Board of Education* decision ending the "separate but equal" doctrine, the 1964 Civil Rights Act outlawing segregation and discrimination, and the 1965 Voting Rights Act helped to usher in a new era of opportunity and prosperity for African Americans. Affirmative Action and Equal Employment Opportunity policies, coupled by growth in the number of African American college graduates, provided access to the mainstream economy that African Americans had not experienced before. Thus, by 1970 a new African American middle class had emerged in the United States (Landry 1987).

While this third phase in the development of the African American middle class has yielded greater comparability between the races, researchers have acknowledged its unique challenges and vulnerabilities. As illustrated in Figures 1.1 and 1.2, over the course of the last century the number of African Americans receiving a college education and securing white-collar employment – two traditional indicators of middle-class status – has followed a trajectory similar to that of European Americans. And Black-White ratios have narrowed in the process.

Median household incomes among African Americans and European Americans have also followed comparable trajectories in recent years, though a persistent gap remains, as shown in Figure 1.3. However, when it comes to the accumulation of wealth, as defined by net worth (i.e., household assets minus debts), there remains a staggering gap between African American and European American households, as illustrated in Figure 1.4.

Furthermore, African Americans across the spectrum have been disproportionately affected by periods of economic turmoil. According to Mishel et al. (2012), the Great Recession that began in 2007–8 "wreaked havoc" on African American households. African American median wealth fell 49.7% compared to 35.8% for European American households. Median household income among African Americans fell 10.1%, compared to 5.4% for European American households. And the annual unemployment rate for African Americans peaked at 15.9% in 2010–11, compared to 8% for European

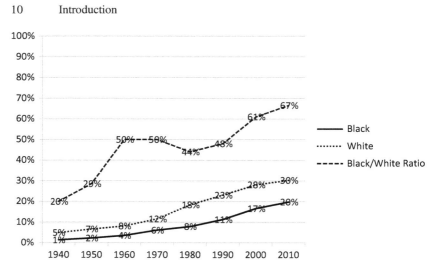

Figure 1.1 Percentage of Blacks and Whites who completed four or more years of college (1940–2010)
Note: Years prior to 1980 include persons of Hispanic origin. Data for 1993 and later years are for persons with a bachelor's degree or higher.
Source: Information Please® Database www.infoplease.com/ipa/A0774057.html[12]

Americans. Even African American college graduates saw their unemployment rates rise from 3.5% in 2007 to 8.2% in 2011.[13]

Thus, while there are many high-profile African American celebrities, politicians, athletes, business executives, etc. who have accumulated significant wealth in today's society, Bowser (2007) contends that there is still no African American upper class, from the perspective of intergenerational wealth, power, and influence, to drive significant social and political change. Furthermore, many middle-class African Americans continue to endure the challenges of racial profiling, discriminatory practices in housing and employment, de facto segregation, and economic and educational disparities, all of

---

[12] Original Sources: US Department of Commerce, Bureau of the Census, US Census of Population, 1960, Vol. 1, part 1; *Current Population Reports*, Series P-20 and unpublished data; and *1960 Census Monograph*, "Education of the American Population," by John K. Folger and Charles B. Nam. From US Dept. of Education, National Center for Education Statistics, *Digest of Education Statistics 2007*, US Census Bureau, *Current Population Survey*, March 2007, US Census Bureau, *Statistical Abstract of the United States: 2011*.

[13] Source: http://stateofworkingamerica.org/fact-sheets/african-americans/.

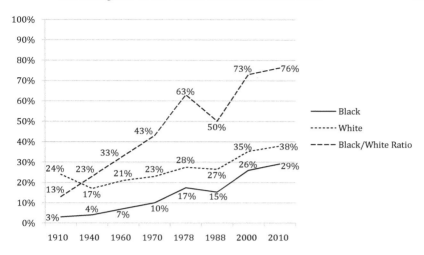

Figure 1.2 White-collar employment percentages for Black and White workers and Black/White ratios (1910–2010)
Note: Figures from 1910 to 1970 represent workers aged fourteen years and over. Figures from 1978 to 2010 represent workers aged sixteen years and over. Numbers exclude those employed in sales and clerical work.
Source: 1910–2000 figures from Bowser (2007), Tables 5.1 (p. 72) and 6.1 (p. 103). 2010 figures from the Bureau of Labor Statistics, "Labor Force Characteristics by Race and Ethnicity, 2010" (PDF), Report 1032, August 2011

which serve to restrict economic mobility and maintain class differences. And as the Affirmative Action policies that helped create the third wave of the African American middle class give way to less clearly defined "diversity" measures, the economic stability of the African American middle class becomes even more precarious (Bowser 2007).

In a 2007 study of middle-class African Americans in the suburbs of Washington, DC, sociologist Karen R. Lacy observed that "Blacks who 'make it' in this country do so against a backdrop of ongoing racial discrimination and persistent black poverty, coupled with the pervasive influence of hip-hop culture – a variant of 'success' that circumvents the assimilationist path toward upward mobility" (xii). To cope with this reality, many middle-class African Americans engage in a process of "strategic assimilation" by which they carve out class-based identities that distinguish them from lower-class African Americans, and race-based identities that separate them from the White main-stream (152). Thus, in spite of their increased integration into the American

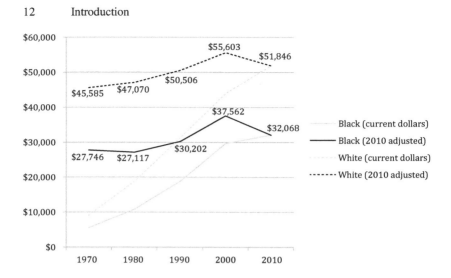

Figure 1.3 Median household income for Blacks and Whites (1970–2010)
Note: Income in 2010 CPI-U-RS adjusted dollars (black) and current dollars
(gray).[14]
Source: Table H-5 "Race and Hispanic Origin of Householder – Households
by Median and Mean Income 1967–2010" (www.census.gov)

mainstream, racial consciousness remains a strong defining characteristic for
many middle-class African Americans today. And language plays a central
role in navigating this unique and complicated terrain.

Defining the African American Middle Class

While traditional measures of socioeconomic status (SES) have looked to
education, occupation, and income as benchmarks for class assignment,
middle-class status in African American communities is often less clearly
defined. As observed by sociologist Mary Pattillo-McCoy in her 1999
study of an African American middle-class neighborhood on the south
side of Chicago:

[14] The US Census Bureau uses the Bureau of Labor Statistics' Consumer Price Index for All
Urban Consumers Research Series (CPI-U-RS) to adjust for cost-of-living changes. In
Figure 1.3, the gray lines display income as "current dollars" (i.e., the "income in the year in
which a person, household, or family receives it"). The black lines display income adjusted for
inflation to 2010 dollars. For more information, visit: www.census.gov/topics/income-poverty/
income/guidance/current-vs-constant-dollars.html.

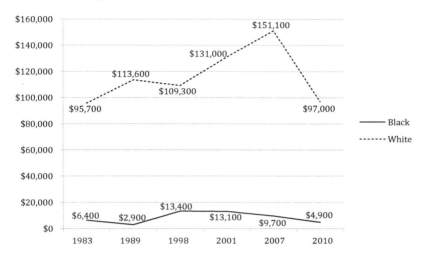

Figure 1.4 Median household wealth for Blacks and Whites (1983–2010)
Note: Wealth, reported here in 2010 dollars, is defined as net worth.
Source: "Table 6.5 Median household wealth and share of household with
zero or negative wealth, by race and ethnicity, 1983–2010" (Mishel et al.
2012, p. 385)

"Middle class" is a notoriously elusive category based on a combination of socioeconomic factors (mostly income, occupation, and education) and normative judgments
(ranging from where people live, to what churches or clubs they belong to, to whether
they plant flowers in their gardens). Among African Americans, where there has
historically been less income and occupational diversity, the question of middle-class
position becomes even more murky. (Pattillo-McCoy 1999: 13–14)

With regard to education, the strictest measures of middle-class status require,
at minimum, a college degree. However, as observed by Lacy (2007), most
studies of the African American middle class have "fudged" on this measure.
As an example, Lacy cites Pattillo-McCoy's (1999) study, where only 20 percent of residents in the community in which she conducted her research were
college educated. Pattillo-McCoy defended this decision by noting that 20
percent, while not a majority, was a much larger proportion than the 12 percent
of African American adults overall who had a college degree in 1990 (1999:
15). Since one of the goals of the current study is to determine the extent to
which speakers with access to Standard English, which is typically associated
with access to (higher) education, employ and evaluate vernacular speech, it
will be useful for my purposes to prioritize education in my consideration of
middle-class status. Accordingly, some form of higher education (either

completed or in progress)[15] will serve as a useful baseline for middle-class status, at least for those aspects of the research where education can be controlled for.[16]

With regard to occupation, middle-class status is typically linked to white-collar employment (e.g., professionals, managers, and supervisors), which will serve as another baseline for middle-class status in this study.[17] It is worth noting, however, that linguistic studies such as Sankoff and Laberge (1978), Nichols (1983), and Eckert (1989) have demonstrated the extent to which the "linguistic marketplace" can also have a significant impact on language usage. In other words, it has been observed that speakers who are involved in, or oriented toward, occupations that require Standard English (e.g., teachers, receptionists, salespeople, etc.) are likely to exhibit more standard language usage, regardless of class status. Where relevant, therefore, consideration will also be given to speakers engaged in occupations that expect (or require) regular use of Standard English, even if they do not fit the typical definition of white-collar employment.

Finally, with regard to income, Pattillo-McCoy (1999) cites a practice commonly employed by economists of using an income-to-needs ratio to define class categories. She explains, "The income-to-needs ratio divides total family income by the federal poverty level based on the family's size. The lower bound of the income-to-needs ratio for middle-class status is frequently set at two; that is, if a family earns two times a poverty-level income, they are middle-class" (Pattillo-McCoy 1999: 14–15). According to the 2010 figures published by the US Census Bureau, the weighted average poverty threshold for a family of four was $22,315, which, according to the formula described above, would place the baseline for middle-class status at $44,630 (i.e., twice the poverty level).[18] Although the income figures reported in Figure 1.3 do not control for family size, recall that the median household income for Black

---

[15] This includes students pursuing degrees at both two-year and four-year institutions, as well as graduate and professional schools.
[16] Data for this study were drawn from a variety of sources, not all of which were elicited specifically for this project. More details about the data examined will be provided in Chapter 2 and, where relevant, in the chapters that follow.
[17] According to Lacy (2007), sociological studies of the middle class have exhibited a tendency to collapse white-collar occupations (e.g., professionals, managers, and supervisors) into the same category as clerical and sales workers (37). Lacy notes that this practice might have made sense historically, particularly in the Black community, where working-class positions such as porters and postal workers were considered to be middle-class occupations. She argues, however, that the Black class structure today has expanded enough to warrant making more fine-tuned occupational distinctions.
[18] As an alternative measure of poverty, the Department of Health and Human Services (HHS) issues a poverty guideline each year in the *Federal Register*. In 2010, the poverty guideline for a family of four was set at $22,050, which would place the baseline for middle-class status at $44,100 (http://aspe.hhs.gov/POVERTY/10poverty.shtml).

families in 2010 was $32,068, which is considerably below this threshold, while the median household income for White families was $51,846, which is considerably above this baseline figure. Thus, while this formula will serve as a useful guide for establishing middle-class status, again for those aspects of the project where income can be measured and controlled for, some allowances will be made for speakers who meet the other criteria discussed above, education in particular, but whose income places them outside the established parameters for middle-class status.

In other words, in the spirit of Bourdieu's concept of symbolic capital and Weber's emphasis on the social psychological component of class identity, some aspects of this project will allow for consideration of speakers who fall above or below the limits of middle-class status as defined by traditional socioeconomic indicators, but whose experiences, practices, and perspectives are otherwise consistent with those who meet these criteria.[19] For studies of sociolinguistic variation, Rickford (1986, 2019), in fact, advocates for such an approach, urging researchers to employ both conflict models and ethnographic perspectives in our approaches to social class.[20]

The Origins and Development of African American English

Early descriptions of African American English were nonlinguistic accounts that attributed the distinctive features of African American language to physiological and linguistic "inadequacies" that were said to prevent people of African descent from fully acquiring the English language.[21] (See, e.g., Bennett 1908; Gonzales 1922.) To counter such racist, linguistically unfounded myths, dialectologists in the early 1900s declared that African American English was in no way special or inferior, but instead that Blacks spoke the same language as Whites with whom they shared comparable socioeconomic and regional backgrounds. (See, e.g., Krapp 1924; Kurath 1928.)

By and large the Southern Negro speaks the language of the White man of his locality or area and of his level of education. But in some respects his speech is more archaic or old-fashioned; not un-English, but retarded because of less schooling. As far as the speech of uneducated Negroes is concerned, it differs little from that of the illiterate

---

[19] While finer-grained distinctions *within* the middle class (e.g., lower-middle vs. upper-middle) are also likely to reveal interesting linguistic patterns (see, e.g., Labov 1966; Wolfram 1969), this project will be largely focused on middle-class status more broadly defined. It is my hope that the findings shared herein will provide fodder for subsequent studies (and, in particular, community-based studies), where more nuanced distinctions can be explored.

[20] For more discussion of sociolinguistic approaches to social class, see Ash (2004), Mallinson (2007), and Dodsworth (2009).

[21] For later statements of this position see Walker (1971) and Morse (1973).

White; that is, it exhibits the same regional and local variations as that of the simple White folk. (Kurath 1949: 6)

Such arguments formed the foundation of the Dialectologist (or Anglicist) Hypothesis, which proposed that AAE descended from British English roots, similar to other American English varieties, including Southern American English, but retained certain features of seventeenth- and eighteenth-century British English that other American English varieties had since lost. While the Dialectologist Hypothesis acknowledged the legitimacy of African American English, on the one hand, it denied any contribution from the African substrate. Krapp (1924) declared: "The Negroes, indeed, in acquiring English have done their work so thoroughly that they have retained not a trace of any African speech. Neither have they transferred anything of importance from their native tongues to the general language" (190). This perspective was later challenged, however, by the research of Melville Herskovits ([1941] 1970), Lorenzo Dow Turner (1949), and others, who observed the retention of African features in the language and culture of African American speakers (see, e.g., Dalby 1971; Dunn 1976; Van Sertima 1976; and Debose and Faraclas 1993). A related position, known as the Creolist Hypothesis, later attributed this influence to a period of creolization in the history of AAE. Noting a number of striking similarities between AAE and Jamaican Creole, Beryl Bailey (1965) argued that the varieties shared a "deep structural relationship" not found among other varieties of English:

I would like to suggest that the Southern Negro "dialect" differs from other Southern speech because its deep structure is different, having its origins as it undoubtedly does in some Proto-Creole grammatical structure. Hence, regardless of the surface resemblances to other dialects of English ... we must look into the system itself for an explanation of seeming confusion of person and tenses. (Bailey 1965: 172)

From this perspective, AAE was said to have derived from a Creole (i.e., contact variety) spoken by persons enslaved on the North American plantations, which, in turn, was said to have derived from a Pidgin English that developed out of the contact between English and various West African languages brought together by the Atlantic slave trade[22] (see also Stewart 1967, 1968, and Dillard 1972).

---

[22] The terms "Pidgin" and "Creole" are used here to describe varieties that emerge in situations of contact between speakers who share no common language among them, but who have an urgent need to communicate. Pidgins are traditionally thought to represent the first stage in the development of this contact variety, during which speakers create a rudimentary system of communication, strictly for purposes of trade or other business-related matters. Speakers draw the vocabulary primarily from the language of those who have the most power in the contact situation (i.e., the superstrate), while transferring features of their own grammar and pronunciation (i.e., the substrate) into the emerging variety. If this Pidgin gets passed on to a generation of speakers as their first (i.e., native) language, thus becoming the primary form of communication for a group of speakers, it is then that it develops into a full-fledged Creole language.

Many supporters of the Creolist Hypothesis argued that Gullah, an African American variety spoken along the coasts of South Carolina and Georgia, represented a fairly direct descendant of the Creole spoken on the North American plantations, which preserved much of its Creole structure because of the geographical and social isolation of the Sea Islands. African American varieties spoken further inland, however, were said to have undergone a process of decreolization (i.e., becoming more English-like under direct contact with other English varieties). The hierarchical division of labor on the plantations themselves would have laid the foundation for a linguistic continuum, with house servants speaking more English-like (i.e., "acrolectal") varieties, field hands speaking more Creole-like (i.e., "basilectal") varieties, and drivers and artisans speaking more intermediate (i.e., "mesolectal") varieties.[23] However, the process of decreolization would not have occurred until the breakdown of the plantation system, following the end of the Civil War. It was at this time that the continuum would have been fully realized, as Blacks gained greater access to English, both through education and more extensive contact with speakers of other English varieties.

Over the last two centuries, the proportion of American Negroes who speak a perfectly standard variety of English has risen from a small group of privileged house slaves and free Negroes to persons numbering in the hundreds of thousands, and perhaps even millions. Yet there is still a sizable number of American Negroes – undoubtedly larger than the number of standard-speaking Negroes – whose speech may be radically nonstandard. The nonstandard features in the speech of such persons may be due in part to the influence of the nonstandard dialects of Whites with whom they or their ancestors have come in contact, but they also may be due to the survival of creolisms from the older Negro field hand speech of the plantations. (Stewart 1967: 26)

While much of the early debate between creolists and dialectologists linked the question of AAE's origins to the question of its synchronic relationship to other varieties, Wolfram (1971, 1974) urged against such tendencies. Eventually, a consensus began to coalesce around the idea that AAE might have originated as a Creole, but that the process of decreolization had progressed to the point that its contemporary grammar was essentially the same as that of other English dialects (see, e.g., Labov 1972a, 1982; Fasold 1976, 1981). This consensus was short-lived, however, as some scholars began to question whether decreolization had actually taken place, noting instead that Black varieties and White varieties appeared to be diverging from one another as a result of the increased segregation and isolation of

---

[23] Charged with the task of managing the labor gangs and slave quarters, drivers were the primary liaisons between the overseers and other enslaved labor (Crum 1940; Clifton 1981). Enslaved artisans, who worked as skilled carpenters, shoemakers, blacksmiths, etc., often trained under White craftsmen (Newton 1977).

speakers (see, e.g., Labov and Harris 1986; Bailey and Maynor 1987). Others argued that this Divergence Hypothesis, as it was called, lacked sufficient linguistic evidence and failed to take into account the full range of social factors that could be involved (see, e.g., Fasold et al. 1987; Butters 1989; Rickford 1992).

Consensus around the Creole Origins Hypothesis was also challenged on the basis of sociodemographic evidence that called into question the likelihood that US plantations ever met the conditions for indigenous creolization anywhere other than in the Southeast region, where Gullah developed (see, e.g., Schneider 1989; Mufwene 1997; Winford 1997; Rickford 1999c).[24] Unlike Jamaica and other Caribbean islands, where African substrate speakers often outnumbered English speakers at a ratio of nine to one (Rickford 1999c), the average number of enslaved persons on most US plantations outside the south was fifteen or fewer (D'Eloia 1973). Such conditions would have permitted most Blacks to acquire closer approximations to English. In fact, studies such as Mufwene (1997) and Winford (1997) have suggested that some early form of African American English likely preceded the formation of a Creole during the first fifty years of settlement in the Carolina colony (1670–1720), as Africans and Europeans interacted regularly on small homestead farms rather than large plantations. By this account, the Creole would not have emerged until around 1720, as institutionalized segregation and the massive importation of Africans to the Carolina colony to meet the needs of the rapidly growing plantation economy would have produced more favorable conditions for Creole formation.[25] Under this scenario, a Creole continuum would already have been in place prior to the breakdown of the plantation system, allowing for the possibility of Creole substratum influence during the formative years of AAE's development via language shift or transfer (cf. Alleyne 1971, 1980; LePage 1960, 1977). In light of this evidence, Winford (1997) offered the following scenario as an alternative to earlier statements of the Creolist Hypothesis:

> We can assume that there was a sizeable body of Africans throughout the southern states in this period whose primary vernacular was a creole English, and many of whom shifted over the years to AAVE as their primary vernacular, "transferring" or preserving in the process certain elements of the creole grammar. I also assume that there was a sizeable body of Africans whose primary vernacular was an earlier form of AAVE

---

[24] According to Bickerton (1981), one of the conditions necessary for Creole formation is that the number of people speaking a superstrate variety should not exceed 20 percent of the total population in a given community. Otherwise, substrate speakers are presumed to have sufficient access to the superstrate to acquire at least some approximation to it.

[25] The Creole would likely have spread to Georgia during the last few decades of the eighteenth century as South Carolina planters migrated to the Georgia coast, taking their enslaved labor with them (Winford 1997; Moody 2011; Weldon and Moody 2015).

which was fashioned after the settler dialects, and which provided the target of the shift. Contact between these groups of Africans on the plantations is likely to have contributed to the development of AAVE. (Winford 1997: 317)

Winford argued that the distinctive features of the vernacular that emerged during this period of contact would have spread to other areas of the country during the post-emancipation period of the nineteenth and twentieth centuries, as increased mobility led to higher contact among African Americans of different regional and social backgrounds.[26] According to Rickford (1999c), however, Creole influence might also have played a role in the formative years of AAE's development outside the South, given the sizeable number of Creole speakers imported from the Caribbean to the Middle and New England colonies in the seventeenth and eighteenth centuries.

To date, no consensus has been reached regarding the emergence of AAE and what role, if any, Creoles played in its formation. There also remains considerable controversy over the current trajectory of African American varieties vis-à-vis their European American counterparts. Many early supporters of the Dialectologist Hypothesis have now adopted a Neo-Anglicist Hypothesis, which asserts that certain distinctive features, particularly in the tense, mood, and aspect (TMA) system of AAE, are creations of the twentieth century, reflecting a growing social and economic divide between African American and European American speakers (see, e.g., Dayton 1996; Labov 1998; Poplack 2000). However, as Rickford (2006) demonstrates, the evidence brought to bear thus far in support of the Neo-Anglicist Hypothesis is far from conclusive, leaving much still to be debated and explored about the origins and development of AAE.[27] More importantly for the purposes of this study, the bulk of the evidence that has been examined thus far has been drawn from working-class speech communities, with little consideration given to the ways in which middle-class speech communities might inform the divergence debate.

Defining African American English

In this book, I will use the term "African American English" to refer to the collection of distinctive American English varieties spoken primarily by and among native-born African Americans (i.e., Americans of African descent who were born in the United States). In other words, I will treat AAE as a collection

---

[26] Early supporters of the Dialectologist Hypothesis also attributed the regional spread of southern AAE to the "Great Black Migration" of the early twentieth century.

[27] Rickford (2006) provides an exhaustive, chapter-by-chapter, critique of Poplack (2000) that urges readers to question some interpretations of the data and to conduct comparable analyses of the examined features in Creole varieties so that more informed conclusions can be reached.

of American English varieties, distinct from (though possibly historically related to) other English varieties, including those of the African diaspora, such as Caribbean English Creoles (CECs) and second-language varieties of English spoken by African immigrants residing in the United States. This definition, which I adopt from Mufwene (2001), is grounded in the "sentiments of [most] lay African Americans" that they are, first and foremost, speakers of English (34).[28] From this perspective, Gullah, the English-based Creole spoken by African Americans on the Sea Islands and along the coasts of South Carolina and Georgia, will also be treated as a variety of AAE.[29] "We can thus articulate the distinction between Gullah and AAVE as basically a regional one, within which other continua are identifiable and associated, in part, with density of their respective basilectal features" (Mufwene 2001: 36).

Given this definition, two important caveats should be noted. First of all, while AAE is spoken primarily by and among African Americans, it is not spoken exclusively by African Americans. Because language is socially constructed, not biologically determined, members of other racial/ethnic groups who live, work, socialize, and identify primarily with AAE speakers, perhaps especially during the formative years of birth to puberty, are also likely to become fluent speakers of AAE (cf. Fix 2011). Furthermore, there is the phenomenon of "linguistic appropriation" (see, e.g., Cutler 1999; Smitherman 2006), by which members of other racial/ethnic groups borrow from AAE, particularly at the level of the lexicon (i.e., vocabulary), in order to, for example, sound "cool" – a concept that has become iconically linked to African Americans and by extension to AAE. Such uses of AAE are not the focus of this book, however, which is primarily concerned with the use of AAE by middle-class African American speakers.

---

[28] It is, nonetheless, important to acknowledge the preference among many linguists today to refer to the variety as "African American Language" (AAL), as opposed to "African American English." For example, in their introduction to *The Oxford Handbook of African American Language*, Lanehart and Malik explain this preference as follows:

> Our preference to use AAL, as opposed to AAE, is to bypass some of the problematic implications of "English" within the socioculture and history of African slave descendants in the United States and the contested connections of their language variety to the motherland and colonization and encompass rhetorical and pragmatic strategies that might not be associated with English. (Lanehart and Malik 2015: 3)

While these are certainly legitimate concerns to which I take no exception, I believe that it is equally important to acknowledge the many essential contributions of African American speakers to the linguistic fabric of American English. My choice to use the AAE label, as opposed to AAL, is largely motivated by this perspective. For more on the continuing evolution of labels used to refer to the variety, see Mufwene (1992), Morgan (1994), Blackshire-Belay (1996), Smitherman (1998), Baugh (2000a), and Green (2002).

[29] But see Spears (1988, 1998, 2008), Kautzsch and Schneider (2000), and Moody (2011) for additional perspectives on this issue.

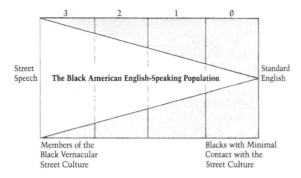

Figure 1.5 The African American speech community
Source: Baugh 1983: 128, Figure 15

A second, related, caveat is that not all African Americans speak AAE. In his 1983 study, *Black Street Speech*, John Baugh offered the diagram shown in Figure 1.5 as an illustration of the wide range of varieties spoken by and among African Americans.[30] As this figure suggests, African Americans who live, work, socialize, and identify primarily with nonvernacular speakers (i.e., those who are far removed from "street culture," to put it in Baugh's terms) may use few to none of the features identified as characteristic of vernacular varieties of AAE. And some will even fail to exhibit regular use of the phonological, prosodic, lexical, and rhetorical features said to characterize more standard varieties of AAE. For this reason, I will make a distinction in this study between SAAE, which is subsumed under the AAE umbrella, and "talking/sounding Proper" (also referred to as "talking/sounding White"), which is a label used in the African American speech community to refer to African American speakers who are not perceived as "talking/sounding Black"[31] (see, e.g., Mitchell-Kernan 1971; Spears 1988). Thus, while my research will be focused primarily on the language of middle-class African Americans, my goal is not to explore the full range of varieties used by and among middle-class African American speakers, but rather to examine the use of African American English by middle-class African American speakers, and to explore attitudes about and perceptions of such uses.

---

[30] Baugh uses the term "Street Speech" to refer to vernacular varieties of African American English.
[31] While there are some nuanced distinctions between "talking Black" and "sounding Black," they are often used interchangeably in the African American community, but with primary emphasis on a speaker's phonology or prosody (i.e., accent) (see Mufwene 2001: 45).

AAVEs --- SAAEs

Figure 1.6 Continuum of standardness for African American English
Source: adapted from Wolfram and Schilling-Estes 1998: 11, Figure 1.1

Consistent with Taylor, Hoover, Spears, and others, I will use African American English as a cover term for a range of varieties distributed along a standard-vernacular continuum. Adopting a model used in Wolfram and Schilling-Estes (1998), I illustrate this concept in the form of a "continuum of standardness," as shown in Figure 1.6.[32] By treating AAE as a continuum of related varieties with endpoints that in and of themselves represent collections of varieties, I acknowledge that at any given point on the AAE continuum, there exists regional variation, as well as variation in terms of other factors such as age, gender, sexuality, and social class (cf. Hoover 1978; Taylor 1983; Rahman 2008).[33] From this perspective, varieties that fall near the vernacular end of the continuum (which I will refer to, for convenience, as "the vernacular") would be expected to exhibit a salient clustering of vernacular structural features, and at the other end (which I will refer to, for convenience, as "the standard"), little to no use of such features. Lexical, prosodic, rhetorical, and, to some extent, phonological and grammatical features that are characteristic of, or even distinctive to, the African American speech community, but are less saliently marked for vernacularity might exist anywhere along the continuum. What brings these varieties together is their systematic indexing of African American identity and culture.

While this model presumes the existence of a racially/ethnically unmarked "American English," for the purposes of this study, it is "Mainstream American English" (MAE), a collection of varieties that is largely defined according to the dominant culture in the USA (i.e., the White middle-class establishment), and which exists closer to the standard end of the continuum, that often serves as a primary point of comparison and contrast for AAE. Nevertheless, we should not lose sight of the fact that MAE also draws on

[32] This model is an adaptation of one proposed by Wolfram and Schilling-Estes (1998) to illustrate their concept of "Informal Standard English." Wolfram and Schilling-Estes explain: "On this informal level, standard English is a pluralistic notion, at least with respect to pronunciation and vocabulary differences. That is, there are regional standards which are recognized within the broad and informal notion of standard American English" (1998: 11).

[33] Those familiar with the history of research on AAE will recognize that this approach moves away from the traditional treatment of AAE as a homogenous, supra-regional variety. While linguists have identified a core set of grammatical features that appear to extend across regional boundaries, recent research has demonstrated the ways in which AAE varies according to region, class, gender, sexuality, etc. This study of middle-class AAE is a contribution to these more recent efforts.

particular sociocultural identities, including White middle-class identities (which are largely unexplored in sociolinguistic research, because they are so often treated as the "norm" against which other identities are measured).[34]

The adoption of a continuum model such as this is useful for extending definitions of AAE beyond vernacular usage. In adopting this model, it is not my intention to arrive at (or depart from) a static list of features associated with middle-class African American English, but rather to explore the range of features, uses, and attitudes associated with the collection of varieties joined under this label. In this regard, my approach is not inconsistent with Benor's (2010) concept of the "ethnolinguistic repertoire,"[35] which is defined as "a fluid set of linguistic resources that members of an ethnic group may use variably as they index their ethnic identities" (160). However, my adoption of the repertoire model differs from Benor's in several significant ways. First, whereas Benor's 2010 description of the African American repertoire model seems primarily focused on vernacular feature usage, I view the repertoire itself as a continuum of features that includes not only vernacular structural features, but also lexical, rhetorical, and prosodic features, as well as camouflaged features (cf. Spears's 2015 DBGFs), that can be "mapped onto" more standard varieties of American English, in order to index racial/ethnic identity.

Also, unlike Benor, who proposes abandoning labels like "African American English" for broader descriptors like "language use among African Americans," I choose to retain the AAE label in recognition of the observation made above that my focus is not on the language of (middle-class) African Americans, some of whom make no use of the African American repertoire at all (a fact that Benor herself acknowledges), but rather on the distinctive uses of English by and among many middle-class African American speakers as a means of indexing African American identity and culture.[36] The AAE label also remains useful for distinguishing what Benor calls "out group" uses of the variety, including imitations, parodies, performances, and appropriations, from

---

[34] To the extent that the current study also uses MAE as a primary point of comparison with AAE, I acknowledge that it too has the potential to perpetuate the normative treatment of White American identity, language, and culture. However, it is my hope that this acknowledgment will at least serve as an invitation to other researchers to more fully interrogate these concepts, as such interrogations go beyond the scope of the current project.

[35] As observed by Benor (2010), the concept of the linguistic repertoire dates back to some of the foundational research on codes and styles used in multilingual and monolingual communities, respectively (see, e.g., Gumperz 1964; Hymes 1967; Blom and Gumperz 1972). In Gumperz (1964) the "verbal repertoire" is defined as "the totality of linguistic forms regularly employed in the course of socially significant interaction" (137). Benor adapts this concept by shifting the analytic focus to "the arsenal of distinctive resources used by a particular [ethnic] group" (161).

[36] In fairness, Benor does concede that "there may be instances where these terms are useful, as long as they are acknowledged as abstractions" (2010: 175).

uses that demonstrate a deeper knowledge of the linguistic constraints and sociocultural norms governing more systematic use of the repertoire. While the repertoire model is useful for capturing the totality of ways in which language can and does index African American identity, it is this systematic knowledge of the repertoire that will be the primary focus of this study.

Also, while the "repertoire" model (cf. Gumperz 1964), which is grounded in a more "third wave" (i.e., social constructionist) approach to variation (see, e.g., Eckert 2008, 2012), focuses largely on the micro-social dynamics that drive individual language choice, my focus in this study will remain largely concerned with the macro-social dynamics of race and class as they intersect with language variation.[37] Nevertheless, I will draw on social constructionist models and perspectives, where appropriate, particularly in my consideration of the stylistic choices that individual speakers make in the performance of identity (cf. Coupland 1980; Irvine 2001). It is my hope that a combined approach such as this will contribute to our understanding of how the individual construction of identity in everyday discourse (i.e., style) serves to create, reflect, and reinforce broader circulating meanings, particularly about race and class, in society (i.e., sociolinguistic variation) (cf. Eckert and Rickford 2001). Thus, in response to Orlando Taylor's call over three decades ago to "re-think and refine" how we define African American English, this study aims to present a broader, more inclusive look at the use and perception of AAE by middle-class speakers. In the next chapter, I provide an overview of the burgeoning line of research that has begun to heed Taylor's call, and I situate my own study therein.

---

[37] As described in Eckert (2012), the study of sociolinguistic variation has undergone three waves (or stages) in its development. In the first wave, sociolinguists used survey methodology to examine how linguistic variables were distributed across macro-social categories such as class, gender, and ethnicity (see, e.g., Labov 1966). In the second wave, ethnographic approaches, such as social networking methodology, were used to explore the local manifestations of these broader social phenomena (see, e.g., Milroy 1980). The third wave focuses on stylistic practice and the "social-semiotic moves" (Eckert 2012: 94) that speakers make in the construction and indexicalization of meaning through language. (See also, e.g., Silverstein 2003; Eckert 2008).

The Study of Middle-Class African
         American English

To be lame means to be outside of the central group and its culture; it is a negative
characterization and does not imply any single set of social characteristics. . . .
What all lames have in common is that they lack the knowledge which is
necessary to run any kind of a game in the vernacular culture.
                                            —William Labov (1972a)

I have had numerous discussions about class and race with middle-class
African Americans. None of them equate being middle-class with an absence
of African American culture and values. . . . [R]acial consciousness continues
to be an important indicator of community membership.
                                            —Marcyliena Morgan (1994)

The Linguistic Consequences of Being a Lame

The concept of the linguistic "lame" emerged out of a tradition in early AAE
research that focused disproportionately on the speech of working-class adolescent boys who were core members of the street or "vernacular" culture of
the inner cities. Labov (1972a) provided a compelling argument for why the
language of this group required the attention of sociolinguists to dispel harmful
myths about verbal deprivation and genetic inferiority (see, e.g., Bereiter and
Englemann 1966; Jensen 1969) and to address the severe reading challenges
faced by many vernacular speakers in schools. (See also Labov et al. 1965,
1968.) Middle-class speakers, among others, were cast aside as linguistic
lames, who were presumed to be too far removed from street culture to be
influenced by the vernacular. And even *within* urban working-class communities, Labov identified as lames certain "isolated individuals" who did not
hang out in peer groups dominated by vernacular culture norms.

In his chapter on "The Linguistic Consequences of Being a Lame," Labov
(1972a) reported the results of a peer group study in Harlem, New York that
compared the speech of inner-city "lames" to that of "members" of the
vernacular culture.[1] Four preadolescent groups, ranging in age from nine to

[1] Peer group membership was determined by level of participation in group activities as well as the
boys' responses to the question "Who are all the cats you hang out with?"

Table 2.1 *Phonological and grammatical features in Harlem study (Labov 1972a)*

Phonological features	
consonant cluster reduction	*past, passed* [s]
fricative stopping	*th*is [d]
post-vocalic [r] absence	*car, four o'clock* Ø
unstressed nasal fronting	*work*ing [n]
Grammatical features	
copula (*is/are*) absence	*He* Ø *working with us.*
existential *it*	*It's a policeman at the door.*
inverted word order in embedded questions	*I asked him* **could he do it.**
negative concord	**Nobody** *knows* **nothing** *about it.*

Note: With the exception of unstressed nasal fronting, all examples in Table 2.1 are from Labov (1972a).

thirteen years old, were observed for their use of several socially diagnostic linguistic features (see Table 2.1), distributed across a range of speech styles. No casual speech data were collected from the "lames," however, who were only recorded in individual interviews.

Labov also compared patterns of subject–verb agreement for *have*, *do*, *want*, *say*, and *was* – five verbs that have been found to exhibit high rates of nonagreement among vernacular speakers. For this comparison, Labov observed adolescent lames and club members, as well as an older peer group, known as the Oscar Brothers (ages eighteen to nineteen), and a White peer group from the Inwood section of upper Manhattan. Compared to the vernacular peer group members, the lames exhibited lower rates of vernacular usage for most of the observed features, often with patterns of linguistic constraint that resembled those found among White speakers. Labov interpreted the lames' patterns as indicative of their removal from Black vernacular culture and a closer adherence to White mainstream norms.

In his analysis of the largest adolescent peer group, Labov also found a strong correlation between status in the group and rates of vernacular usage. Specifically, core members exhibited the most consistent use of vernacular features, compared to peripheral members, older members, and lames, who produced significantly lower frequencies of most vernacular forms. Furthermore, the Oscar Brothers, described as "older and wiser" than the other adolescent groups, were beginning to show signs of modifying their speech in the direction of more standard norms, particularly in their use of *were* with plural and second-person singular subjects. Also, a group of adults who were interviewed in the study produced vernacular frequencies that were much more consistent with those of the adolescent lames. Given these observations, Labov suggested that vernacular speakers might become more "lame" as they approach adulthood and become increasingly isolated from the influence of vernacular street culture. However, he also acknowledged the possibility that, over time, adults simply become more adept at shifting into more standard styles of speaking in formal contexts (1972a: 285). Unfortunately, because the adults in this study, like the younger lames, were only observed in interview settings, there was no opportunity for Labov to observe their styleshifting ability in this way.[2]

Based on his findings, Labov concluded that lames suffered "a loss of some magnitude" in not being able to draw upon the "rich verbal culture" of the vernacular and the prestige of peer group membership. Consequently, they were deemed to be unreliable subjects in studies of the vernacular. "If we are interested in toasts, jokes, sounds, the dozens, riffing, or capping, we cannot turn to the lames. They have heard sounding from a distance, but proficiency at these verbal skills is achieved only by daily practice and constant immersion in the flow of speech" (Labov 1972a: 288). What followed were decades of research focused on the "authentic Other," contributing to the perception that the vernacular was only spoken by those who were "hip, male, adolescent, street, or gang-related" (Morgan 1994: 135). This tradition of research left little room for consideration of the ways in which many middle-class African Americans use the vernacular to construct their own racial/ethnic identities and to counterbalance the effects of mainstream assimilation. As observed by Marcyliena Morgan,

I have had numerous discussions about class and race with middle-class African Americans. None of them equate being middle-class with an absence of African American culture and values. They argue that the street culture (as defined by sociologists) is integral to the community, and they object to any attempt to identify it as either representative or separate. Thus, though the representation of class may be changing in the African American community – and quite likely the significance of education as an indicator of social class – racial consciousness continues to be an important indicator of community membership. (Morgan 1994: 136)

---

[2] According to Keith Gilyard (1991), a closer examination of the "lames" in a variety of social and stylistic contexts might have revealed a more complex verbal range than that observed by Labov.

There were shrewd youngsters out there who were not in traditional gangs but were, nonetheless, fashioning and reinforcing and projecting intricate selves through complex manipulations of Black English and Standard English. By over romanticizing the basilect often heard in the street clubs and viewing the language of the so-called lames as diametrically opposed to that of the gang members, Labov may have missed an opportunity to describe those intriguing processes. (119)

As noted in Chapter 1, researchers in recent years have begun to extend the study of AAE beyond working-class speech communities, yielding a small body of research on middle-class AAE that includes studies of social stratification, intraspeaker variation, performative language practices, and attitudes and perceptions. In the sections to follow, I discuss some of these pioneering studies and position the current project within the context of this burgeoning line of research.

Social Stratification

Traditional approaches to sociolinguistic variation focused on the stratification (or social differentiation) of linguistic variables across a given speech community. Of primary interest were the relative frequencies of particular linguistic features, or *markers*, as they were distributed across social classes and along a formality continuum, thus reflecting the varying levels of prestige (or status) assigned to them (see, e.g., Labov 1966). While stratification studies such as these were foundational to sociolinguistic research, there were relatively few such studies conducted in African American speech communities. Using dialect atlas methodology to classify speakers by level of education, Williamson (1968) provided an early examination of the social distribution of phonological and morphological features among African American speakers in Memphis, Tennessee. However, her study provided no quantitative analysis of the relative frequencies of these features among the various groups. The first quantitative approach to social stratification in AAE was Wolfram (1969), which examined the use of four phonological variables and four grammatical variables (Table 2.2) in the speech of forty-eight African American participants in Detroit, Michigan. The speakers were evenly distributed across four social class categories (Lower Working, Upper Working, Lower Middle, and Upper Middle).

In this study, Wolfram observed relatively consistent use of standard variants among his middle-class speakers, though younger speakers showed some individual variation, and women across all social class categories exhibited more standard usage than men. He also observed that the grammatical variables were sharply stratified across social classes, compared to the phonological variables, three of which were gradiently stratified.[3] While Wolfram's findings did not necessarily challenge the depiction of middle-class speakers as "lames," they did draw attention to the complicating effects

---

[3] The pronunciation of /θ/ as [f] (e.g., *tooth*, *nothing*) was the exception here, where fourteen of the twenty-four middle-class participants produced no [f] variants at all, compared to working-class participants, for whom [f] was the most frequent variant (Wolfram 1969: 85).

Table 2.2 *Phonological and grammatical features in the Detroit study (Wolfram 1969)*

Phonological features	
consonant cluster reduction	*test* [s], *laughed* [f]
medial and final /ɵ/ as [f], [t], or Ø (i.e., zero realization)	*tooth* [f]
	nothing [f]/[t]/Ø
	with [f]/[t]/Ø
post-vocalic [r] absence	*work, brother* Ø
syllable-final /d/ as [t̚] (i.e., unreleased [t]), [ʔ] or Ø	*good* [t̚]/[ʔ]/ Ø

Grammatical features	
–s absence in third singular present, possessive, and plural environments	*He stand_ on his hind legs. (third singular present)*
	He was really my grandfather_ dog. (possessive)
	I wish I had a million dollar_. (plural)
copula (*is/are*) absence	*Dolores Ø the vice-president.*
	We Ø going Friday night.
invariant *be* in habitual or future contexts	*Sometime she **be** fighting in school. (habitual)*
	*I **be** twelve February seven. (future)*
multiple negation	*I **couldn't hardly** pick him up.*
	*I **don't** bother **nobody**.*
	*They **didn't** have **no** gym.*

Note: All examples in Table 2.2 are from Wolfram (1969).

of gender, age, and linguistic salience on the social stratification of the observed variables.[4]

Nguyen (2006) extended the focus on the social stratification of phonological variables, using data from the 1966 corpus on which Wolfram (1969) was based and contemporary interview data that she and others collected between 1999 and 2004 in Detroit, Michigan. Nguyen examined two consonantal variables analyzed by Wolfram – post-vocalic /r/ and syllable-final /d/ – as well as the glide reduction of /ai/ before voiced and voiceless consonants (e.g., *ride* as [rad], *right* as [rat]) and the fronting of /ʊ/ (e.g., in *could, look*). Several of Nguyen's findings challenged traditional perceptions of middle-class speakers as "lames." For example, in her examination of syllable-final /d/,

---

[4] Though restricted to a Black inner-city working-class community in Detroit, Michigan, Edwards (1992) observed similar trends with regard to age, gender, linguistic salience, levels of social isolation, and attitudinal factors.

Nguyen found that both the "high status" and "low status" speakers in her study exhibited a preference for the "AAE variants" [ʔ] and Ø over the "non-AAE variant" [d], which both groups reportedly used with low, but relatively equal frequency.[5] In her study, "high status" speakers used [ʔ] more frequently, while "low status" speakers preferred Ø. Nguyen also observed that, contrary to conventional wisdom, the higher-status speakers had, in fact, *led* in a change toward a context-dependent pattern of [ʊ] fronting,[6] suggesting that middle-class speakers were not categorically disconnected from vernacular culture, but were, instead, speakers who "can and do introduce new features into AAE that may be adopted by speakers of all social status backgrounds" (2006: 178).

In a social stratification study of the vowel systems of working- and middle-class African Americans in Lansing, Michigan, Jones and Preston (2011) observed that young upper-middle-class women were making use of a "divided vocalic system" that was "at once reflective of on-going local changes in the front vowel system, in this case, the Northern Cities Chain Shift (Labov et al. 1972), but at the same time reflective of older African American norms in the back vowel system" (2). Upper-middle-class speakers in their study participated in the local pattern of /ae/-raising (e.g., "cad" [kæd] as [kɛd] or [kɪd]), which was described as "a regional but not ethnic characteristic" that was gradiently stratified across social classes. However, they resisted the local pattern of /a/-fronting (e.g., "cod" [kɑd] as [kæd]), which, according to Jones and Preston, was resisted by almost all of the African American speakers in their study, resulting in a sharp stratification across *ethnic* (rather than social class) boundaries. Based on these findings, Jones and Preston concluded that /a/-fronting was "a phonological marker of ethnic identity, and perhaps . . . even an avoided white sound" (17). They also suggested that this linguistic behavior might reflect what Smitherman (1977) called a "push-pull" effect, by which African Americans, and perhaps middle-class African Americans in particular, participated in local linguistic changes while simultaneously retaining a symbolic African American identity through the manipulation of finely tuned phonological features. While limited in their generalizability, given that both were conducted in Michigan, these contemporary studies by Jones and Preston and by Nguyen challenged some previously held assumptions about middle-class African American speakers that emerged from the early sociolinguistic tradition. They also shed light on the importance of ethnically marked, but less

---

[5] Nguyen used the notation [alv] to refer to the non-AAE variant, which included any alveolar stop closure on the coda, voiced or voiceless (2006: 75). For purposes of readability (and given the relative infrequency of [t] in her study), she gave me license (via personal communication) to refer to the non-AAE variant simply as [d].

[6] Specifically, Nguyen observed here a pattern by which [ʊ] was fronted more in pre-alveolar contexts (e.g., *put*) than in pre-velar ones (e.g., *look*).

overtly stigmatized, phonological features as a means of "sounding Black" at higher levels of the socioeconomic spectrum.

In *The Language of Professional Blackness*, Grieser (2014) found that final stop devoicing, which was treated in her study as a continuous variable (cf. syllable-final /d/ in Wolfram 1969 and Nguyen 2006), was used by young female "professional-class (PC) aligned" African American speakers in Southeast, Washington, DC to simultaneously index both African American and Professional Class identities.[7] Using Silverstein's (2003) model of indexicality, Grieser explained:

> Final consonant devoicing is a longtime documented feature of AAE, thus one first order meaning arising from this connection is the group-associational meaning of "African American." . . . But final consonant devoicing, by departing from the expected pronunciation, shares the iconized connection between "pronounced" and "precise" that drives the patterning with other hyper-articulated features. Because of this, it gains a competing second-order meaning of "correct" or "precise," which helps explain its presence in the speech of PC-aligned speakers who otherwise have low rates of features of AAE. (Grieser 2014: 134)

Furthermore, Grieser observed that both the PC-aligned and PC-nonaligned speakers interviewed for her study exhibited an increase in final consonant devoicing with "talk about race," demonstrating its status as an "ethnoracially marked" feature. And yet, for some PC-aligned speakers, there was also an increase in final consonant devoicing with "talk about talk" (i.e., metalinguistic commentary), where the *salience* of "correctness" in the topic of the discourse appeared to correlate with the *performance* of "correctness" or "professionalness" through the same phonological feature. Variable shifts of this sort have also been the focus of a related line of research on Middle-Class AAE, namely intraspeaker variation.

Intraspeaker Variation

In the study of AAE, intraspeaker variation has been the subject of considerable debate as it pertains to the nature of the system(s) at work. For years, linguists have debated whether such variation reflects "dialect mixture," with speakers drawing from two separate and autonomous linguistic systems, or whether the variation is inherent to a single system. As discussed in Chapter 1, much of the early debate on this topic was linked to the question of AAE's origins, with supporters of the Creolist Hypothesis arguing that the variation spanned two separate systems (see, e.g., Bailey 1965; Stewart 1967, 1968;

---

[7] Grieser used the terms "PC-aligned" and "PC-nonaligned" to distinguish between those participants in her study who affiliated with the professional class through their education, occupation, social network, and self-identification and those who did not (2014: 82).

Dillard 1972), while Dialectologists argued that the variation was inherent to a single system (see, e.g., Krapp 1924; Kurath 1928). Labov (1972a) endorsed a one-system model, citing linguistic phenomena such as the interrelatedness of contracted and deleted forms of the copula as evidence of its inherent variability.[8] Mitchell-Kernan (1971) came to a similar conclusion in her study of an urban working-class community in West Oakland, California, noting the lack of strict co-occurrence restrictions[9] between standard and vernacular forms, as well as the ideological treatment of standard and vernacular forms along a "single ranked system" of grammaticality (50). And in a comparison of the sociolinguistic interviews and public presentations of three African American political leaders in the rural South, Kendall and Wolfram (2009) noted the absence of any "discrete shifts" in diagnostic features across styles, concluding that:

> these structures are part of a core vernacular variety that seems immune to code switching. In effect, there is a default or "matrix" variety (Myers-Scotton 1998) that may show some sensitivity to stylistic shifting or may even be switched from momentarily for performative effect (Schilling-Estes 1998), but there is no indication of coexisting dialect codes that can be readily accessed by the speakers. (Kendall and Wolfram 2009: 325)

According to Debose (1992), it is owing to the prevalence of the inherent variability model that so little attention has been given to individual codeswitching in the African American speech community.

> Labov's theoretical claims regarding the inherent variability of American English presuppose a monolingual language situation in the African-American speech community ... Dillard, while acknowledging a "bidialectal" linguistic repertoire for African-Americans seems to under-estimate the prevalence of bilingual speakers. He seems to believe that most middle-class blacks are monolingual speakers of SE, whereas most poor blacks are monolingual BE speakers; and that middle class African-Americans rely upon "ethnic slang" for the purpose of maintaining linguistic identity with their group. (Debose 1992: 158)

In his analysis of the conversational strategies of a middle-class African American woman from the San Francisco/Oakland Bay area, whom he described as a "balanced bilingual speaker of BE [Black English] and SE [Standard English]," Debose employed a codeswitching model, as described below:

---

[8] In his chapter on "Contraction, Deletion, and Inherent Variability of the English Copula," Labov observed that "the population upon which the deletion rule operates is limited to the pool of forms already contracted" suggesting that the rules are inherent to a single system (1972a: 87).
[9] Mitchell-Kernan did suggest, however, that such co-occurrence restrictions might be more commonly found in Black middle-class communities than they were in the working-class community that she was studying (1971: 85).

In this paper, BE and SE are treated as two different closely-related linguistic systems which coexist in the African American linguistic repertoire. Each system is defined as an autonomous grammar, and the interaction between them is considered to be governed by the same principles as those that govern languages in contact (Weinreich 1953) generally. Such a model does not rule out [Orlando] Taylor's claim of standard/ vernacular variation within BE, but it allows for the separate existence of an ethnically-unmarked standard English as a superposed variety. (Debose 1992: 159)

In a more recent treatment of this issue, Labov (1998) proposed a similar model, by which he described the coexistence of an African American (AA) component and a General English (GE) component in African American Vernacular English (AAVE). Like Debose, Labov distinguished the GE component of AAVE from the GE component of Other American Dialects (OAD), though his primary focus was on the ways in which the GE and AA components of AAVE impose mutual influence on one another. Unlike Debose, however, Labov did not view the AA system as an "autonomous grammar" but instead maintained his position that the AA component, which consists largely of a distinct tense/aspect system, is interdependently linked to the GE component.

AAVE consists of two distinct components: the General English (GE) component, which is similar to the grammar of OAD, and the African-American (AA) component . . . On the one hand, GE is a fairly complete set of syntactic, morphological, and phonological structures, which can function independently . . . The AA component is not a complete grammar, but a subset of grammatical and lexical forms that are used in combination with much but not all of the grammatical inventory of GE. (Labov 1998: 117–18)

This more recent approach to intraspeaker variation proposed by Labov is perhaps most closely aligned with Benor's (2010) model of the ethnolinguistic repertoire, which abandoned the concept of an ethnic dialect (or "ethnolect"), in favor of a "tool kit" model in which speakers "deploy linguistic resources" in order to construct various ethnic and other identities (161). As observed by Benor, traditional conceptions of intraspeaker (as well as intragroup) variation, whether viewed as existing across or within the boundaries of a given variety, become complicated by the question of *how much* variation is required in order for the phenomenon to be described as styleshifting versus codeswitching. Benor explained, "The question arises: how many distinctive features must be present for a given stretch of speech to be considered part of the ethnolect rather than the standard?[10] . . . Should an African American who often speaks without distinctively African American features be seen as switching into

---

[10] To the extent that I adopt a repertoire approach in the current study, it is important to recall that my own conception of the African American ethnolinguistic repertoire differs from Benor's in that it encompasses both standard and vernacular features along a continuum of standardness.

AAVE when she uses one token of remote *been?*" (2010: 166). Benor proposed that, instead of focusing on the variety itself, researchers treat such variation in terms of the extent to which a speaker draws on the repertoire in a given stretch of speech. Using a passage from Jacobs-Huey (2006), in which the "selective use of elements of an 'ethnolect' confounds the notion of codeswitching," Benor offered the following alternative analysis,

> In the repertoire approach, this problem disappears. We would say that in this excerpt Mrs. Collins is speaking in one code, but she is making increased use of a distinctly African American repertoire in lines 8–11 and then decreased use of the repertoire in the last section. There is clearly a stylistic shift, but the three sections are not different codes or dialects. (2010: 166–67)

While the repertoire model perhaps renders moot the long-term debate over the nature of the system(s) at work, it still allows for a consideration of the various functions and motivations that the repertoire serves for individual speakers. As noted by Ervin-Tripp (2001), shifts in dialect features often resemble bilingual codeswitching phenomena in that both "invok[e] contrastive implications of the linguistic features" (47). It, therefore, remains instructive to consider the kinds of motivations that trigger the use of certain features, the various meanings that get invoked through such uses, and the kinds of functions that such uses serve. Within sociolinguistics, there have been three main approaches to the study of intraspeaker variation.[11] The "attention-to-speech" model introduced in Labov (1966) explores intraspeaker variation as it is distributed along a formality continuum, such that the use of a given feature is said to vary according to the formality of the situation and the extent to which a speaker is aware of their speech. A key consideration in such studies is tapping into the "vernacular," defined in this context as "the style which is most regular in its structure and in its relation to the evaluation of the language" and "in which the minimum attention is paid to speech" (Labov 1972b: 112). Studies emerging out of this tradition have observed that speakers typically increase their use of socially prestigious features as the formality of the event increases, and the amount of attention to speech increases, thus reflecting a sense of "linguistic insecurity" on the part of speakers (Labov 1966). Accordingly, women and speakers located more centrally along the socioeconomic continuum have been found to exhibit a heightened sensitivity to such formality constraints, presumably reflecting their precarious position in society (Labov 1966; Trudgill 1983).

From this perspective, the distinction that Benor invokes between "the ethnolect and the standard" represents a false dichotomy, as the ethnolect encompasses the standard.
[11] For a succinct overview of these three approaches, see Wolfram and Schilling (2016).

Alternative approaches have challenged the unidimensional nature of the attention-to-speech model and the primacy of the vernacular as the ultimate goal of sociolinguistic inquiry. One such approach, the "audience design" model explores intraspeaker variation as a function of a speaker's reaction to their audience, including both ratified and nonratified conversational participants (Bell 1984).[12] Emerging out of a tradition of study known as "accommodation theory" (Giles 1984; Giles et al. 1991), this model presumes that speakers *converge* with their conversational partners and other audience members in order to build solidarity and *diverge* from them in order to create distance.

Finally, a third approach looks at intraspeaker variation, not as a *response* to formality or audience, but rather as a way of *proactively* constructing identity through language (Eckert 2008, 2012; Silverstein 2003). This approach, described by Wolfram and Schilling (2016) as the "speaker design" model, shifts the focus to the speakers themselves and the ways in which speakers use language to index various meanings and to actively construct their individual identities or personas through styleshifting.

In contrast to the traditional "attention-to-speech" models in which variation has been measured primarily along the dimensions of formality and social status, many studies of middle-class AAE have taken a more nuanced approach to intraspeaker variation. For example, in a study of the codeswitching strategies of two middle-class African American women in a northeastern US city, Stanback (1984) observed a considerable amount of individual variation that appeared to be governed by the race and gender of the speaker's conversational partner, as well as "the circumstances under which she learned the code, how proficient she [was] in using the code, her attitude toward the code, and her opportunities to use the code in her everyday life" (Stanback 1984: 192). In a comparison of the styleshifting practices of middle-class AAVE speakers and German-English bilinguals in Houston, Texas, Linnes (1998) observed a broad diglossic relationship between AAVE and Standard English, by which ethnic themes were linked to the vernacular, while more mainstream themes were tied to the standard. In their analysis of interview data from a 65-year-old middle-class African American woman from Seattle, Washington, Scanlon and Wassink (2010) found that both /ay/ monophthongization and *pen/pin* merging showed signs of shift according to interlocutor ethnicity and familiarity, as well as some accommodation to interlocutor speech (cf. Baugh 1983; Rickford and McNair-Knox 1994). And, in her 2014 study in Southeast, Washington, DC, Grieser observed professional class-aligned participants engaging in styleshifting

---

[12] See Rickford and McNair-Knox (1994) for a test of this theory, using AAVE data.

triggered by topics such as race, personal history, and individual stances toward neighborhood gentrification.

Performative Language Practices

As some of above-mentioned studies of intraspeaker variation demonstrate, middle-class African American English has also been explored through the lens of public performance, with a particular focus on the public-speaking styles of some prominent African American public figures. While the social standing of some of these individuals far exceeds traditional measures of middle-class status, the linguistic practices exhibited through their public performances and the linguistic ideologies reflected therein have informed our understanding of the indexical meanings (Eckert 2008, 2012) associated with certain linguistic features and the parameters that govern their use in public settings.

For example, in a study of the televised speech of African American talk-show host Oprah Winfrey, Hay et al. (1999) found that Winfrey used higher rates of /ay/ monophthongization in words with high lexical frequency and when discussing African American referees (usually upcoming guests whom Winfrey referenced on her show). Rahman (2007) also found that /ay/ mono-phthongization was a tool used by some African American narrative comedians to contrast the "down-home common sense and resourcefulness" of African American characters with the "conservativeness [and] naivete" of White middle-class establishment characters (67). Studies such as these speak to the salience of the (ay) variable as a means of indexing racial/ethnic identities (and more specifically African American vs. European American identities) and the characteristics and values associated with these respective groups.

In a study of rhetorical "style switching," Ervin-Tripp (2001) observed the performative practices of civil rights activist Stokely Carmichael and political comedian Dick Gregory, who strategically juxtaposed certain standard and vernacular features in order to accommodate to different audiences and high-light the contrasting ideologies of various social groups (e.g., "rioters versus sophisticated protesters," "colonists versus British") (56). And Johnstone (1996) described how the careful and consistent style of former Texas senator and U.S congresswoman Barbara Jordan compared to the situational versatility of novelist, historian, and jazz singer Sunny Nash in the construction and presentation of their individual personas.

My own entrée into the study of middle-class AAE began with an examin-ation of television and radio personality Tavis Smiley's 2004 "State of the Black Union" (SOBU) symposium, in which a panel of nationally recognized public figures exhibited a variety of linguistic behaviors, ranging from those with almost no vernacular structural usage to those employing a wide array of phonological, grammatical, lexical, and rhetorical features. As the moderator of the event, Smiley used vernacular features to build solidarity with the predominately African American audience assembled before him, while also shifting into more formal styles of speaking in order to appeal to the larger television viewing audience (Weldon 2004).

In an analysis of Smiley's 2008 symposium, Britt (2011a, 2011b) observed the panelists' strategic use of "Black preaching style" to "establish rapport between the speaker and the audience, especially in moments of controversy, or in the moment-by-moment presentation of a specific point of view" (2011a: 229). Black preaching style was also observed by Alim and Smitherman (2012) in their analysis of US President Barack Obama's presentation style, which they argued played a critical role in his election as the country's first African American president. And in an analysis of the styleshifting practices of civil rights activist Reverend Martin Luther King, Jr., Wolfram et al. (2016) described the ways in which King "consistently embodied his Southern-based, African American preacherly stance while fluidly shifting features that indexed performance and formality based on audience, interaction, and intentional purpose" (269).

Attitudes and Perceptions

While there has been considerable discussion in the linguistic literature about attitudes toward AAE and its speakers, only a few studies have focused on the language attitudes of middle-class speakers and even fewer have explored the perceptions of middle-class speakers' *use* of the variety. As discussed at the beginning of this chapter, much of the early linguistic research on AAE perpetuated the perception of middle-class and other upwardly mobile African American speakers as mainstream-oriented "lames," who were removed from, and largely disapproving of, Black vernacular language and culture (see, e.g., Stewart 1975). Indeed, as the now infamous "pound cake" speech[13] delivered by comedian and actor Bill Cosby epitomizes, middle- and upper-class African Americans have been among some of the fiercest critics of the vernacular (see, e.g., Morgan 1994, 2002; Rickford and Rickford 2000).

---

[13] The "pound cake" speech was delivered by Cosby in May of 2004 at a National Association for the Advancement of Colored People (NAACP) awards ceremony in Washington, DC, on the occasion of the fiftieth anniversary of *Brown* v. *Board of Education* – the 1954 US Supreme Court decision ruling against school segregation. The pound cake reference comes from a section of the speech in which Cosby lambasts thieves who risk incarceration for petty crimes such as stealing a piece of pound cake in contrast to those civil rights activists who were jailed in their fight for racial equality and justice.

It's standing on the corner. It can't speak English. It doesn't want to speak English. I can't even talk the way these people talk. "Why you ain't where you is go, ra," I don't know who these people are. And I blamed the kid until I heard the mother talk (laughter). Then I heard the father talk. This is all in the house. You used to talk a certain way on the corner and you got into the house and switched to English. Everybody knows it's important to speak English except these knuckleheads. You can't land a plane with "why you ain't ..." You can't be a doctor with that kind of crap coming out of your mouth. (Cosby 2004)[14]

In a stinging rebuke of Cosby's elitist attitude toward the vernacular, Dyson (2005) suggested that "[p]erhaps there is a deep element of shame that Cosby has not yet overcome in the use of black style and Black English" (77). He also pointed out the hypocrisy of Cosby's blatant rejection of the very language and culture that helped to catapult him to fame, from the vernacular-rich dialogue of *Fat Albert and the Cosby Kids* to the scat-singing improvisations featured in the theme song of *The Cosby Show* (75). (See also Coates 2004). Similar displays of internal conflict have been demonstrated by other prominent African American public figures as well, including poet Maya Angelou, political and religious leader Reverend Jesse Jackson, and talk-show host and entertainment mogul Oprah Winfrey (see, e.g., Lippi-Green 1997, 2012; Rickford and Rickford 2000).[15]

The broader in-group stigma associated with AAVE, however, might be more appropriately viewed through the lens of what Higginbotham (1993) coined "the politics of respectability" – the idea that, in order to achieve success and acceptance in the American mainstream, certain cultural practices should be eschewed in favor of White, middle-class norms and behaviors. According to Higginbotham, this assimilationist perspective grew out of the Black Baptist church women's movement that began at the turn of the twentieth century, led by the formation of the Woman's Convention (WC), an Auxiliary to the National Baptist Convention. The WC brought together Black women from across the country, who were committed to articulating a counternarrative to the depiction of Black people as dirty, lazy, violent, and morally depraved, and of Black women, in particular, as sexually promiscuous and unworthy of respect. Such negative stereotyping was bolstered by scholarly literature promoting Social Darwinist claims of Black inferiority, as well as pop cultural representations of Blacks as violent, immoral, sexual deviants, as depicted in films such as *Birth of a Nation* (1915). Caricatures such as these permeated the American psyche, spreading racist propaganda that promoted

[14] Source: www.rci.rutgers.edu/~schochet/101/Cosby_Speech.htm.
[15] Rickford and Rickford (2000) also explicitly demonstrated Cosby's hypocrisy vis-à-vis the vernacular by citing his use of the vernacular in a 1972 routine, "The Lower Tract," juxtaposed by his ardent critique of the vernacular during this same time period in discussions of language usage in educational contexts (64–65).

myths of White supremacy and Black inferiority and fueling the racial hatred and strict segregationist policies of the Jim Crow era. To contest these narratives, the WC urged working-class Blacks to behave in a "respectable" manner and to conform to purported hegemonic values of cleanliness and temperance in order to gain acceptance in the eyes of White America. In so doing, however, they inadvertently facilitated the internalization of these views among certain members of the African American community itself, creating a lasting fissure between "assimilated" and "unassimilated" Blacks that has had far-reaching effects. As observed by Higginbotham,

> Although white society perceived blacks as an undifferentiated mass and confined them together in segregated neighborhoods, blacks – including those of the working poor – relied upon values and behavior in distinguishing class and status differences among themselves. Indeed, social scientists as well as members of the black community invariably focused on adherence to bourgeois standards of respectability and morality in designating social status. Because of the limited economic options available to all blacks and especially black women, early twentieth century leaders rarely alluded to income or occupation when referring, as they frequently did, to the "better class of Negroes." (Higginbotham 1993: 204–5)

It is, arguably, owing to "respectability politics" that terms such as "country," "ghetto," "hood," and "ratchet" have emerged in juxtaposition to terms like "bougie" (cf. bourgeoisie) and "proper" in the description and assessment of African American dress, temperament, manners, and of course, language.

  Despite the widespread invective against the vernacular, some African American public figures have, in fact, defended and even celebrated AAE, particularly in artistic venues such as poetry, literature, and music (Rickford and Rickford 2000). In a celebration of the beauty and creativity of Black English, James Baldwin wrote:

> Now, if this passion, this skill, this (to quote Toni Morrison) "sheer intelligence," this incredible music, the mighty achievement of having brought a people utterly unknown to, or despised by "history" – to have brought this people to their present, troubled, troubling, and unassailable and unanswerable place – if this absolutely unprecedented journey does not indicate that black English is a language, I am curious to know what definition of language is to be trusted. (Baldwin 1979)[16]

And, in an interview published by Thomas LeClair, Toni Morrison ardently defended the richness, complexity, and cultural significance of Black language practices, exclaiming:

> The worst of all possible things that could happen would be to lose that language. There are certain things I cannot say without recourse to my language. It's terrible to think that a child with five different present tenses comes to school to be faced with books that are

---

[16] Source: www.nytimes.com/books/98/03/29/specials/baldwin-english.html.

less than his own language. And then to be told things about his language, which is him, that are sometimes permanently damaging. He may never know the etymology of Africanisms in his language, not even know that "hip" is a real word or that "the dozens" meant something. This is a really cruel fallout of racism. I know the Standard English. I want to use it to help restore the other language, the lingua franca. (LeClair 1981)[17]

While it is, perhaps, ironic that many prominent African Americans have publicly denounced AAE, even as they have used it to advance their own careers and public personas, this "love-hate" relationship with African American language is in no way unique to public figures. Rather it is a conflict that resonates with African Americans from all walks of life. Borrowing from W.E.B. Du Bois's concept of "double consciousness," Smitherman (2006) described such conflicting attitudes in terms of the concept of "linguistic push-pull" – a term that she coined in the 1970s to describe "Black folk loving, embracing, using Black Talk, while simultaneously rejecting and hatin on it" (6). (See also Smitherman 1977). Nowhere has this linguistic push-pull been more pronounced than in the conflicting attitudes of the African American community, and middle-class African Americans in particular, toward efforts to recognize AAE in educational contexts. In 1979, when a judge in Ann Arbor, Michigan ruled in favor of a group of African American parents from Martin Luther King Junior elementary school, who accused the school of failing to take into account their children's home language in classroom instruction, many middle-class African Americans protested, claiming that such a ruling would encourage segregation and "continue oppression through miseducation by teaching AAE in the schools" (Morgan 1994: 125). However, ten years later, when linguistic debate ensued over claims by William Labov and others that increased linguistic divergence between Black and White speakers resulting from residential segregation was an impediment to the success of African American students in schools (see Stevens 1985; Labov and Harris 1986), many in the African American speech community took exception to these claims as well. Morgan (1994) explained,

Considering the position taken by the middle class on the King case, perhaps the most surprising reaction to the divergence controversy appeared in Kenneth M. Jones's September 1986 article in *EM: Ebony Man*, a middle class publication devoted to African American men. In this article, Jones maintained that many sociolinguists simply did not understand the community's notion of pride or power. He argued that AAE is the language variety of choice throughout the African American community and cites language use in rap and hip-hop music as an example of the expressive character and "African beat" inherent in African American speech styles. (Morgan 1994: 127)

---

[17] Source: https://newrepublic.com/article/95923/the-language-must-not-sweat.

Another decade later, there were similarly mixed reactions expressed by many in the African American community to the Oakland, California school board resolution that recognized "Ebonics" as the primary language of many African American students and endorsed instructional use of the home language as a bridge to teaching Standard English in schools.[18] While the media played a critical role in dispensing misinformation and fueling negative reactions to these and other such efforts (see, e.g., Baugh 2000a; Rickford and Rickford 2000; Morgan 2002), Morgan (1994) suggested that sociolinguists should also be held accountable for failing to "incorporate the language and educational values and beliefs of the African American community within language and education plans" (123).

Of course, conflicting attitudes toward AAE are not limited to the African American community either, but can instead be found in all corners of American society. While it is largely through the "gaze" of White America that Black cultural and linguistic practices have been maligned by the public-at-large (Du Bois 1903), the imitation, appropriation, and commodification of many of these same practices stand in stark contrast to the negative depictions that continue to permeate society. As noted by Rickford and Rickford (2000), "Americans of all types tend to bad-talk soul talk, even though it is the guts of the black music they so relish, and even though this would be a much duller country without it" (74). Alongside nonverbal cultural practices such as high fives, fist bumps, dabs, and twerks, members of the dominant culture regularly adopt African American linguistic practices in order to index identities of "coolness," "toughness," or "street savvy," often with little to no acknowledgment of their African American origins (Cutler 1999; Smitherman 2006). The prevalence of such appropriations in American society is a testament to the fact that the stigma associated with African American language varieties is not really about the language at all, but rather about the speakers who use it. As observed by Rosina Lippi-Green,

The real problem with AAVE is a general unwillingness to accept the speakers of that language and the social choices they have made as viable and functional. Instead we relegate their experiences and capabilities and, most damaging, their potential to spheres which are secondary and out of the public eye. We are ashamed of them and because they are a part of us, we are ashamed of ourselves. (2012: 209; see also Lippi-Green 1997)

While few linguistic studies have examined the complex range of social, emotional, and psychological dynamics that influence the attitudes and perceptions of middle-class African American speakers, two notable exceptions

---

[18] For a documentary depiction of the Oakland Ebonics controversy, see the "E-word," directed and produced by Jonathan Gayles (www.ewordfilm.com).

are the research of Mary Rhodes Hoover (1975, 1978) and Jacqueline Rahman (2008). In Hoover's study, a group of African American parents in East Palo Alto, California were asked about their attitudes toward their children's use of three different levels of Black English, identified as Standard Black English, Vernacular Black English, and Superstandard Black English (cf. "talking Proper").[19] In this study, Hoover found that Standard Black English was accepted by an average of 85 percent of parents in "all domains, channels, and contexts" (1978: 78). However, the parents in her study also accepted Vernacular Black English, depending on the domain, channel, and topic. They found the vernacular to be acceptable for certain types of listening and speaking channels, but not for reading and writing. They accepted its use in the home and in some community contexts, but typically not in schools. And they accepted its use in informal settings, but rarely in formal ones. Vernacular Black English was valued by the parents in Hoover's study for purposes of solidarity and cultural identity. And both standard and vernacular varieties of Black English were valued for purposes of survival and communication. "Talking Proper," on the other hand, was not endorsed by the parents in Hoover's study. Based on these findings, Hoover concluded that:

Parents with high occupational levels – professionals, students, skilled workers – generally control standard Black English and so do not object to their children being exposed to vernacular. The standard level can be learned from them at home. The lower-occupation parents do not have such an advantage, and so depend on the schools to stress the standard level which they generally do not control. (Hoover 1978: 81)

Rahman (2008) looked at the attitudes and perceptions of AAE by middle-class African American students and employees at a "prestigious university in California." Rahman used subjective reaction tests, interviews, and an online survey to test participants' judgments about the linguistic indexing of ethnicity, standardness, and social class, as well as the appropriateness of AAVE, Black Standard English (BSE), and Mainstream Standard English (MSE) in various contexts. Rahman found that dense use of AAVE grammatical and phonological features was strongly correlated with African American ethnicity, nonstandardness, and working-class identity, while heavy use of MSE was strongly correlated with whiteness, standardness, and middle- to upper-middle-class identity. Like Hoover, Rahman found that speakers who exhibited standard grammatical usage and only moderate use of non-overtly stigmatized AAVE phonological features were judged to be standard, African American, and middle class (i.e., BSE speakers). And like Hoover, the

---

[19] Unlike the current study, where "talking Proper" is treated as existing outside the AAE continuum, Hoover (1978) characterized "talking Proper" in terms of "'network' grammar and attempted 'network' phonology" but with an intonation pattern that is "decidedly black" (74). (See also Mitchell-Kernan 1971).

participants in Rahman's study found BSE to be appropriate in all contexts, unlike AAVE and MSE, which were only perceived to be appropriate in certain contexts and for certain sectors of society. Rahman observed, "By meeting the conflicting linguistic demands of establishment institutions and the African American community, BSE is a tool that works to resolve the linguistic push-pull that middle-class African Americans often face" (Rahman 2008: 170).

A related line of research in the area of social psychology corroborates many of the findings reported in these linguistic studies. In an examination of the attitudes and perceptions of middle-class Blacks toward Black English and Standard English, Garner and Rubin (1986) observed a group of southern African American attorneys who regularly shifted between standard and vernacular styles of speaking in order to navigate various personal and professional domains. They reportedly valued the expressiveness of the vernacular in more relaxed settings, while at the same time acknowledging the importance of Standard English as a means of garnering respect in the workplace. Some also described times when more vernacular styles of speaking were useful in conveying "solidarity and humility" in the courtroom, as illustrated by the following anecdote, shared by one of their study participants:

There is a brand of lawyer that my associates and I might jokingly call "Cornbread lawyers." These are the people that say "I'm just an ole country lawyer" and they may be as sophisticated as anybody you want to see. But they're gonna adopt a drawl and adopt the colloquialisms to make themselves human to the jury, to get their point over to those that they're trying to persuade. (Garner and Rubin 1986: 38–39)

Another important observation made by Garner and Rubin was that while their participants had difficulty describing what might constitute "formal Black English," they rejected the idea that Standard English was a "White dialect." Some participants observed that many of the southern Whites with whom they came in contact on a regular basis were not Standard English speakers at all, while many of the Blacks spoke primarily Standard English. Garner and Rubin argued that by separating Standard English from whiteness in this way, these lawyers were able to employ more standard ways of speaking without compromising their sense of racial and cultural attachment. "Since SE [Standard English] is not white English, and is rather an educated person's tool for survival, these professionals have found a way to maintain cultural identity while at the same time communicating credibility in the dominant culture" (Garner and Rubin 1986: 46).

In another study, Koch et al. (2001) reported the results of a matched-guise experiment that tested the perceptions of African American college students to Black English, Standard English, and to "appropriate" and "inappropriate" codeswitching (as defined by social norms) in casual and formal settings. The results pointed to a positive evaluation of both Standard English and "appropriate codeswitching" (ACS) guises over Black English and "inappropriate codeswitching" (ICS). However, Koch et al. did not interpret these results as an outright rejection of Black English, but rather an indication that Black English tends to be viewed negatively when used in situations that require more formal ways of speaking. Codeswitching was, therefore, seen as an important mechanism for achieving mainstream success while still maintaining ties with the African American community.[20] (See also Doss and Gross 1994.) Studies such as these highlight the importance of examining the role and perception of African American English at all points along the standard-vernacular continuum and exploring the many and varied ways in which it is used and evaluated by middle-class speakers as a symbol of racial pride, solidarity, and consciousness.

The Present Study

In the chapters to follow, I use a variety of methodological approaches to pursue several lines of inquiry inspired by these pioneering studies and to raise new questions about the current status of middle-class AAE and its trajectory vis-à-vis other varieties of American English. In Chapter 3, I present an updated analysis of my 2004 study of Tavis Smiley's "State of the Black Union" symposium, in which I explore the performative use of AAE as a marker of racial and ethnic identity and consider the implications of such stylized uses for traditional definitions of "lame" linguistic behavior (cf. Labov 1972a). I also consider the implications of such performances for our understanding of intraspeaker variation. I continue this focus on intraspeaker variation in Chapter 4, with a self-study, in which I provide an autoethnographic account of the use of AAE in the "stylistic construction of a self" (Eckert 2001: 123) and reflect on some of the tensions and expectations that inform my own identity performance in everyday interactions as a middle-

---

[20] Some scholars, however, have taken exception to the argument that codeswitching represents the "happy medium" between accommodating to the demands of mainstream America and satisfying the expectations of the African American community, since it places all of the burden for change on members of the nondominant culture. Keith Gilyard writes, "I have often chosen to switch, rather than fight, but the routine hasn't always implied any emotional ease" (1991: 31). An alternative to codeswitching that is gaining some currency in educational settings, and particularly in the field of Rhetoric and Composition, is the concept of "codemeshing," which Young (2009) describes as "the blending and concurrent use of American English dialects" (51). Codemeshing allows students to strategically incorporate their home varieties into their academic writing rather than switching them off when they enter the classroom. (See also Canagarajah 2006; Young and Martinez 2011). Codemeshing has also been demonstrated in the writing styles of linguists Geneva Smitherman and Samy Alim (see, e.g., Smitherman 1977; Alim and Smitherman 2012).

class speaker of AAE. I also examine the quantitative distribution of several salient AAE features within my own stylistic repertoire and discuss how such distributions inform our assumptions about middle-class AAE as well as our understanding of intraspeaker variation.

In Chapter 5, I use survey methodology to explore the use and interpretation of camouflaged features (identified by Labov [1998] as a central element of the AA component of AAVE) and consider how the displayed patterns contribute to our understanding of the relative trajectories of African American and European American varieties today, particularly among speakers positioned along the middle of the socioeconomic continuum. Chapter 6 makes use of social psychological techniques that explore the attitudes and perceptions of college students regarding the concept of "sounding Black" and how various circulating labels both reflect and inform such perceptions. Finally, in Chapter 7, I consider the future of middle-class AAE and future directions of sociolinguistic research on this topic, both in light of the findings presented in this book, and in the context of the current social, racial, economic, and political climate in the United States.

3   "Talking Black" as Public Performance

Not So Lame

This is all the stuff that we sent to the panelists to prepare them for this conversation today, 'cause it's gon be rich up in here. Yeah. That's a– that's a Black thing, ain't it? You always up in something. (Audience responds) Up in the church, up in the barbershop, up in the beauty salon. Off up in college. Up in folk business. Oops! You always up in something. I'm glad y'all up in here today. How 'bout you?

—Tavis Smiley (2004)
"The State of the Black Union"

Introduction

. . . Sojourner Truth
Frederick Douglass
Booker T. Washington
Fannie Lou Hamer
Malcolm X
Martin Luther King, Jr.
Barbara Jordan
Shirley Chisholm
Angela Davis
Barack Obama . . .

The linguistic agility and oratorical talents of African American public figures have long been celebrated and imitated by the public-at-large. And yet, such figures have been largely excluded from prevailing sociolinguistic definitions of the African American speech community. Furthermore, the celebration of Black oratorical talent often stands in stark contrast to the prevailing public stigma associated with vernacular language usage. As discussed in Chapter 2, a growing number of linguistic studies have begun to explore the performative styles of African American celebrities, political activists, religious leaders, and scholars, many of whom draw extensively on the African American rhetorical tradition in order to signal solidarity with the African American community (see, e.g., Johnstone 1996; Hay et al. 1999; Ervin-Tripp 2001; Weldon 2004; Rahman 2007; Kendall and Wolfram 2009; Britt 2011a, 2011b; Alim and

46

Smitherman 2012; Wolfram et al. 2016). However, there has been little acknowledgment of the paradoxical tension that exists between the widespread stigma of African American Vernacular English (AAVE) and the widespread appeal of the African American rhetorical tradition. Understanding more about the ways in which many prominent African American public figures incorporate vernacular features into their public presentations, as well as the extent to which certain distinctive aspects of the African American repertoire both draw upon and extend beyond the vernacular can help to elucidate this paradox. In this chapter, I interrogate traditional sociolinguistic assumptions about "lame" linguistic behavior, by examining the role of African American English (AAE) as a public-speaking mechanism used by a panel of prominent African American public figures in Tavis Smiley's 2004 "State of the Black Union" (SOBU) symposium.

Two key considerations in this investigation are (1) what kinds of AAE features get employed in public performances such as this and (2) what role *awareness*, *salience*, and *control* play in the selection and use of such features.[1] In his seminal research on the social stratification of linguistic variables in New York City, William Labov (1972c) identified three categories of sociolinguistic features, distinguished according to the varying levels of speaker awareness and commentary that they invoke. *Indicators* are features that are socially and/or regionally stratified, but which fall *below* the level of conscious awareness, such that individual speakers fail to styleshift in ways that would suggest any conscious evaluation of their meaning or significance. *Markers* are stable sociolinguistic variables that are socially and/or regionally stratified, and also subject to individual styleshifts along a formality continuum. And *stereotypes* are features for which speakers exhibit such a heightened awareness that the features become the subject of overt social commentary, and, over time, can become "increasingly divorced from the forms which are actually used in speech" (Labov 1972c: 180). Subsequent approaches to style, while challenging the unidimensional nature of the formality continuum itself, have drawn on various aspects of this distinction. For example, in Bell's (1984) "audience design" model, it is noted that the intraspeaker (i.e., stylistic) variation that *markers* are subject to "derives from and echoes" the interspeaker (i.e., social) variation of *indicators* (151). And Silverstein's (2003) "indexicality" model describes *indicators* in terms of a *first-order index*, which indicates membership in a group, and *markers* as a *second-order index* that individual speakers can adopt in order to associate themselves with various aspects of a given group. (See also Eckert 2008) According to Preston (1996), "folk linguistic" (i.e., nonspecialist) accounts of

---

[1] For a book-length treatment on awareness, salience, and control, see Babel (2016).

language vary according to the *availability* of the features, the *accuracy* with which they are described, the level of linguistic *detail* that speakers are able to provide about them, and the level of *control* that speakers have in imitating or performing them. The performative styles of the SOBU participants thus provide an opportunity to observe how speakers at higher levels of the socio-economic spectrum negotiate these and other factors as they draw upon the African American repertoire in the construction and presentation of their public personas.

This event also provides an opportunity to reflect upon the paradox described at the start of this chapter, by considering how vernacular features get taken up in more formal contexts. Typically, standard features, which tend to be associated with higher-status groups and/or more formal contexts, are considered socially *prestigious*, while vernacular features, which tend to be associated with lower-status groups and/or more informal contexts, are considered socially *stigmatized*. As observed by Wolfram and Schilling (2016), the *overt prestige* (Labov 1966) associated with standard features derives from a "consensus-based model of social class, in which everyone in all social status groups orients toward the norms of higher status groups, including linguistic norms" (175). There is, however, another type of prestige, known as *covert prestige* (Labov 1966), that gets associated with peer group membership and vernacular feature usage, and often stands in opposition to these mainstream norms and expectations. The tension between these opposing norms can become particularly pronounced for middle-class African Americans who experience the linguistic "push-pull" (Smitherman 1977) of overt prestige norms by virtue of their social class standing, and covert prestige norms by virtue of their racial/ethnic identification and affiliation. In this chapter, I consider how the SOBU participants navigate these potentially conflicting norms in the construction of both race-based and class-based identities and what role vernacular features and other AAE features play in such public performances.

Finally, I also consider the ways in which the stylized performances of the SOBU participants inform our understanding of intraspeaker variation. As described in Chapter 2, much of the early research on intraspeaker variation in AAE was motivated by a debate over the nature of the variation between standard and vernacular forms and the question of whether such variation represents dialect mixture or inherent variability within a single system. While the model that I have adopted for the purposes of this study privileges a one-system approach, by which speakers are viewed as shifting along a standard-vernacular continuum, it does not preclude consideration of the nature of the variation observed. For example, in a study of the "rhetorical switching" of civil rights figures Stokely Carmichael and Dick Gregory, Ervin-Tripp (2001) observed the strategic use of both standard and vernacular features to index a wide range of complex ideological contrasts in performative contexts. She explained, "The functions of dialect feature shifts are probably similar to those found in bilingual code-switches – change of domain or stance, emphasis, or emotion, for example. Functions identified in the many code-switching studies have included getting attention, persuasion, asides, elaboration, personalization, dialogue in a narrative, and marking identity" (Ervin-Tripp 2001: 49). Similarly, in this study, I will consider the various functions performed by the SOBU participants in their use of the African American repertoire and consider what such uses suggest about the nature of intraspeaker variation at higher levels of the socioeconomic spectrum.

The State of the Black Union

The "State of the Black Union" symposium was an annual event organized by radio and television talk show host and political activist Tavis Smiley, who assembled panels of nationally recognized public figures for the purpose of addressing the social, political, and economic state of affairs in Black America. This event, which took place each February from 2000 to 2009, was aired live on CSPAN (a television network dedicated to national politics and public affairs) and drew an average of 7,000 to 10,000 participants each year.[2] The data presented in this chapter were drawn from the 2004 symposium on *Strengthening the Black Family*, which was held at New Birth Baptist Church in Miami, Florida. While the full symposium ran a little over eight hours and consisted of two separate panels of participants, the findings reported here come from the first panel, which was approximately four and a half hours long.[3] The participants (listed in Table 3.1) included six female panelists, six male panelists, and Tavis Smiley, who was the lead moderator.[4]

Introduced by Tavis Smiley as "the best and brightest that Black America has to offer," the panelists assembled for this event represented a highly accomplished group of individuals, including lawyers, doctors, educators,

---

[2] Source: www.huffingtonpost.com/2010/01/06/tavis-smiley-ends-black-state-of-the-union_n_ 412825.html.

[3] The symposium began with opening remarks by Tavis Smiley and the introduction of the panelists. After a few preliminary presentations, the first panel started with a round of unscripted monologues by each of the participants, moderated by Tavis Smiley. This round was followed by a question and answer session, during which the moderators read questions from the audience. Each panelist then gave a brief closing monologue.

[4] Five participants from the first panel were excluded from the study because their participation differed in significant ways from those of the other participants. Excluded from this study were Evangelist Joyce Smiley, who only gave the opening and closing prayers; Bishop Victor T. Curry, who primarily read from a prepared text; Jamaican-born Dr. Orlando Patterson, who was not a native speaker of American English; and radio personalities Rodney Baltimore and Tom Joyner, who assisted as panel moderators, but mostly read biographies and/or questions submitted from the audience.

Table 3.1 *2004 SOBU Panel 1 participants by occupation, year/place of birth*[5]

	Occupation (in Feb. 2004)	Year of Birth	Place of Birth
Female Participants			
MW = Myrlie Evers-Williams	Chair, NAACP, Board of Directors	1933	Vicksburg, Mississippi
MC = Marva Collins	President, Collins Math Institute; Founder, Westside Preparatory School	1936	Monroeville, Alabama
JH = Julia Hare	Author; Motivational Speaker; National Executive Director, The Black Think Tank	1939	Tulsa, Oklahoma
ST = Susan Taylor	Editor-in-Chief, *Essence* Magazine	1946	Harlem, New York
VM = Vashti M. McKenzie	Bishop, African Methodist Episcopal Church	1947	Baltimore, Maryland
SL = Sheila Jackson-Lee	US Representative, D-Texas	1950	Queens, New York
Male Participants			
DS = David Satcher	MD, Kaiser Foundation Fellow; Former US Surgeon General	1941	Anniston, Alabama
NA = Na'im Akbar	Professor of Psychology, Florida State University	1944	Tallahassee, Florida
JJ = Jeffery Johnson	President and CEO of the National Partnership for Community Leadership	1952[*]	Maryland[*]
CW = Cornel West	Professor of African American Studies, Princeton University	1953	Tulsa, Oklahoma (raised in Sacramento, California)
GM = Greg Mathis	Judge, Wayne County, Michigan, 36th District Court; Star, The *Judge Mathis Show*	1960	Detroit, Michigan
JAH = Jordan A. Harris	President, Youth Action; Sophomore, Millersville University	1984[*]	Philadelphia, Pennsylvania
Lead Moderator			
TS = Tavis Smiley	Talk Show Host, NPR, PBS, The *Tavis Smiley Show*	1964	Gulfport, Mississippi (raised in Bunker Hill, Indiana)

Note: * Dates and places marked by an asterisk represent unconfirmed biographical information, gleaned from secondary sources.

[5] The biographical information reported here comes from Wikipedia (https://en.wikipedia.org/wiki/Main_Page) and other such internet sources and, thus, cannot be deemed 100 percent accurate. The information for Jeffrey Johnson and Jordan A. Harris that is marked by an asterisk in Table 3.1 could not be verified online.

politicians, journalists, radio and television personalities, and members of the clergy. With the exception of Jordan A. Harris, who was a sophomore at Millersville University at the time of the symposium, all of the participants had completed their college education, and many had completed advanced and/or terminal degrees.[6] Also with the exception of Harris, who was approximately twenty years old at the time of the symposium, all of the participants were middle-aged or older. The female participants ranged in age from fifty-four to seventy-one, and the male participants were between the ages of forty and sixty-three. And while the participants represented a variety of regional backgrounds, most hailed from parts of the East Coast, the South, or the Midwest.

Based on traditional socioeconomic indicators, as described in Chapter 1, these participants all met or exceeded the minimum standards for middle-class status. One might even apply Eugene Robinson's "transcendent elites" nomenclature to distinguish such prominent public figures, who have enjoyed exceptional levels of recognition and accomplishment, from the "mainstream middle-class majority" (2010: 5) (cf. Grieser 2014). More importantly, as high-profile, college-educated adults, working in professional fields, all of these participants would have satisfied Labov's (1972a) criteria for linguistic "lames," though the demographic information alone tells little of their individual ideologies, family histories, and life experiences.

Given the nature of this event – a televised public forum addressing topics like education, health, politics, and the economy – one might have expected the participants to make consistent use of a relatively formal style of speaking. However, this event (like others of its kind) yielded a range of linguistic behaviors, reflecting both intragroup and intraspeaker variation along the standard-vernacular continuum. One factor that likely contributed to this variation was the "dual audience" that the participants were addressing – the predominately Black audience assembled in the church itself and the CSPAN television viewing audience, which potentially included viewers from a variety of racial/ethnic backgrounds. During the symposium, Tavis Smiley commented on this imagined dual audience, describing the event as "a gathering of us, being watched by them." And he continued to draw on this "us/them" dichotomy at various times over the course of the event, as in this

---

[6] Harris completed his BA in 2006 and a Master of Education degree in 2008. At the time that this chapter was being written, he was reportedly enrolled in a Doctoral program in Educational Leadership at Neumann University. Harris worked as a teacher in the Philadelphia public schools for several years and was elected to the Pennsylvania House of Representatives in 2013, representing the 186th legislative district. His accomplishments since the 2004 symposium are thus on par with those of the other panelists assembled, in spite of the age difference at the time of the event. (Sources: http://en.wikipedia.org/wiki/Jordan_A._Harris and www.legis.state.pa.us/cfdocs/legis/home/member_information/house_bio.cfm?id=1633).

metalinguistic observation, shown in Excerpt 3.1, about his co-moderator Tom Joyner's nickname "the fly jock":[7]

Excerpt 3.1

There're a lot of our White brothers and sisters watching right now around the country saying, "Who is the fly jock? And what is a fly jock?" I'll explain that in just a second [TS].

The "Black family" narrative was, in fact, a theme woven throughout the program, featured in the title of the symposium itself, and invoked at the outset, as Smiley provided an overview of the topics to be addressed (Excerpt 3.2):

Excerpt 3.2

And today we want to talk about the Black family, the state of the Black union, strengthening the Black family, preserving the African American imprint on America [TS].

The setting itself also likely played a role in the variation observed. While large African American public gatherings such as this one often blur the lines between the sacred and the secular (Knowles-Borishade 1991), the "mega-church"[8] where this event was held invited, and perhaps even obliged, the participants to engage in a certain amount of "talkin and testifyin." As observed by Geneva Smitherman, "To speak of the "traditional" black church is to speak of holy-rolling, bench-walking, spirit-getting, tongue-speaking, vision-receiving, intuitive-directing, Amen saying, sing-song preaching, holy dancing, and God-sending church" (Smitherman 1977: 90). Consistent with

---

[7] Joyner reportedly got this nickname at a time when he was hosting a morning radio show in Dallas, Texas and then flying to Chicago, Illinois to do an afternoon show (source: www.star-telegram.com/entertainment/music/article179285546.html).

[8] Consistent with the Hartford Institute for Religion Research, the term "megachurch" is used here to refer to a large Protestant congregation that averages 2,000 or more attendees in weekly worship services. Other distinctive characteristics of megachurches include a charismatic senior minister, an active seven-days-a-week congregational community, various outreach ministries, an innovative worship format, and a complex organizational structure (http://hirr.hartsem.edu/megachurch/megachurches.html). According to a 2003 article in the *Orlando Sentinel*, New Birth Baptist Church claimed 15,000 members in 2002, "making it the largest Black church in Florida and one of the 10 largest congregations in the state." In addition to its African American membership, the congregation reportedly included "Haitians, Jamaicans, Bahamians, Nigerians and South Africans, as well as a sprinkling of whites and Hispanics" (http://articles.orlandosentinel.com/2003-12-15/news/0312150038_1_megachurch-congregations-birth-baptist-church).

these observations, several participants drew heavily on the language of the Black church in their presentations (cf. Britt 2011a, 2011b). Smiley, in fact, acknowledged the significance of the church setting and its connection to the Black family in his introductory remarks (Excerpt 3.3).

Excerpt 3.3

Talking now about the Black church. It is without question one of the most abiding institutions in our community. And so we talked at last year's heated symposium, you'll recall, a very– last year's honest symposium about the role and responsibility of the African American church. And so there is no institution that has done more for us than the Black church. Always on the vanguard, on the cutting edge of the issues that matter to Black America. Always the conscience of our community, indeed, in many ways, the conscience of this country. But there would not be a Black church if there were no Black family. So in this important election year again, we decided that this year was the best time to have a critical conversation in the community about the importance of Black family [TS].

Thus, in spite of the formality of the event, factors such the dual audience, the Black family theme, the church setting, and the expectation that the panelists assembled would not only be skilled orators, but orators skilled in the practice of African American rhetorical style and presentation provided an ideal opportunity for observing the ways in which African American public figures draw on the resources of the African American repertoire in the construction and negotiation of their public personas. Smiley set the stage for this oratorical display by regularly drawing on the vernacular himself, as illustrated by the bolded text in Excerpt 3.4.[9]

Excerpt 3.4

*Now, y'all know me from radio and television. I could pontificate ad nauseum, but **I got some talkuhs up in here wit me today**. So I want– I wanna move as expeditiously as I can to give them all the time that they need here this morning to make their case, to address the issues that are important to America, to Black America in particular, and give you a chance at the end of this first panel to engage in some Q & A, some dialogue, with the most brilliant minds in Black America [TS].*

---

[9] Here and elsewhere, an effort is made to highlight relevant nonstandard or otherwise nonmainstream pronunciations via alternative spellings. When more specificity is required, phonetic symbols are used instead. While I am aware that alternative spellings have the potential to exoticize the text in ways that can bias reader perceptions, a full reliance on phonetic transcription would also be potentially alienating and heavy-handed, given the number of excerpts that are presented.

In the sections to follow, I present an inventory of the SOBU participants' vernacular feature usage and consider the quantitative distributions of a few select phonological and grammatical features in order to determine how the use of these features compares to that typically observed in working-class speech communities, which have, thus far, served as the benchmark for assessments of vernacularity in sociolinguistic research.[10] I also consider how the participants' use of lexical, rhetorical, and discourse features characteristic of the African American rhetorical tradition (Smitherman 1977, 1994, 2000) help to extend definitions of African American English and the African American speech community beyond the vernacular.[11] Finally, I discuss the kinds of variation exhibited by the participants and consider the implications of such patterns for our understanding of intraspeaker variation along the standard-vernacular continuum and the role of awareness, salience, and control, as well as prestige and stigma in the actualization of these practices.

Taking Inventory on Vernacular Feature Usage

Grammatical Features

Table 3.2 provides an inventory of the vernacular grammatical features that were used by the SOBU participants. As the checklist shows, vernacular grammatical features were not widely distributed among the participants. The male participants used a wider range of features, on average, than the female participants, with the widest range of features being used by moderator Tavis Smiley – an observation that I will return to later in this chapter.

Nouns/Pronouns Among the nominal/pronominal features, there were two instances of demonstrative *them*, shown in sentences 1 and 2, and five instances of existential *it*, illustrated by sentences 3 and 4.

---

[10] For reviews of some of the phonological and grammatical features that have been identified as characteristic of AAVE, see Fasold and Wolfram (1970), Labov (1972a), Baugh (1983), Mufwene et al. (1998), Rickford (1999b), and Green (2002).

[11] While a full consideration of the participants' AAE usage should also include an examination of prosodic feature usage, given the broad definition presented in Chapter 1, such an analysis goes beyond the scope of this chapter. Some aspects of AAE prosody are discussed in Chapters 5 and 6.

Table 3.2 AAVE grammatical feature inventory

Features	Female Panelists						Male Panelists						Mod.	PT
	MW	ST	VM	JH	SL	MC	NA	DS	CW	JJ	GM	JAH	TS	
Nouns/Pronouns														
Plural –s absence								√					√	2
Associative plural						√							√	2
Demonstrative *them*											√		√	2
Null expletive											√		√	2
Existential *it*												√	√	2
Possessive –s absence										√		√	√	3
Negation														
Negative inversion													√	1
Ain't											√	√	√	3
Multiple negation			√								√	√	√	4
Verbal Marking														
Aspectual *done*											√		√	2
Do-support absence													√	1
Past as past participle												√	√	2
Subj-verb non-agreement					√	√				√	√	√	√	6
Is/are absence		√		√	√	√			√		√	√	√	8
Have/has absence			√	√		√		√	√	√	√	√	√	9
FT	0	1	2	2	2	4	0	2	2	3	8	8	15	

Notes: PT = Total number of participants using a given feature; FT = Total number of features used by a given individual.

Demonstrative *them* (N = 2)[12]
1. *You ain't getting no damn respect until you take care of **them** kids that you're producing. [GM]*
2. *When y'all see John Kerry, I want you to ask him **them** questions, okay? [TS]*

Existential *it* (N = 5)
3. *I began to realize **it** was nothing wrong with working hard. [JAH]*
4. *And I wouldn't be mad at you, except for **it's** a whole lot of y'all up in here. So please reach in your bags. You'll find an index card on which you can write your question. [TS]*

As features that AAVE shares with other varieties of American English, the use of these features in the data is not particularly marked in terms of race/ethnicity.

By contrast, the associative plural and null expletive constructions, shown in sentences 5–10, are less common in White varieties, especially those spoken outside the South, but similar to constructions found in some Caribbean English Creoles (Mufwene 1998; Rickford 1999b; Nicolis 2008). As such, they represent more saliently marked constructions from the perspective of race/ethnicity.

Associative plural (N = 3)
5. *But Yale, Princeton **and those** are privileged to have these people. [MC]*
6. *Right now, I don't think we see in our communities that entertainers **and those** are – are becoming the superstars in our community. [MC]*
7. *We'll even come stand next to you so your mama **'nem** can see you on TV. [TS]*

Null expletive (N = 3)
8. *Ø ain't no love coming until you show some love to your family, until you show some love to the children that you bear. [GM]*[13]
9. *Well, first of all, Ø seem like Jeff was a little hesitant to lay the blame where it lies. [GM]*

---

[12] The data were transcribed and coded using an audio recording of the symposium. The original video recording was consulted, when needed, for extra-linguistic input. Multiple transcribers and coders were used to improve inter-rater reliability. Here and in the examples to follow, the numbers in parentheses beside each label indicate the feature frequencies (i.e., the number of times that a given feature is used). And the initials in square brackets at the end of each sentence indicate who produced the given utterance. As noted earlier, alternative spellings are used to highlight marked phonological features, where relevant. Otherwise, all excerpts are presented using standard orthography.

[13] While sentences 8 and 10 are listed as null expletives, they could also be interpreted as instances of negative inversion (cf. *No love ain't coming...*). (See Labov 1972a; Sells et al. 1996; Martin and Wolfram 1998 for more on the ambiguity of these types of constructions.) Sentence 9 is the only unambiguous use of a null expletive observed in these data.

10. *Mathis said, "Ø ain't no love coming." Susan said, "where is the love." Somebody else said, "what love got to do with it." Are we getting micro enough for you yet? [TS]*

The salience of these features in the SOBU data, however, is tempered not only by their low frequency, but also by how the constructions are used by the participants. For example, Marva Collins's use of *and those* rather than the more typical associative plural construction *and them* in examples 5 and 6 creates a kind of camouflage effect, by which the construction comes to resemble the type of syntactic ellipsis that one might encounter in more mainstream varieties (cf. *Yale, Princeton, and those (folks)*). And Smiley's use of the expression *mama 'nem* in example 7 is couched in a performative styleshift designed to make the audience laugh and mitigate the face-threatening act of asking them to submit their questions in writing for the moderators to read. Smiley also uses the null expletive performatively in example 10 to parrot Greg Mathis's earlier use of the construction. Such stylized uses of these constructions emphasize their intentionality and functionality, thus mitigating their vernacular salience to some extent.

Sentences 11–14 are illustrative of plural –*s* absence in the SOBU data.

Plural –*s* absence (N = 3; *folk* N = 62)

11. *This is the fifth anniversary, the fifth year that we have done these annual Black think* **tank**_, *these conversations in the community, these, uh, these symposiums, to talk about issues that we are grappling with every day in Black America. [TS]*

12. *Let me– let me just say, and I'm not gon cast* **aspersion**_ *on nobody, but I know you will feel me on this. [TS]*

13. *Tommy Thompson, the Secretary of Health and Human Services, responded to all of these* **criticism**_ *[DS]*

14. *We've got two or three other* **folk**_ *we got to hear from here. Then we'll get this round robin thing going. But, two or three other* **folk**_ *who have not spoken, who have a great deal to say. [TS]*

The word *folk(s)* was separated out from the overall count for plural –*s* absence because of its frequency in the data (N = 71), as well as its frequency as an unmarked noun 87.3% of the time (N = 62/71). Furthermore, Tavis Smiley produced fifty-six of the sixty-two instances of unmarked *folk*, thus accounting for the majority of these instances. Apart from *folk*, there were only three other instances of plural –*s* absence, illustrated by sentences 11–13 above, which represented 0.23% frequency (N = 3/1,289) in the overall data.

Possessive –*s* absence was also relatively rare in the SOBU data, occurring with 7.4% frequency (N = 4/54), as illustrated by sentences 15–18.

Possessive –s absence (N = 4)

15. *Up in the church, up in the barbershop, up in the beauty salon. Off up in college. Up in **folk_** business. Oops! You always up in something. [TS]*
16. *Please stop going on Maury, finding your **baby_** daddy. [JAH]*
17. *The **baby_** mama's mamas was telling him that, "You could do bad by yourself." [JJ]*
18. *And the reality is is that baby's **mama_** mama, if she got some contacts, and she thinks that this guy needs a job, let's use those contacts to get him a job. . . [JJ]*

The examples of possessive –s absence also occurred in fixed colloquial expressions (i.e., *folk* and *baby mama/baby daddy*) and, as such, did not seem indicative of productive processes of –s deletion.[14]

In comparison to rates typically observed in working-class speech communities, the low rates of –s absence illustrated here would, indeed, be considered "lame" by traditional measures. Wolfram (1969) reported an average of 5.8% plural –s absence and 26.8% possessive –s absence among Lower Working Class speakers in his Detroit study (141, 143). And Baugh (1983) reported probability ratings of 0.173 for plural –s absence and 0.611 for possessive –s absence in his study of Black Street Speech in Los Angeles and other urban areas across the USA. (95). The SOBU figures are comparable to those reported by Labov et al. (1968) for his NYC "lames," who produced eight tokens of plural –s absence, compared to the forty tokens produced by the Thunderbird (or T-bird) vernacular peer group members (163). They are also comparable to the frequencies reported in Wolfram (1969) for Upper Middle Class speakers in Detroit, who produced an average of 0.5% plural –s absence and 0.0% possessive –s absence.

Negation Sentence 19, produced by Smiley, was the only instance of negative inversion observed in the SOBU data.[15]

Negative inversion (1)

19. *But **ain't nobody** put no gun to these Black men's heads, and said, "Don't come." Well, maybe some of y'all have. I ain't gon ask for a show of hands. [TS]*

---

[14] Note in Example 17, though not in Example 18, that Jeffrey Johnson attached a possessive –s to the end of "baby mama," even though "baby" itself was not marked for possession, thus lending support to the argument that "baby mama" can behave like a fixed lexical expression.

[15] Like sentences 8 and 10, there is also the possibility that sentence 19 could be interpreted as a null expletive construction (cf. *[There] ain't nobody [who] put no gun to these Black men's heads. . .*). If this sentence were a null expletive, however, it would likely have been followed by an existential-type construction such as *Well, maybe there is.* Instead, the sentence that follows, *Well, maybe some of y'all have*, seems to support the interpretation of this construction as an inverted auxiliary.

The other two vernacular negation structures – *ain't* and multiple negation – were more frequent at N = 45 and N = 17, respectively.

Ain't (45)

20. *And you laugh, but when you have a young lady that has to go on the show three or four times and test eight, to nine, to ten guys to find out who her baby's father is, that **ain't** cute. [JAH]*
21. *You **ain't** getting no damn respect until you take care of them kids that you're producing. [GM]*
22. *I'm tripping 'cause we **ain't** even started yet. [TS]*

Multiple negation (17)

23. *A church is a place where, like Bishop Curry, a place where, now, I can learn how to manage my finances. I can live debt free. I can owe **no** man **nothing** but love. [VM]*
24. *You **don't** deserve **no** respect. [GM]*
25. *But trust me, if your knee break, if your hip break, you **don't** have **nothing** to fall back on but your mind. [JAH]*
26. *Let me, let me just say, and I'm **not** gon cast aspersion on **nobody**, but I know you will feel me on this. [TS]*

The disproportionate number of *ain't* tokens in the data, compared to other vernacular grammatical features, seems to reflect its status as an iconic marker of vernacular speech (cf. Labov's 1972c *stereotypes*). Similar to the stylized uses of the *associative plural* and *null expletive* constructions discussed above, *ain't* is used by Smiley a total of thirty-eight times, to perform a variety of functions in his role as moderator. In the excerpts below, for example, Smiley uses *ain't*, in conjunction with other vernacular features, to banter with the audience (Excerpt 3.5):

Excerpt 3.5

*There is – there are instructions once you leave the room here, for those who are going to stay, and I know most of you are, 'cause y'all **ain't** giving up these seats, are you? I feel sorry for the folk outside trying to get in, 'cause y'all **ain't** tryina leave. [TS]*

---

to mitigate face-threatening acts (Excerpt 3.6):

Excerpt 3.6

*We are in a sanctuary. So you know that means no eating, no drinking, no smoking. I know I **ain't** got to tell you that. [TS]*

---

to issue thinly veiled criticisms (also known as "throwin' shade") (Excerpt 3.7):

Excerpt 3.7

*Let me– let me just say, and I'm not gon cast aspersion on nobody, but I know you will feel me on this. But there're a whole lot of other networks that ought to be carrying this that **ain't**. I'm gon leave that alone. I'm gon leave that alone up in here this morning. [TS]*

---

and to directly challenge the claims of others (Excerpt 3.8):

Excerpt 3.8

*I hear you talking 'bout psychology. But don't tell me – I know you **ain't** tryina tell me that you don't believe that there has been something that's gone wrong with the Black family as we have known it. [TS]*

Despite its frequency, the only instances of *ain't* observed in these data were those that equated to *be + not* (n = 27) and *have + not* (n = 18)[16] – uses that are also found in other vernacular varieties of English. The use of *ain't* to mean *didn't* (e.g., *I ain't see you there* "I didn't see you there"), which has been identified as a more ethnically marked construction (see, e.g., Fasold and Wolfram 1970; Wolfram 1973; Rickford 1977; Feagin 1979; Weldon 1994) was not used by any of the SOBU participants in this forum.

   Verbal Marking Among the verbal constructions, there were four instances of aspectual *done*, illustrated by sentences 27–29.

Aspectual *done* (4)
27. *We **done** closed the candy store. [TS]*
28. *You **done** started something, Judge Mathis. [TS]*
29. *When I go back in the 'hood, lotta brothers say, "Oh judge, ain't– we ain't went nowhere. You **done** came up. You **done** done something for yourself. But we ain't got no opportunities." [GM]*

   In 27, Smiley uses *done* to allude to Bishop Vashti McKenzie's earlier suggestion that women withhold sex (i.e., the candy store) until marriage – an

---

[16] The *ain't = have + not* count also includes all instances of *ain't _got(ta)*, although it is acknowledged that such instances could conceivably also be interpreted as the equivalent of *do + not*, given the ambiguity of *got* in AAVE as both a participle and a main verb (see Berdan 1977; Weldon 1994). However, there were no overt instances of *don't _got(ta)* in the SOBU data that would support this latter interpretation.

example that Smiley uses to demonstrate how "real" (i.e., unfiltered) the discussion has become. In 28, Smiley observes how Judge Greg Mathis's directive to Black men to "man up" has been taken up as a refrain by so many members of the panel that the audience is able to produce it readily in a call-response exchange. And in 29, Mathis's use of *done* is voiced from the perspective of imagined speakers who reportedly regularly contrast his success with their own lack of opportunity.[17] Such uses of *done* appear to mark a resultative state, similar (though not identical) to present perfect *have* in Mainstream Standard English (MSE) (cf. Dayton 1996; Labov 1998; Winford 1998; Green 2002), thus representing a less ethnically marked use of this particular vernacular construction. It is worth noting, however, that in addition to the aspectual function that it serves, *done*, in these examples, seems to bolster a modal context that in the case of Smiley's utterances equates to something akin to amused bewilderment and in the case of Mathis's comment communicates respect or reverence for an accomplishment. The salience of these meanings gets considerably diminished, perhaps even lost, if *done* is replaced by *have*.

Also observed among the SOBU participants were the use of past forms in past participle contexts (sentences 30–32) and *do*-support absence (sentences 33–35).

Past as past participle (6)
30. *So what we have done is we've **came** together... [JAH]*
31. *We ain't **forgot** y'all. We have not **forgot** what happened. [TS]*
32. *I keep saying he is my abiding friend, and I say that because there've been times that his job has been on the line for stuff that I said on his show, and he ain't **gave** me a pink slip yet. [TS]*

***Do*-support absence (3)**
33. *Susan Taylor, Ø you want some of this? [TS]*
34. *Marva Collins, Ø you want some of this? [TS]*
35. *What Ø they tell you to do? [TS]*

Given the instability of the perfect in contemporary American English, the use of past forms in past participle contexts occurs in many nonstandard varieties of English and occasionally in the speech of Mainstream Standard English (MSE) speakers as well. Similarly, instances of *do*-support absence such as those shown in 33 and 34, where question intonation does the work of the deleted auxiliary, are found in many varieties of American English, including

---

[17] The examples by Mathis were included in the overall *done* count in spite of the fact that they occurred in the context of Mathis "voicing" imagined speakers. Here and elsewhere, I include such constructions because they demonstrate the speaker's ability to produce the given features in ways that are both grammatically and contextually appropriate, thus demonstrating familiarity with the rules of usage.

MSE. As such, these grammatical constructions are not particularly marked. The absence of *do*-support in embedded clauses, as shown in example 35, is more marked from the perspective of MSE. However, there is only one such instance in the data.

There were nineteen instances of subject-verb nonagreement in the data, including eight tokens of third-person singular –*s* absence and eleven tokens of other types of verbal nonconcord.

Subject-verb nonagreement (19)
Third singular –s absence (8)
36. *I see myself reflected in the eyes of a Christ who* **know**_ *exactly who I am... [VM]*
37. *He really* **don't** *need no introduction. [TS]*

Other subject-verb nonagreement (11)
38. *I'm gonna give you some simple things that* **does** *work [MC]*
39. *There's too many brothers who've been brought up without men in the home. [JJ]*
40. *Oh, you* **wasn't** *there? [JAH]*

While subject-verb nonagreement was more frequent and more widely distributed among the SOBU participants than any other grammatical feature observed in the data, its use was still negligible compared to rates typically observed in working-class speech communities, where certain types of subject-verb nonagreement appear to be the norm. For example, Labov acknowledged the pervasiveness of this feature in his NYC study, making the following observation:

In general, we can say that the black vernacular has no agreement between subject and verb. There is one exception: some agreement is clearly registered in the finite forms of *be*. Here the 1st person singular regularly has contracted '*m*, 3rd person singular has *is* or '*s* when realized, and other persons when realized mostly have *are*, sometimes *is*. Aside from this, we have invariant verb forms with no relation to the person and number of the subject. Forms in –*s* are rarely found for *have*, *do*, *don't*, *want*, or *say*. The invariant form for *be* in the past is *was*, not *were*. (Labov 1972a: 271)

With regard to third-person singular contexts in particular, Baugh (1983) reported a 0.753 probability of –*s* absence among his Black Street Speech participants (95). And Wolfram reported an average of 71.4% third singular –*s* absence among Lower Working Class speakers in his Detroit study (1969: 136). In the SOBU data, third singular –*s* absence occurred with only 4.8% frequency (N = 8/166), a rate that would be described as "lame" by comparison with such working-class norms, but more or less on par with rates reported for Upper Middle Class (UMC) speakers elsewhere. In Wolfram's Detroit study, for example, UMC speakers exhibited only 1.4% third singular –*s* absence.

Similarly, while *have/has* auxiliary absence was the most common and most frequent grammatical feature observed in the SOBU data (N = 84), most of the tokens (N = 76) occurred before *got(ta)*, as in examples 41 and 42.[18]

Have/has absence (84)
41. We Ø gotta get the brothas to grow up. [CW]
42. You've got email, you Ø got phones, you Ø got letter-writing ability. [SL]
43. She Ø been doing this good work for a long time. [TS]

The absence of *have/has* before *got(ta)* is a feature that is found in other varieties of American English as well, including the casual speech styles of some MSE speakers. As such, it does not appear to be a highly marked vernacular feature in these data.

The absence of *is/are* (N = 51), however, while slightly less frequent in the data than *have/has* absence, deserves more attention here, given that its variable distribution has been said to have implications for the debate over the relationshp between AAVE and other varieties of English.

Is/are absence (51)
44. I know we Ø gonna get these other questions. [SL]
45. We Ø in a war for our survival. [GM]
46. She Ø 'bout to be president. [TS]

Table 3.3 shows the distribution of full, contracted, and zero tokens of *is/are* in the SOBU data. In these data, *is* appears categorically in full or contracted form among all participants except Tavis Smiley, who exhibits 7.8% *is* absence (N = 4). The low amount of *is* absence in these data is significant because *is* absence has been identified as a predominately "Black pattern," compared to *are* absence, which also occurs in other vernacular varieties of American English (Labov 1972a: 268).[19] In the SOBU data, however, the absence of *are* is more frequent and more common among the participants

---

[18] An alternative interpretation of these constructions would equate *got(ta)* to *have(ta)*, in which case there would be no auxiliary deletion involved. However, as noted above with regard to *ain't _ got(ta)*, there were no overt instances of *do*-support in these data (e.g., We gotta get the brothas to grow up, don't we?) that might support such an interpretation. There were, however, instances of overt *have/has* alternating with Ø _ *got(ta)*, as in example 42, that would support the analysis of variable *have/has* deletion in this environment.

[19] In an examination of copula absence among White speakers in Franklin County, Mississippi, Wolfram (1974) observed 64.2% *are* absence in the environment of pronominal subjects (i.e., Pro__) compared to just 6.5% *is* absence in all environments (1974: 504, 513). He noted that the majority of speakers who exhibited both *is* absence and high rates of *are* absence were "the children of farm or logging laborers whose income [was] below the poverty level" (505), compared to those at the other end of the spectrum, which included schoolteachers and the children of college-educated professionals. Based on his findings, Wolfram concluded that "copula absence in white Southern speech may have been assimilated from Southern black speech" (524), resulting in a continuum of lects, some of which exhibited qualitatively similar patterns to those found in comparable Black varieties.

Table 3.3 *Rates of* is/are *absence among SOBU participants*

	Is			Are		
	Is	's	Zero	Are	're	Zero
Female Panelists	45/49 (91.8%)	4/49 (8.2%)	0/49 (0.0%)	89/160 (55.6%)	59/160 (36.9%)	12/160 (7.5%)
Male Panelists	39/56 (69.6%)	17/56 (30.4%)	0/56 (0.0%)	37/79 (46.8%)	34/79 (43%)	8/79 (10.1%)
Moderator (TS)	16/51 (31.4%)	31/51 (60.8%)	4/51 (7.8%)	48/97 (49.5%)	22/97 (22.7%)	27/97 (27.8%)
Totals	100/156 (64.1%)	52/156 (33.3%)	**4/156 (2.6%)**	174/336 (51.8%)	115/336 (34.2%)	**47/336 (14%)**

than *is* absence. While Smiley produced twenty-seven of the forty-seven tokens of *are* absence, the remaining twenty tokens were distributed across seven other participants.

Beyond the frequencies themselves, the distribution of the copula has also been said to have implications for the debate over AAE's origins and development. In Labov's NYC study, patterns of *is* absence among the "lames" were not only low compared to vernacular peer group members, they also failed to exhibit the same sensitivity to subject type and following grammatical environment exhibited by these groups (see Figure 3.1).[20]

Furthermore, the syntactic distribution of the copula that Labov observed among the T-birds was replicated in other seminal studies of the AAVE copula (see, e.g., Wolfram 1969; Mitchell-Kernan 1971; Baugh 1980, 1983), as well as studies of the copula in Creole varieties such as Jamaican Creole and Gullah (Holm [1976] 1984). And yet, these patterns were not regularly found in comparable White varieties – an observation that spoke to the robustness of these patterns among Black speakers and was interpreted by some as lending weight to the Creole Origins Hypothesis for AAVE.[21] Given such observations, Labov concluded that the patterns of copula absence demonstrated by the "lames" in his study were more closely aligned with that of White speakers than with Black vernacular norms (1972a: 269).

While rates of *is* absence in the SOBU data were too low to observe for their grammatical distribution vis-à-vis these vernacular norms, the distribution of

[20] For a seminal treatment of copula variability in AAVE, see Labov (1969).
[21] For more on copula variability and the Creole Origins debate, see Poplack and Sankoff (1987), Rickford and Blake (1990), Bailey et al. (1991), Poplack and Tagliamonte (1991), Rickford et al. (1991), Singler (1991), Winford (1992a), Rickford (1996, 1998), Hannah (1997), Weldon (1998), Walker (2000), and Weldon (2003a, 2003b).

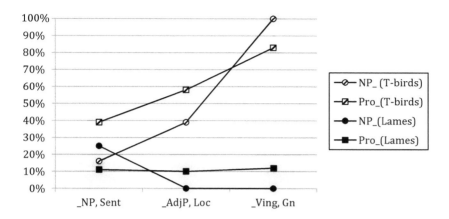

Figure 3.1 Grammatical constraints on *is* absence among preadolescent Thunderbirds and 1390 lames in Labov (1972a).
Source: figures drawn from Table 7.3, p. 269

are absence, illustrated by Figures 3.2 and 3.3, *does* show an adherence to the vernacular constraints found in earlier studies.[22] Especially notable in Figure 3.3 is the high rate of copula absence before *gon(na)*, a pattern that AAVE shares with English-based Creoles (see, e.g., Weldon 1998). Wolfram (1969) reported similar results in his study of upper-middle-class African American speakers in Detroit (see Figures 3.4 and 3.5), although *is* and *are* were combined in Wolfram's study and the following grammatical environment results were only calculated for those instances of copula absence that were preceded by a subject pronoun.[23]

Given the high rate of copula absence before *gonna* among middle-class speakers in his study, Wolfram concluded that "zero realization preceding *gonna* is less stigmatized than zero realization in other environments" (1969:

---

[22] In Labov (1972a), the overall rates of *are* absence by the Lames and T-birds were plotted as points of reference in comparison to *is* (cf. Figure 7.3, p. 270). However, the distribution of *are* by subject type and following grammatical environment was not provided. As such, there were no comparable data from the NYC study by which to judge the SOBU patterns shown in Figures 3.2 and 3.3. Furthermore, different formulas were used to calculate contraction and deletion in Labov's study. Based on his observation that only those forms of the copula that were candidates for contraction could be deleted, Labov counted deletion as a subset of contraction – a formula that has come to be known as "Labov deletion" (Rickford et al. 1991). For the SOBU data, however, I applied a "straight deletion" formula, by which instances of copula absence were counted out of all possible forms (full, contacted, and zero), so as not to impose any such assumptions on the data.

[23] As in the SOBU data, Wolfram's results were calculated using a "straight deletion" formula.

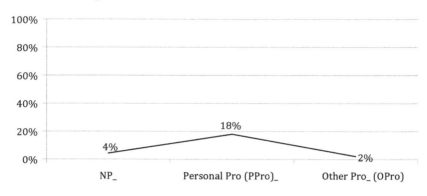

Figure 3.2 Rates of *are* absence by subject type among SOBU participants

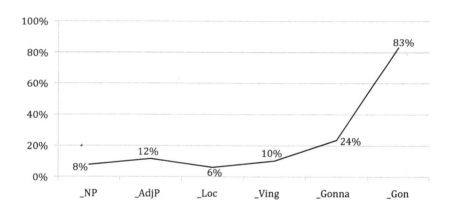

Figure 3.3 Rates of *are* absence by following grammatical environment among SOBU participants

172–73). Thus, while the rates of vernacular grammatical feature usage are low among the SOBU participants, the linguistic patterning of the copula suggests that there is some collective awareness of the vernacular norms that govern its usage – an indication that the use of these features goes beyond mere superficial borrowing or imitation.

One possible explanation for the participants' tempered use of vernacular grammatical features in this performative context might be the salience of grammatical forms in guiding perceptions of standardness in American English. As observed by Wolfram and Schilling-Estes (1998),

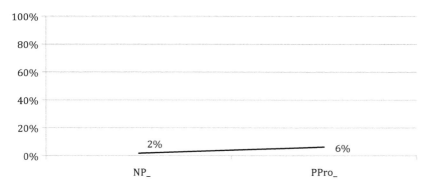

Figure 3.4 Rates of *is/are* absence by subject type among Upper Middle Class African American speakers in Detroit.
Source: adapted from Wolfram 1969: 170, Fig. 48

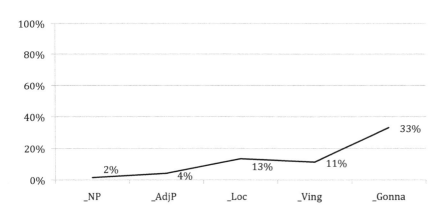

Figure 3.5 Rates of *is/are* absence by following grammatical environment (subject pronoun environments only) among Upper Middle Class African American speakers in Detroit.
Source: adapted from Wolfram 1969: 172, Fig. 49[24]

To a large extent, American English speech samples rated as standard English by a cross-section of listeners exhibit a range of regional variation in pronunciation and vocabulary items but they do not contain grammatical structures that are socially

---

[24] These numbers were drawn from the bar graph in Figure 49 of Wolfram (1969), as there appeared to be a typo that reversed the figures for nominative and adjectival grammatical environments in the table itself.

stigmatized. If native speakers from Michigan, New England, and Arkansas avoid the use of socially stigmatized grammatical structures such as "double negatives" (e.g., *They didn't do nothing*), different verb agreement patterns (e.g., *They's okay*), and different irregular verb forms (e.g., *She done it*), there is a good chance they will be considered standard English speakers even though they may have distinct regional pronunciations. (Wolfram and Schilling-Estes 1998: 12)

Furthermore, it has been observed that vernacular grammatical features are more salient among African American listeners than Whites, for whom certain phonological features appear to carry more salience and stigma. In her chapter, "The real trouble with Black English," Rosina Lippi-Green observed that White listeners "seem to be most comfortable voicing overt criticism about phonological matters" like the pronunciation of *ask* as [æks], in comparison to African American listeners, who "focus almost exclusively on grammatical issues" (1997: 179). (See also Lippi-Green 2012). The participants' use of vernacular phonological features is discussed in the next section.

Phonological Features

Table 3.4 shows the inventory of phonological features observed in the SOBU data.[25] Compared to the grammatical feature inventory, the inventory of phonological features shown in Table 3.4 is more widely distributed among the SOBU participants. Because the participants represent a variety of regional backgrounds (recall Table 3.1), the range of pronunciation features listed in Table 3.4 undoubtedly reflects the regional heterogeneity of this group.[26] However, there are some phonological features shared by speakers *across* regional backgrounds that seem to signal an ethnic, rather than regional, significance, as observed below.

Vowels Table 3.5 provides examples of the vowel features observed in the SOBU data. Several of the features listed in Table 3.5 involved the laxing of tense vowels, either before [l] (e.g., *feel*, *available*) or in word-final, unstressed syllables (e.g., *issue*, *family*, *tomorrow*). While laxing before [l] occurs in a number of American English dialects, it has been identified as more common among African American speakers in certain regions of the country (see, e.g., Gordon 2000; Thomas 2001, 2007; Labov et al. 2006). Similarly, the

---

[25] Phonological features were identified perceptually (not acoustically). While every effort was made to present an exhaustive list of any (ethnically) distinctive phonological features in the data, some of the more subtle features, particularly those involving vowel shifts that are not easily tracked perceptually, might not have been identified.

[26] The regional heterogeneity of the group had less of an effect on the grammatical features discussed above, most of which have been found to extend across regional boundaries.

Table 3.4 *AAVE phonological feature inventory*

Features[a]	Female Panelists						Male Panelists						Mod.	PT
	MW	ST	JH	VM	SL	MC	NA	JJ	GM	DS	JAH	CW	TS	
Vowels														
[i]→[e]/ _[ŋ]												✓	✓	2
[æ]→ [e] in *can't*			✓										✓	2
[ɑ] →[ɔ]/ _nasals												✓	✓	3
Vowel laxing/ _ [l]					✓				✓	✓	✓	✓		5
[ɪ]/[ɛ] merging _ nasals; in *get*		✓	✓	✓			✓	✓	✓	✓		✓	✓	9
Vowel laxing in unstressed syllables	✓	✓	✓	✓		✓	✓	✓	✓	✓			✓	10
/ay/ monophthongization	✓	✓	✓	✓	✓	✓	✓	✓	✓	✓	✓	✓	✓	13
Consonants														
[sk] metathesis in *asked*									✓					1
Deletion of [r] in *library*											✓			1
[r] deletion in initial [θr] clusters												✓	✓	2
Post-vocalic [l] deletion/vocalization				✓						✓				2
[y] deletion in [Cy] clusters					✓	✓								2
[nd] → [nt] word-finally											✓		✓	2
Labialization of [θ]→[f]							✓					✓		2
Deletion of initial [d]/[g] in TMA aux.					✓	✓			✓		✓	✓		5
Word-final deletion of [v]		✓				✓	✓	✓	✓	✓	✓	✓	✓	9

69

Table 3.4 (*cont.*)

Features	Female Panelists						Male Panelists						Mod.	PT
	MW	ST	JH	VM	SL	MC	NA	JJ	GM	DS	JAH	CW	TS	
Loss of [t] in contractions	✓					✓	✓	✓	✓	✓	✓	✓	✓	11
Fricative stopping		✓	✓	✓	✓	✓		✓	✓	✓	✓	✓	✓	11
Unstressed nasal fronting		✓	✓	✓	✓	✓	✓	✓	✓	✓	✓	✓	✓	12
Post-vocalic [r] deletion/vocalization	✓	✓	✓	✓	✓	✓	✓	✓	✓	✓	✓	✓	✓	13
Word-final consonant cluster reduction	✓	✓	✓	✓	✓	✓	✓	✓	✓	✓	✓	✓	✓	13
Other Phonological Features														
Stress shift from second to first syllable					✓	✓				✓		✓		3
a + vowel-initial word					✓	✓		✓		✓	✓		✓	5
Unstressed syllable deletion					✓	✓				✓	✓	✓	✓	7
FT	**5**	**7**	**8**	**9**	**11**	**13**	**7**	**11**	**13**	**13**	**14**	**16**	**18**	

Notes: PT = Total number of participants using a given feature; FT = Total number of features used by a given individual.

[a] Not included in this table were pronunciations of *says* and *again* with a tense vowel [e]. Such pronunciations might be described as spelling pronunciations (cf. pronunciation of [t] in *often*) or even hypercorrections. However, it was not entirely clear whether these would be perceived as vernacular pronunciations. So they were excluded for this reason.

Table 3.5 *Vowel features*

Vowel Features	Examples
[ɑ] →[o]/ _nasals	*wrong* [roŋ], *on* [on], *want* [wont]
[æ]→ [e] in *can't*	*can't* [kent]
/ay/ monophthongization	*lives* [la:vz], *side* [sa:d], *why* [wa:]
[i]→[e]/ _[ŋ]	*thing* [θeŋ]
[ɪ]/[ɛ] merging _nasals; in *get*	*been* [bɪn], *ten* [tɪn], *get* [gɪt]
Vowel laxing/_[l]	
[i] → [ɪ]	*feel* [fɪl], *really* [rɪli]
[e] → [ɛ]	*available* [əvɛləbəl], *jails* [jɛlz]
Vowel laxing in unstressed syllables	
[u]→[ʊ]	*issues* [ɪʃʊz]
[i]→[ɪ]	*army* [ɑrmɪ], *family* [fæmlɪ]
[o]→[ə]	*tomorrow* [təmɑrə]

laxing of word-final [i] is a feature of American English that seems to have been preserved particularly among older African American speakers (Denning 1989; Thomas 2007). This feature has also been observed in the public speeches of many well-known African American orators, including iconic figures such as civil rights activist Reverend Martin Luther King, Jr. and US President Barack Obama.

The SOBU participants also used several vowel features characteristic of Southern American English, including the shifting of [i]→[e] (as in *thing*), [æ]→[e] (as in *can't*), and [ɑ]→[o] (as in *want*), as well as the merging of [ɪ] and [ɛ] (as in *been* and *get*), a feature that was used by a majority of the participants in the forum. While the [ɪ]/[ɛ] merger is a common feature of Southern American English, it was used by both Southerners and non-Southerners in the SOBU data, suggesting an ethnic rather than regional significance (cf. Labov et al. 2006).

The most common vowel feature in the SOBU data, however, was mono-phthongization of /ay/, which was used by all of the participants. While /ay/ monophthongization among White speakers is primarily a Southern feature, it extends across regional boundaries among African American speakers, par-ticularly in open syllables and before voiced consonants (see, e.g., Kurath and McDavid 1961; Bernstein 1993; Thomas 2001, 2007; Labov et al. 2006). Table 3.6 displays the rates of /ay/ monophthongization in prevoiced environ-ments and open syllables in the SOBU data.

While the female panelists exhibited an observable range of frequencies, from Susan Taylor (27.7%) to Julia Hare (75%), the overall rates of /ay/ monophthongization in prevoiced environments and open syllables in the SOBU data were relatively high, averaging over 50% among the female

Table 3.6 *Rates of /ay/ monophthongization in prevoiced environments and open syllables*[27]

Female Panelists	[a:]		Male Panelists	[a:]		Lead Moderator	[a:]	
ST	13/47	27.7%	GM	37/52	71.2%	TS	262/348	75.3%
MC	42/110	38.2%	JAH	51/64	79.7%			
MW	18/45	40%	DS	48/57	84.2%			
VM	34/57	59.6%	NA	24/28	85.7%			
SL	62/100	62%	JJ	26/30	86.7%			
JH	39/52	75%	CW	35/40	87.5%			
Female Average	208/411	**50.6%**	Male Average	221/271	**81.5%**	Lead Moderator	262/348	**75.3%**

panelists and over 80% among the male panelists. These rates were somewhat unexpected, given that studies such as Thomas (2001) and Nguyen (2006) have reported relatively low rates of /ay/ monophthongization among African American middle-class speakers (and women in particular) in comparison to their working-class peers. However, as noted earlier, Rahman (2007) has demonstrated the racial markedness of the (ay) variable in performative contexts, where the monophthongal variant, [a:], has been used by African American comedians to "mark" (i.e., imitate) African American characters in opposition to the diphthongal variant, [ay], which has been used to mark members of the White middle-class establishment (74). (See also Preston 1992; Rahman 2004.) Given the predominately Black audience assembled in the church, and the forum's emphasis on the "Black family" theme, noted earlier, the prevalence and frequency of this feature among the SOBU participants might reflect its utility as a means of "sounding Black" or, more specifically, the avoidance of "sounding (too) White" or "Proper" (cf. Jones and Preston 2011) in this racialized setting.

By contrast, in prevoiceless environments, the participants were almost categorically diphthongal, as shown in Table 3.7. Given the overwhelming association of prevoiceless [a:] with poor, Southern, rural White speech (see, e.g., Pederson 1983; Hazen and Fluharty 2004; Bernstein 2006; Irons 2007;

---

[27] While it has been demonstrated that /ay/ ungilding is a continuous phenomenon with variable realizations that can be measured acoustically (see, e.g., Nguyen 2006; Reed 2016), for the purposes of this analysis, the variable was coded perceptually and treated as a binary distinction between [ay] and [a:]. Any tokens that were perceived as monophthongal to the "naked ear" were coded as [a:]. Tokens of "I" were excluded from the overall count because of their frequency in the data, though derived forms (e.g., I'll, I'm, I've, etc.) were included.

Table 3.7 *Rates of /ay/ monophthongization in prevoiceless environments*

Female Panelists	[a:]		Male Panelists	[a:]		Lead Moderator	[a:]	
ST	0/16	0%	GM	0/23	0%	TS	34/141	24.1%
MW	0/5	0%	JAH	0/14	0%			
VM	0/12	0%	DS	0/14	0%			
SL	0/34	0%	NA	0/5	0%			
JH	0/33	0%	CW	0/12	0%			
MC	2/33	6.1%	JJ	1/11	9.1%			
Female Average	2/133	**1.5%**	Male Average	1/79	**1.3%**	Lead Moderator	34/141	**24.1%**

Greene 2010; Reed 2016), the participants' lack of monophthongization in this environment probably also reflected an effort of avoidance (likely below the level of conscious awareness).[28] The only panelists who produced monophthongs in prevoiceless environments were Marva Collins and Jeffrey Johnson, who exhibited trace amounts of the feature at 6.1% (N = 2) and 9.1% (N = 1), respectively. Tavis Smiley produced higher rates of monophthongization in prevoiceless environments (24.1%, N = 34) compared to the other participants, but significantly lower than what he exhibited in prevoiced environments (75.3%, N = 262). Though Smiley was raised in Indiana, his Mississippi roots might have motivated the comparatively higher use of this feature in prevoiceless environments, similar to Anderson's 2002 study in Detroit, Michigan, where it was noted that a speaker's positive orientation to the South and/or rejection of northern pronunciation norms resulted in increased use of this feature. (See also Anderson 2003.)

Consonants Table 3.8 is illustrative of the consonantal features observed in the data. Several of the features listed in Table 3.8 were lexically and/or phonologically restricted pronunciations, used by just 1–2 speakers each. These included [sk] metathesis in *asked*, deletion of [r] in syllable-initial clusters (e.g., *library* and *through*), deletion/vocalization of post-vocalic [l] (e.g., *myself*), and [y] deletion in [Cy] clusters, (e.g., *distribute*, *figured*, and *particular*). Also observed among a couple of the participants was the devoicing of [d]

[28] I would conjecture, further, that the lack of /ay/ monophthongization in prevoiceless contexts likely extends beyond this particular performative context for most of the panel participants and may even constitute an "avoided White sound," similar to that observed by Jones and Preston (2011) for /a/ fronting in Michigan.

Table 3.8 *Consonant features*

Consonant Features	Examples
consonant cluster reduction	*subject* [səbʤek], *old* [ol], *kept* [kɛp], *esteemed* [ɛstim]
deletion of [r] in syllable-initial clusters	*library* [laybɛri], *through* [θu]
deletion of initial [d]/[g] in TMA auxiliaries	*don't* [õnt], *gon* [õn]/[õ]
deletion of [y] in [Cy] clusters	*distribute* [dɪstrɪbət], *figured* [fɪgərd], *particular* [pətɪkələr]
fricative stopping	*them* [dɛm], *with* [wɪt], *business* [bɪdnɛs]
labialization of [θ]→[f]	*birth* [bɪ̯f], *both* [bof]
loss of [t] in contractions	*it's* [ɪs], *that's* [ðæs], *what's* [wʌs], *let's* [lɛs]
[nd] → [nt] word-finally	*found* [fawnt], *second* [sɛkənt]
post-vocalic [r] deletion/vocalization	*store* [sto], *card* [kɑːd], *sister* [sɪstə]
post-vocalic [l] deletion/vocalization	*myself* [maysɛf]
[sk] metathesis in *asked*	*asked* [ækst]
unstressed nasal fronting	*taking* [tekɪn]
word-final deletion of [v]	*give* [gɪ]

in word-final [nd] clusters such as *second* and *found* (cf. Grieser 2014) and the labialization of [θ]→[f] (as in *both*, *birth*). The relatively narrow distribution of these features among the SOBU participants might be indicative of their greater salience and stigma compared to other consonant features found in the data.[29] The pronunciation of *ask* as [aeks] – a derivation of Old English *acsian* – represents one of the most stigmatized features of AAVE, perceived by many non-AAVE speakers as a marker of ignorance or lack of education[30] (Lippi-Green 1997, 2012). And with regard to the labialization of [θ], Wolfram (1969) observed a sharp stratification along class lines in his Detroit study, where the feature was used frequently by working-class speakers, but infrequently by middle-class speakers.

---

[29] In Grieser (2014) word-final devoicing was more pervasive. However, it was found to serve a dual function, indexing both African American and Professional Class identities, the latter through a second-order indexical association with "precise" or "pronounced" articulations (134).

[30] According to Lippi-Green (1997),

> The *Oxford English Dictionary* establishes this variation between [æsk] and [æks] as very old, a result of the Old English metathesis *asc-, acs-*. From this followed Middle English variation with many possible forms: *ox, ax, ex, ask, esk, ash, esh, ass, ess*. Finally, *ax* (aks) survived to almost 1600 as the regular literary form, when *ask* became the literary prefer-ence. Most people know nothing of the history of this form, and believe the *aks* variant to be an innovation of the AAVE community. In fact, it is found in Appalachian speech, in some urban dialects in the New York metropolitan area, and outside the US in some regional varieties of British English. (179)

More common, particularly among the male speakers, was the deletion of initial [d] or [g] in tense-mood-aspect (TMA) auxiliaries (as in *don't*, *gon*), a feature that has also been observed in Gullah and other English-based Creoles (Rickford 1999b), and the deletion of word-final consonants (as in *give*), which has been identified as a feature that is unique to AAVE (Bailey and Thomas 1998). While these features are ethnically marked, they appear to be less salient, and perhaps less stigmatized (cf., Labov's 1972c *indicators*) in comparison to some of the consonant features discussed above, which tend to trigger much more overt social commentary and judgment on the part of listeners.

The most common consonant features in the SOBU data, however, were the loss of [t] in *it's*, *that's*, *what's*, and *let's* contractions, fricative stopping (e.g., *them*, *with*, or *business*), unstressed nasal fronting (e.g., *taking*), post-vocalic [r] deletion (e.g., *store*, *card*, and *sister*), and word-final consonant cluster reduction (e.g., *subject*, *old*, and *esteemed*). With the possible exception of the loss of [t] in contracted forms, which Labov (1972a) identified as a distinguishing feature of Black varieties (11), all of these features are shared with other varieties of American English (see Labov 1972a; Wolfram 1969). Their use in the SOBU data is discussed in more detail in the paragraphs that follow.

The most common type of fricative stopping observed in the SOBU data was *th-* stopping, which ranged from 0.6% by the female participants to 14.6% by moderator Tavis Smiley, as shown in Table 3.9. In his NYC study, Labov calculated the (dh) variable, in other words the frequency of the voiced fricative, [ð], as a stop or affricate in word-initial position (e.g., *this*, *then*), using an index formula that situated the variable on a scale of 0–200.[31] For comparative purposes, the (dh) variable, which represented the bulk of the tokens shown in Table 3.9, was extracted from the SOBU data and compared to Labov's NYC results for "interview style" (Style B), using this same index formula. According to Labov, the (dh) variable did not exhibit as regular a pattern as some of the other variables in his study. However, the rates of fricative stopping produced by the "lames" ((dh) index = 84) were consistently lower than those produced by the vernacular peer group members, whose (dh) indices ranged from 114 to 144 (1972a: 264). The SOBU participants' rates, which ranged from (dh)-1 among female SOBU participants, to (dh)-13 among male SOBU participants, and (dh)-24 for Tavis Smiley, were even lower than those produced by the NYC "lames."

[31] In his NYC study, Labov identified three distinct variants for the (dh) variable – the fricative [ð] (the "prestige" variant), which was assigned a value of 0, the affricate [dð] (a regional pronunciation), which was assigned a value of 1, and the stop [d], which was assigned a value of 2. The index score was calculated by dividing the total number of points by the total number of occurrences of the variable and multiplying by 100. The higher the index score, the more stigmatized the pronunciation (Labov et al. 1968, 1: 95).

Table 3.9 *Rates of* th-*stopping*

Female Panelists	[d]/[t]		Male Panelists	[d]/[t]		Lead Moderator	[d]/[t]	
MW	0/163	0%	NA	0/127	0%	TS	190/1,304	14.6%
MC	1/386	0.3%	JJ	11/222	5%			
SL	1/324	0.3%	DS	15/229	6.5%			
ST	1/189	0.5%	JAH	12/186	6.5%			
VM	1/171	0.6%	CW	15/160	9.4%			
JH	5/277	1.8%	GM	33/259	12.7%			
Female Average	9/1510	0.6%	Male Average	86/1,183	7.3%	Lead Moderator	190/1,304	14.6%

Table 3.10 *Rates of unstressed nasal fronting*

Female Panelists	[n]		Male Panelists	[n]		Lead Moderator	[n]	
MW	0/43	0%	NA	1/32	3.1%	TS	128/312	41%
ST	7/72	9.7%	DS	8/45	17.8%			
VM	7/37	18.9%	JJ	11/36	30.6%			
JH	14/71	19.7%	CW	17/43	39.5%			
SL	19/86	22.1%	GM	26/57	45.6%			
MC	20/84	23.8%	JAH	28/55	50.9%			
Female Average	67/393	17%	Male Average	91/268	34%	Lead Moderator	128/312	41%

More frequent among the SOBU participants were the rates of unstressed nasal fronting, which ranged from 17% among the female participants to 41% by Smiley, as shown in Table 3.10. Described by Labov (1972a) as "perhaps the most sensitive sociolinguistic variable for BEV [Black English Vernacular] groups," the (ing) variable reportedly exhibited sharp styleshifting among the NYC preadolescent peer group members, whose rates of [n] usage ranged from near 100% frequency in casual conversation to near 0% frequency in reading and word-list (i.e., more formal) styles (266). In "interview style" (Style B), vernacular peer group members produced nasal fronting rates ranging from 76% to 100% frequency and the "lames" produced nasal fronting with 78% frequency.[32] In comparison to these vernacular norms, the SOBU rates were notably lower, but higher than those observed for the (dh) variable. To the

---

[32] In Labov (1972a), the (ing) variable was plotted according to the "prestige" variant [ŋ]. The percentages reported here represent the "nonprestige" variant [n].

Table 3.11 *Rates of post-vocalic [r]-lessness (_##V)*[33]

Female Panelists		Ø	Male Panelists		Ø	Lead Moderator		Ø
MC	11/60	18.3%	GM	8/26	30.8%	TS	68/209	32.5%
ST	8/32	25%	JJ	12/26	46.2%			
SL	17/57	29.8%	NA	10/18	55.6%			
JH	15/28	53.6%	JAH	14/24	58.3%			
MW	12/19	63.2%	CW	12/20	60%			
VM	28/43	65.1%	DS	27/39	69.2%			
Female Average	91/239	38.1%	Male Average	83/153	54.2%	Lead Moderator	68/209	32.5%

extent that higher rates of the "prestige" variant, [ŋ], might have been perceived as "sounding White/Proper" by the audience members, particularly in Black public spaces such as this one, the participants might have used the [n] variant more frequently in order to shield themselves from such perceptions.

Similarly, while post-vocalic [r]-lessness is a regionally marked feature, associated with speakers in NYC, Boston, and various pockets of the South, Labov observed that the (r) variable holds particular significance in the African American community, where the "prestige" variant, [r], functions as an indicator of formal, educated speech (1972a: 264). Furthermore, Labov observed that rates of post-vocalic [r]-lessness in word-final position, followed by a vowel-initial word (i.e., _##V), as in *four o'clock*, were reportedly low among White speakers, but high among vernacular peer group members, whose [r]-less rates ranged from 93% to 96% frequency in interview style (Style B). At 79% frequency, the "lames" exhibited slightly lower rates of [r]-lessness in this environment.[34] In the SOBU data, rates of post-vocalic [r]-lessness ranged from 32.5% by Tavis Smiley to 38.1% among the female panelists and 54.2% among the male panelists, as shown in Table 3.11.

However, a glance at the individual data reveals a range of frequencies for this variable as well, particularly among the female panelists, from Marva Collins with 18.3% [r]-lessness to Vashti McKenzie with 65.1%. While none of the SOBU participants approached the vernacular levels reported by Labov in his NYC study or even the [r]-less rates exhibited by the NYC "lames," the

---

[33] In the SOBU data, instances of vocalization as well as deletion were counted as [r]-less.

[34] In Labov (1972a), the (r) variable was plotted according to the "prestige" variant [r]. The percentages reported here represent the "nonprestige" variant Ø.

rates of [r]-lessness were higher, on average, than both *th*-stopping and nasal fronting in the SOBU data. The intragroup variation observed for the (r) variable was, undoubtedly, influenced by the regional heterogeneity of the group. However, the salience of this variable as a formality marker was a likely factor here as well.

Finally, while consonant cluster reduction occurs in many varieties of American English, including MSE, it is more prevalent in AAVE than in other varieties (Wolfram and Schilling-Estes 1998; Thomas 2007). This feature varies, however, in terms of the linguistic constraints that govern it. In Labov's NYC study, vernacular peer group members showed greater sensitivity to the following phonological environment, where a following consonant favored reduction over a following vowel, whereas the "lames" were more sensitive to morpheme type, where monomorphemic clusters (e.g., *past*) showed higher rates of reduction than bi-morphemic clusters (e.g., *passed*), as illustrated in Figure 3.6.

Among the SOBU participants, the rates of consonant cluster reduction, shown in Figure 3.7, also exhibited mixed patterns of constraint. Whereas moderator Tavis Smiley exhibited higher rates of reduction in preconsonantal environments, regardless of morphemic status, consistent with Labov's vernacular peer group members, the other participants reduced clusters with greater frequency in monomorphemic clusters, regardless of the following phonological environment, consistent with the "lames" in Labov's study.

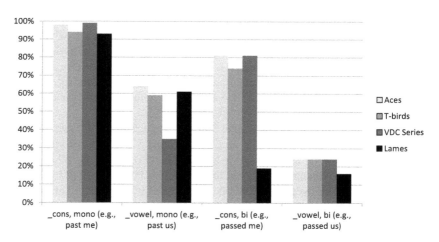

Figure 3.6 Frequencies of consonant cluster reduction in Labov's (1972a) preadolescent interviews (Style B).
Source: adapted from Table 7.2, p. 264

Table 3.12 *Chi-square results for consonant cluster reduction among the SOBU participants*

	Female Panelists		Male Panelists		Lead Moderator	
Morphemic Structure						
mono	163/274	59.5%	148/204	72.5%	173/309	56%
bi	26/121	21.5%	27/56	48.2%	17/68	25%
Pearson Chi-square results	X^2 (1) = 48.574,		X^2 (1) = 11.825,		X^2 (1) = 21.408,	
	p = 0.000		p = 0.001		p = 0.000	
Following Phonological Environment						
_cons	133/208	63.9%	120/168	71.4%	150/240	62.5%
_non-cons	56/187	29.9%	55/92	59.8%	40/137	29.2%
Pearson Chi-square results	X^2 (1) = 45.606,		X^2 (1) = 3.664,		X^2 (1) = 38.694,	
	p = 0.000		p = 0.056 (ns)		p = 0.000	

Note: *Results marked by (ns) did not meet the $p \leq 0.05$ threshold for significance.

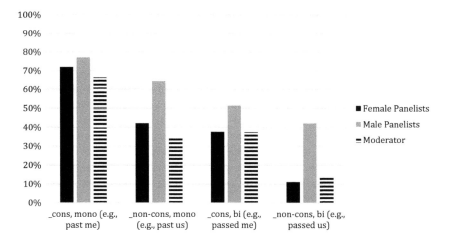

Figure 3.7 Frequencies of consonant cluster reduction among SOBU participants[35]

Nevertheless, as shown in Table 3.12, the Pearson chi-square results from a Two-Proportions test show that both sets of linguistic constraints had a significant effect on the rate of consonant cluster reduction among the SOBU

---

[35] Tokens of "and" were excluded from the overall count because of their frequency in the data.

Table 3.13 *Other phonological features*

Other Phonological Features	Examples
a + vowel-initial word	*he's **a** athlete; **a** off-switch; get **a** education; **a** exodus*
stress shift to first syllable	*cément* (verb), *prétend*
unstressed syllable deletion	*remember→'member, little→li'l, Carolina→Car'lina*

participants, with the exception of the male panelists, where the effect of following phonological environment fell just shy of the $p \leq 0.05$ threshold for significance.

Finally, a few additional phonological features observed among the SOBU participants are listed in Table 3.13. The shifting of primary stress from the second syllable to the first is a feature that AAE shares with many Southern varieties. The other two features – *a* before vowel-initial words and unstressed syllable deletion in initial and medial positions – occur in other American English varieties as well, though the latter has been described as an age-graded feature in AAE (i.e., used more frequently among older speakers than younger speakers) (Vaughn-Cooke 1986; Rickford 1999b; Thomas 2007).

As with the grammatical features, the SOBU participants appear to make strategic use of phonological features that are ethnically marked (i.e., perceived as "sounding Black") but relatively low in salience and stigma. Some of the most common features used by the SOBU participants (e.g., nasal fronting, monophthongization, post-vocalic [r]-lessness, and consonant cluster reduction) occur in other vernacular varieties, as well as the relaxed speech styles of MSE, thus reducing their stigma from the perspective of more mainstream audiences. And yet, the patterns of usage among the participants suggest at least some knowledge (likely below the level of conscious awareness) of the social and linguistic constraints that govern their use in the African American speech community. By minimizing the frequencies of "prestige" variants such as [ŋ], [ay], and [r], and making greater use of their vernacular equivalents, the participants are able to "sound Black" or at least reduce the likelihood of "sounding (too) White/Proper" without drawing excessively on overtly stigmatized features that would increase the likelihood of being perceived as sounding "uneducated." Similarly, features such as vowel laxing and word-final [v] deletion, which are more ethnically marked but less overtly stigmatized, were used by a greater number of participants. However, more overtly stigmatized pronunciations, such as fricative stopping (an ethnic *marker*) and [sk] metathesis (an ethnic *stereotype*) were used sparingly or avoided altogether. The greater prevalence of vernacular phonological features compared to vernacular grammatical features among the SOBU participants also speaks to the lower relative stigma associated with phonological feature usage. A similar observation is made with regard to the participants' use of lexical and rhetorical features, discussed below.

Beyond the Vernacular: Lexical and Rhetorical Feature Usage

Table 3.14 shows the distribution of African American lexical and rhetorical features observed in the data. While the African American speech community has been a primary generator of slang terminology in the USA (see, e.g., Major 1994; Smitherman 1994, 2000, 2006; Kearse 2006; Widawski 2015), it is the colorful, trendy, sometimes defiant, vocabulary of young speakers that typically gets the attention of mainstream America. However, there are also more stable in-group terms that are shared by a wider spectrum of the African American speech community. As Smitherman (1998) observes, "the lexicon of the Black speech community crosses boundaries, [including] sex, age, religion, social class [and] region" and, in doing so "reflects the dynamic, colorful span of language used by African Americans from all walks of life" (204–5). Table 3.15 lists some of the AAE slang terms and other lexical items that were used by the SOBU participants.

While some expressions, like *shout out, You go, girl, baby daddy/baby mama, man up,* and *up in here* are terms that have crossed over into more mainstream usage, many of the items listed in Table 3.15 represent the kind of stable, in-group vocabulary that Smitherman describes. Terms like *light skinned/light skinded* to refer to African Americans who have a lighter skin complexion, "fictive kinship" terms like *folk, auntie,* and *sista/brotha*[36] that emphasize the (Black) family narrative, as well as other colloquial expressions like *check someone, play yourself, feel me, go there,* or *call someone out of one's name* are items that have largely resisted the processes of mainstream appropriation and subsequent in-group abandonment that so often occur with the AAE lexicon (see Smitherman 1998). They are also terms that have eluded much of the pejoration often directed at trendier slang terms by those who view slang vocabulary with disdain. The fact that such items were used by this group of regionally heterogeneous, high-status, (primarily) middle-aged speakers, in a televised public forum held in a church underscores Smitherman's observation about the unifying effect of the African American

---

[36] While terms like "bro" or "bruh" (as variants of "brother") have undergone a certain degree of crossover into mainstream usage, the particular uses of fictive kinship terms exhibited by the SOBU participants, as illustrated in Table 3.15, have remained relatively in-group.

Table 3.14 *AAE lexical and rhetorical feature inventory*

Features	Female Panelists						Male Panelists						Mod.	PT
	MW	MC	ST	VM	SL	JH	NA	DS	JJ	CW	GM	JAH	TS	
Lexical			√	√	√	√			√	√	√	√	√	9
Rhetorical		√	√	√	√	√		√	√	√	√	√	√	11
FT	0	1	2	2	2	2	0	1	2	2	2	2	2	

Notes: PT = Total number of participants using a given feature; FT = Total number of features used by a given individual.

Table 3.15 *Slang and other lexical items used by the SOBU participants*

Slang and Other Lexical Items	Examples
a shout out = *an acknowledgment*	*Can Black folk get **a shout out** once a year? [TS]*
auntie = *aunt (or aunt-like figure)*	*When I'm in Africa, there are **aunties** who mother my daughters and my son. [VM]*
baby('s) daddy/mama = *child's father/mother*	➤ *Please stop going on Maury, finding your **baby daddy**. [JAH]*
	➤ *The **baby mama's** mamas was telling them that, "You could do bad by yourself." [JJ]*
being real/keeping it real = *being authentic; telling the truth*	➤ *I go to a White school, a predominantly White institution. No disrespect to the HBCUs [Historically Black Colleges or Universities]. But, I couldn't afford it. Let's **be real**, I couldn't afford it. [JAH]*
	➤ *Now you know that's why I love Tom Joyner. He always **keeping it real**. [TS]*
called out of one's name = *referred to in a disrespectful way*	*Black women are **called out of our names**. [ST]*
don't get it twisted = *don't be mistaken*	*But [you've only got] a little time . . . So **don't get it twisted**. [TS]*
dubs/tens = *20 inch/10 inch car rims*	*I'm not sitting on **dubs**. I got **tens**, but I keep them clean. . . [JAH]*
feel me = *understand and/or agree with me*	*I'm not gon cast aspersion on nobody, but I know you will **feel me** on this. [TS]*
folk = *people*	*We're back in our corners, disgruntled, talking 'bout **folk** taking jobs. [SL]*
'gators = *alligator shoes*	*One of the few judges I know that wears a short set under his robe with a pair of **'gators**. [TS]*
going down = *happening*	*These are the things that are **going down** here. [JH]*
'hood = *neighborhood*	*When I go back in the **'hood**, lot of brothas say "Oh judge, we ain't went nowhere. . ." [GM]*
I ain't mad at X = *X is okay with me; I don't have a problem with X*	*If they can quote or regurgitate anything Dr. West said, they bad anyway. So **I ain't mad at 'em**. [TS]*
light-skinded = *Black person with light complexion*	*You want the **light-skinded** ones too? I didn't want Cornel left out. [TS]*
play yourself = *embarrass yourself*	*So you don't **play yourself** up in here, please reach right now and turn off your pagers. . . [TS]*
right quick = *quickly*	*A few things I have to do **right quick**, and then I want to bring out my abiding friend and co-moderator. [TS]*
sho' 'nuff = *sure enough, surely*	*And if you a Negro in America, you can **sho' 'nuff** get paid in February. [TS]*

Table 3.15 *(cont.)*

Slang and Other Lexical Items	Examples
sista/brotha = *(usu.) Black female/male* (used as titles, terms of address, or third-person references)	➢ **Sista** *Julia wants you to tell that person... [JH]* ➢ **Brotha's**, *it's time to man up! [GM]* ➢ *He's a special kind of* **brotha**. *[CW]*
to check someone = *to correct or educate someone*	*But I always* **check** *folk. I say to them, "You may be my second biggest fan, but my first fan is my mama."[TS]*
to go there = *to talk about a touchy subject or hot topic*	*And while I'm talking about BET, let me say this, since you don't work for them anymore ... They don't sign your paychecks, so we can* **go there**. *[JAH]*
to pimp X = *to take advantage of X*	*When you receive too much love sometimes, if your heart and your mind is not ready to receive it, you will abuse it. You will* **pimp** *it. [GM]*
up in X = *to be in something in a way that makes your presence known*	*I got some talkers* **up in here** *with me today. [TS]*
X up = *to epitomize some quality* e.g., *man up* = *be a good man* e.g., *marry up* = *be a good spouse* e.g., *father up* = *be a good father*	*How you gonna* **man up** *when you don't know how ta be a man? How you gonna* **father up** *when you don't know how to be a father? How you gonna* **marry up** *when you don't know what it takes to be married? [JJ]*
you go (on), X = *good job; continued success*	*I'm told she 'bout to be president of the Bishop's Council. So Bishop McKenzie,* **you go on, girl!** *[TS]*

lexicon.[37] Furthermore, as observed by Smitherman, "there are correct ways of saying these words, of talking Black, which depend on knowledge of the rules of AAVE grammar and pronunciation" (1998: 207). The absence of possessive *-s* in *baby mama/baby daddy*, the reduplication of the past participle in *light skinded*,[38] the post-vocalic [r]-lessness in *sista/brotha*, and the post-vocalic [r]-lessness and unstressed syllable deletion in *sho' 'nuff* are illustrative of the

---

[37] A similar observation is made by Rickford and Rickford (2000), who note that "One of the many fascinating features of black vocabulary is how sharply it can divide blacks and whites, and how solidly it can connect blacks from different social classes .... [F]amiliarity with distinctive black vocabulary is one of the ways in which virtually every African American can be said to speak some form of Ebonics, or Spoken Soul" (93–94).

[38] While *light-skinded* represents a reduplication of the past participle, it is also a strategy for maintaining the *-ed* suffix, which would, otherwise, be a candidate for deletion via consonant cluster reduction (i.e., *skinned* [skɪnd]->[skin]. Among middle-class speakers, however, this reduplicative structure, which is sometimes even extended to *skindeded*, is often used stylistically to emphasize its marked vernacular status (thus simultaneously signaling one's knowledge of and distance from the vernacular). Smiley appears to use the construction in this performative manner, as he playfully signifies on Cornel West about his light complexion.

synergism that exists between the AAE lexicon and many of the phonological and grammatical rules discussed in the preceding sections.

In addition to lexical usage, the SOBU participants also drew heavily on a number of African American rhetorical devices in their presentations. In fact, "talk about talk" was a recurring theme in the panel. Emphasizing the importance of the oral tradition in African American culture, Tavis Smiley opened the symposium with the following *metalinguistic commentary*, as shown in Excerpt 3.9.

Excerpt 3.9

This is all the stuff that we sent to the panelists to prepare them for this conversation today, 'cause it's gon be rich up in here. Yeah. That's a– that's a Black thing, ain't it? You always up in something. (Audience response) Up in the church, up in the barbershop, up in the beauty salon. Off up in college. Up in folk business. Oops! You always up in something. I'm glad y'all up in here today. How 'bout you? [TS]

And he offered the commentary shown in Excerpt 3.10 as a way of educating the CSPAN television viewing audience about the slang interpretation of the term *dope*.

Excerpt 3.10

You a young brother, why is it so dope, and for those who are Ebonically challenged watching us on CSPAN, why is it hip, why is it cool, why is it okay, to be dumb in yo' generation? [TS]

As noted earlier, the fact that this symposium was held in a church, rather than a more secular setting, speaks to the central role that religion and spirituality often play in African American public events (Smitherman 1977, 1994, 2000). According to Knowles-Borishade (1991), "There is no line of demarcation between the spiritual and the secular in African oratorical events" (490–91). Accordingly, the SOBU participants drew on the sacred-secular continuum throughout the symposium. For example, in Excerpt 3.11, Smiley used a *call-response* ritual that is often used by African American preachers to get members of the congregation to interact with one another.

Excerpt 3.11 Call-Response

TS: *I figured there'd be an occasion for this up in the Black church at some point during this symposium, for me to say, turn to your neighbor. So I want you to turn to your neighbor and say, "It's time."*

(cont.)

AUDIENCE:	*It's time.*
TS:	*If you watchin' at home, you can do it too. It's time.*
AUDIENCE:	*It's time.*
TS:	*To man up.*
AUDIENCE:	*To man up.*

And many of the female panelists also supported the comments of others through back-channeling (e.g., *that's right, there you are, that's how it goes, come on,* etc.) or the repetition and/or uptake of others' comments to indicate their support or agreement for what was being said, as illustrated by Excerpts 3.12 and 3.13.

Excerpt 3.12 Back-Channeling

ST:	*You know, I'm not an apologist for black men, but they have been demonized.*
FEMALE PANELIST:	*They have been. They have been.*

Excerpt 3.13 Back-Channeling

ST:	*You know, the churches that are empty during the week.*
FEMALE PANELIST:	*Seven days a week.*

Such exchanges are a common phenomenon in many African American churches, where the "Amen corner" serves to support the pastor or other speakers through feedback such as this.

Several of the SOBU participants also cited *scriptural* or *hymnal quotations*, as demonstrated by Congresswoman Sheila Jackson Lee in Excerpt 3.14.

Excerpt 3.14 Hymnal Quote

Thank you, my brotha, very much. Allow me to express the humble spirit of which I feel this morning, and just say to this great church and all that are gathered here, "There is a sweet, sweet spirit in this place." [SJL]

As noted in Chapter 2, Britt (2011a, 2011b) examined the various ways in which panelists in the 2008 SOBU symposium (regardless of whether they were members of the clergy) drew on the sacred-secular continuum in their use of *preaching register*, particularly as they attempted to negotiate difficult or confrontational stances. This technique was also observed in the 2004 panel, as demonstrated by Bishop Vashti McKenzie in Excerpt 3.15.

Excerpt 3.15 Preaching Register

I step out of that environment, who has taken my dignity and my integrity, and has defined who I am. But I step in the context of church. And I see myself, not reflected. Huh? Oh watch me now! Not reflected, not reflected in the eyes of someone who does not respect me, who does not care whether I live or die. But now I see myself reflected in the eyes of a Christ who know exactly who I am, and who I can become. Huh? [VM]

As discussed in Chapter 2, Labov (1972a) expressed doubt that the "lames" in his NYC study were capable of engaging in rhetorical practices such as these, given their presumed distance from vernacular language and culture. "If we are interested in toasts, jokes, sounds, the dozens, riffing, or capping, we cannot turn to the lames. They have heard sounding from a distance, but proficiency at these verbal skills is achieved only by daily practice and constant immersion in the flow of speech" (1972a: 288). However, the SOBU participants actually employed a wide range of African American rhetorical techniques, including various forms of *signifying* and other *indirect discourse*, achieved through *boasting and bragging*, *insults*, *verbal dueling*, and *word play* (cf. Mitchell-Kernan 1971; Smitherman 1977; Rickford and Rickford 2000; Morgan 2002).

For example, in Excerpt 3.16, Jordan A. Harris boasted about his own academic accomplishments, while signifying on those who endorse anti-intellectual ideologies and "calling out" the state of Florida for its controversial racial politics.

Excerpt 3.16 Boasting and Bragging

And then I began to be around all these other great men, and then I began to see that being an intellectual Black man, it's nothing wrong with it, but that actually, you benefit more from doing that. I'm in Florida, free, because I'm an intellectual Black man. [JAH]

Julia Hare engaged in a series of indirect insults and witty word play, as she appealed to the audience for more time to talk (Excerpt 3.17)...

Excerpt 3.17 Indirect Insult

Okay, I know it is late and I promise not to keep you as long as Whitney Houston has kept Bobby Brown. [JH]

... chided ineffective elected officials and other Black leaders (Excerpts 3.18 and 3.19)...

Excerpt 3.18 Indirect Insult

I know I might be stepping on somebody's pedicures, that may be happening, but we cannot continue to have a party that represents us and we work for them lock, stock, and barrel and give all of our votes to them, and then they will not stand up... [JH]

Excerpt 3.19 Indirect Insult and Word Play

Black people still confuse Black leaders with leading Blacks. And you can't make that mistake. We all know leading Blacks. They preach every Sunday morning at 11 o'clock. But Black leaders are like this pastor, this church, who's out there in the trenches... [JH]

... and lamented a state of affairs that she perceived to be symbolic of the breakdown of the "Black family" structure (Excerpt 3.20)...

Excerpt 3.20 Word Play

And my last thing, I think it is, finally, important for us to know that, while these families are pulled apart like this, we have millions of Black men in jail, waiting for justice, and millions of Black women in church every Sunday, waiting for Jesus. [JH]

In Excerpt 3.21, Tavis Smiley and Sheila Jackson Lee engaged in a friendly banter over the amount of time that Jackson Lee would be allowed to hold the floor.

Excerpt 3.21 Verbal Dueling

SL: *Brotha Smiley, thank you. I could listen to all of these panelists all day long. And I know that there is a second panel. Dr. West has rubbed off on me. I got a lot on my mind and a lot on the plate.*
TS: *But a little– but a little time.*
SL: *A little time.*
TS: *So don't get it twisted.*
SL: *And little patience.*
TS: *I love you.*
SL: *And little patience, but I notice he does not have a gavel. But any event ...*

There were also several examples of *directed discourse*, including *verbal readings* (to be discussed more in Chapter 5), in which a speaker demeans another "in an unsubtle and unambiguous manner" (Morgan 2002: 53). In Excerpt 3.22, Judge Greg Mathis touted his own "street credibility" while chastising men who shirk their parental responsibilities. And he called out fellow panelist Jeff Johnson for not taking as direct a stand on the issue.

Excerpt 3.22 Verbal Reading

And then we'll have a brotha who's out on the corner with his chest stuck out talking 'bout he's the man, he want his respect. You ain't gettin' no damn respect until you take care of them kids that you're producing. You don't deserve no respect. We have to fight back. We have to fight back. There's the bottom line. We– we have to fight back. And I'm not some self-righteous brotha that's preaching. I'm a brother with the street credibility who fought back. And so I can check 'em like that. And maybe Jeff was a little hesitant. But I'ma check 'em. Brothas, it's time to man up. [GM]

And in Excerpt 3.23, Jordan A. Harris "read" (i.e., called out) mothers who have children out of wedlock and then go on reality talk shows to determine their children's paternity.

Excerpt 3.23 Verbal Reading

Please stop going on Maury, finding your baby daddy. I'm serious. And you laugh. But when you have a young lady that has to go on the show three and four times and test eight, to nine, to ten guys to find out who her baby's father is, that ain't cute. [JAH]

Compared to the grammatical and phonological feature inventories presented earlier, there was a much wider distribution of lexical and rhetorical
feature usage among the SOBU participants. The only participants who used
no such features were Myrlie Evers-Williams and Na'im Akbar, both of whom
were notably reserved in their use of vernacular structural features as well.
Neither participant used any vernacular grammatical features. And they each
used the fewest vernacular phonological features within their respective gender
cohorts. Evers-Williams and Akbar did employ a few colloquial expressions
like *been there, done that* [MW], *from the get-go* (i.e., from the beginning)
[MW], and *Podunk* (i.e., small town) [NA], but none that were particularly
innovative or even particularly "marked" in any way that would link them
specifically to the African American speech community. In what might be
considered a subtle form of signifying, Evers-Williams did make reference to
former Vice-President Dan Quayle's infamous gaffe when he attempted to
recite the National Association for the Advancement of Colored People
(NAACP)'s motto "A mind is a terrible thing to waste" (Excerpt 3.24).

Excerpt 3.24

*As was said, education, the mind. I'm not gonna be a Don Quayle– a Dan Quayle, it
is a terrible thing to waste and we must use it. [MW]*

In Excerpt 3.25, she even alluded to her lack of familiarity with current slang
terminology.

Excerpt 3.25

*What came in my mind was "mama." We have been mamas in the loving, nurturing
sense. We have also been "hey, mama," that kind of thing ... You don't become
"mama" in the honorable sense. You become "hey, hot mama" or whatever it is
that is said now. [MW]*

Also relatively reserved in terms of lexical and rhetorical usage were David
Satcher and Marva Collins, who employed no slang terms and exhibited only
limited use of African American rhetorical devices in their presentations. At
one point, as illustrated in Excerpt 3.26, David Satcher commented on how
quiet the audience was in response to his presentation, compared to many of
the other panelists, whose presentations were met with generous applause and
ovation.

> **Excerpt 3.26**
>
> DS: *And I– you know, this is sobering. So if you don't wanna applaud,*
>   *I understand that.*
> TS: (Laughs) *Don't– don't– don't take it personally.*
> DS: *No, I have no problem. This– this is sobering.*

While Satcher attributed the lack of audience response to the subject matter itself, his toned-down delivery likely played some role in the more muted reaction that he received. Given the synergistic relationship between lexical and rhetorical usage and the vernacular structural features discussed earlier, Collins's reserved performance might seem somewhat incommensurate with the relatively high number of structural features that she produced in comparison to the other female panelists. However, given her role as an educator, and her prescriptivist approach to language, as exemplified in Excerpt 3.27, it is likely that much of Collins's vernacular feature usage was performed below the level of conscious awareness, while more salient features at the level of the lexicon or discourse might have been more consciously muted.

> **Excerpt 3.27**
>
> *Take the time to correct the grammar that you do know with your children. Every*
> *conversation is an English lesson.*

Many of the panelists, however, seemed to draw upon these lexical and rhetorical strategies with intentionality, in order to entertain, inform, and build solidarity with the immediate audience. Among the female panelists, Julia Hare and Vashti Mackenzie were particular crowd favorites. And among the male panelists, Cornel West, Greg Mathis, and Jordan A. Harris garnered considerable applause for their rhetorical prowess. However, it was Tavis Smiley, in his role as lead moderator and facilitator, who was most adept at drawing on the African American repertoire to engage the audience. In the final section, I consider the implications of these observations for our understanding of intraspeaker variation along the standard-vernacular continuum.

Intraspeaker Variation in Performative Contexts

The feature inventories presented in this chapter reveal a range of linguistic behaviors, from Myrlie Evers-Williams (MW) and Na'im Akbar (NA), who used almost no vernacular features, to Tavis Smiley (TS), who used a wide

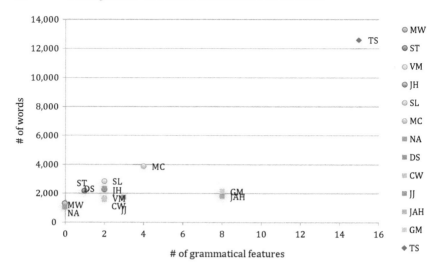

Figure 3.8 Number of grammatical features used per number of words spoken ($rs(13) = 0.550$, p = 0.052)

range of phonological, grammatical, lexical, and rhetorical features. The broad inventory of features used by Smiley, compared to the other participants, could be at least partly reflective of the greater number of words that he used as the lead moderator of the symposium. As indicated in Figures 3.8 and 3.9, a Spearman's Rho correlation coefficient test revealed a positive relationship between the number of words spoken and the number of grammatical and phonological features used, respectively, though neither association fell within the p ≤ 0.05 threshold for significance.

Note that Smiley led the SOBU participants both in terms of the number of words spoken and the inventory of grammatical and phonological features used. However, when the inventory of features for each individual is calculated as a fraction of the number of words spoken (i.e., number of features used/ number of words spoken), we see that Smiley actually had the lowest overall "density" of vernacular feature usage among the SOBU participants, as well as the lowest density of phonological features. And he fell near the middle of the group in terms of grammatical feature usage (cf. Craig and Washington 2006; Renn 2007, 2010; Van Hofwegen and Wolfram 2010).[39]

[39] This method of calculating vernacular feature usage is a variation on the Dialect Density Measure (DDM) introduced by Craig and Washington (2006) and employed in studies such as Renn (2007, 2010) and Van Hofwegen and Wolfram (2010) for the purpose of assessing vernacularity levels and styleshift. It is important to note here, however, that the calculations shown in Figure 3.10 only track the *inventory* of features used, not the actual feature frequencies.

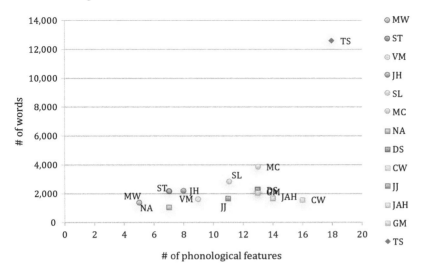

Figure 3.9 Number of phonological features used per number of words spoken ($rs(13) = 0.440$, p = 0.132)

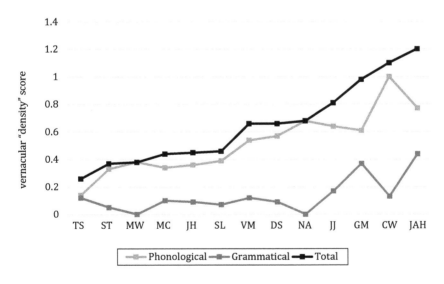

Figure 3.10 Density of vernacular feature usage per # of words spoken

Verbosity alone also fails to account for the gender differences observed in the data. Note in Figure 3.10 that, Tavis Smiley notwithstanding, the density of vernacular feature usage, while low overall, was consistently lower among the female participants (ST, MW, MC, JH, SL, and VM) in comparison to the male

Table 3.16 *Average number of phonological and grammatical features used per speaker and per number of words spoken*

	Female Panelists	Male Panelists	Lead Moderator (TS)
Grammatical			
Total # of features	11	23	15
Average # of features/speaker	1.8	3.8	n/a
Phonological			
Total # of features	53	74	18
Average # of features/speaker	8.8	12.3	n/a
Total # of Phonological + Grammatical Features	64	97	33
Total # of words spoken	14,091	10,550	12,597
Density of feature usage/words spoken	0.45%	0.92%	0.26%

participants (DS, NA, JJ, GM, CW, and JAH). As shown in Table 3.16, female panelists averaged 1.8 grammatical features and 8.8 phonological features per speaker, compared to the male panelists (again excluding Tavis Smiley), who averaged 3.8 grammatical features and 12.3 phonological features per speaker.

While the women used a higher overall number of words (N = 14,091) compared to the men (N = 10,550), the average density of vernacular feature usage per number of words spoken among the women (0.45%) was lower than that of the men (0.92%) at a statistically significant rate ($X^2(1)$ = 20.117, p = 0.000). And among the variables that were observed for actual frequency of usage, the rate of vernacular feature usage among the female panelists was consistently lower than that exhibited by their male counterparts, as illustrated in Figure 3.11.

Thus, despite the relatively low rates of vernacular usage observed among the SOBU participants, the patterns of distribution observed across gender groups were consistent with the traditional observation made in the linguistic literature that women tend to adhere more closely to mainstream prestige norms than men. As discussed earlier, social stratification studies tended to attribute such patterns to the "linguistic conservatism" or even "linguistic insecurity" of female speakers, who might have felt compelled to seek social capital through their use of language in the absence of opportunities to accumulate material wealth and status through occupational endeavors (see, e.g., Trudgill 1983). Given the professional accomplishments of the SOBU participants, however, it is likely that such traditional explanations fall short of fully accounting for the gender divide observed. Other studies have pointed to the effects of the linguistic marketplace, which has offered women greater exposure to Standard English in certain communities (see, e.g., Nichols 1983;

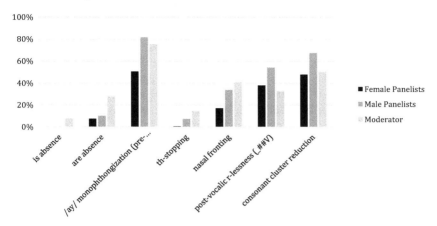

Figure 3.11 Vernacular frequencies for select phonological and grammatical features

Eckert 1989). But given the professional status of the SOBU participants, it is likely that such factors would have been more or less equalized across gender groups.

Another consideration is the extent to which the male participants might have felt greater pressure to demonstrate their vernacular fluency in this performative context. In a study of the language attitudes of African American attorneys in the South, Garner and Rubin (1986) observed that men reportedly experienced greater pressure than their female counterparts to styleshift. They explained,

[Men] generally agreed that peers had a great impact on speech behaviour in everday life. The most common thread that runs throughout male responses was articulated by one respondent who said that a black youth coming up must have "a command of both languages." That linguistic flexibility included a command of SE which he equated with those "on the higher end of the social scale," and a command of BE which he associated with those "lower socio-economic situations." (Garner and Rubin 1986: 45)

To the extent that the men in the SOBU forum felt similar pressures to demonstrate such fluency in a context focused heavily on Black rhetorical skill, such expectations might have contributed to the observed gender patterns.

These pressures might also have been compounded by the effects of age, given that Jordan A. Harris (JAH), the youngest participant on the SOBU panel, exhibited the highest overall density of vernacular feature usage per words spoken, as well as the highest density of grammatical features used

(Figure 3.10). This age dynamic is consistent with Labov's observation in his 1972a study that younger speakers tend to be more closely connected to vernacular language and culture than older speakers, who become more adept at styleshifting over time as they become more fully integrated into the mainstream. For the SOBU participants, this adeptness seemed particularly salient at the level of the grammar, where the most stigmatized features were largely reserved for controlled, performative styleshifts. As demonstrated in Figures 3.10 and 3.11, vernacular grammatical features were consistently lower than vernacular phonological features both in terms of their density and frequency of usage. And most of the performative work of the SOBU participants was done at the level of the AAE lexicon or discourse, where there was high salience, relatively low overt (i.e., mainstream) stigma, and relatively high covert (i.e., in-group) prestige (cf. Labov 1972a). While phonological feature usage appeared to be less susceptible to conscious awareness and control, there was evidence of at least some manipulation of stigma and prestige even at this level, as speakers seemed to avoid the most stigmatized pronunciations, while making greater use of features that were ethnically marked, but with low overt stigma and/or high in-group prestige. Such patterns of usage are consistent with the concept of Standard African American English (SAAE) described earlier.[40] Note in Figure 3.10 that the speaker with the highest density of phonological features per number of words spoken was Cornel West (CW), who conversely had one of the lowest grammatical density rates, particularly among the male participants. Similar patterns were also exhibited by Myrlie Evers-Williams and Na'im Akbar, who employed no vernacular grammatical features at all. In fact, with exception of Tavis Smiley, all of the SOBU participants drew more heavily on phonological, lexical, and rhetorical features than grammatical features in their performances, thus illustrating the efficacy of SAAE in signaling solidarity with the African American community, particularly in Black intellectual spaces such as the SOBU forum where Standard Language Ideology (i.e., overt prestige) and racial/ethnic identification (i.e., covert prestige) had the potential to invoke competing norms and expectations.

Unique among the SOBU participants, however, was Tavis Smiley whose inventory of phonological and grammatical features was remarkably balanced and comparatively broad. As noted several times throughout the chapter, Smiley drew on the vernacular to perform a variety of functions in his role as moderator, e.g., mitigating face-threatening acts, speaking candidly/force-fully, boasting about someone's accomplishments, building solidarity with the

---

[40] Not considered here, of course, is the relative salience of certain prosodic AAE features and the extent to which they are also subject to awareness and control in performative contexts (cf. Tarone 1973; Thomas 2015; Holliday 2016).

audience, etc. Typically, Smiley's vernacular feature usage involved a salient clustering of phonological, grammatical, lexical and rhetorical features (cf. Mitchell-Kernan 1971), as illustrated by Excerpt 3.28, where Smiley playfully signified on Greg Mathis, while introducing him as the next speaker.

Excerpt 3.28

I saw– uh I– I was goin' there anyway. I was goin' there anyway, because we been friends for a lot o' years an' I know his story. And, interestingly, I just looked out the– looked out the side of my eye over here, and uh saw him jump up in the forefront of his seat. Now he walked out nice and clean and cool wit' dat brown pin-striped suit on, sittin' back in his chair wit his legs crossed, rockin' his outfit. And look at him now. He all leaned forward, got his elbows on his knees. I think Judge Mathis is ready to go. An' I– an' I know why he's ready to go. I'm– I'm glad I'm not, I'm glad he ain't on 'e bench right now wit' me standin' in front of him, 'cause he ready to get– he– he ready, he ready to get goin' here. But I know why you ready to go, Greg. And I won't take it any further than that. But your story mirrors exactly what Jeffery was talkin' about. So, again, I ain't gon ask a question, just start layin' it out. [TS]

When observed in isolation, an excerpt such as this one might give the impression that Smiley is a relatively robust and consistent vernacular speaker. However, there were also long stretches of speech like that illustrated by Excerpt 3.29, in which Smiley employed few to no vernacular features.

Excerpt 3.29

So we'll be on CSPAN for this panel, we'll be on CSPAN for panel number two as well. And again, we thank CSPAN for caring enough about these conversations in this all-important political year to share this conversation with America, and indeed the world. Now, it is my pleasure and my privilege, it is my honor, indeed, to every year commence these symposiums with a word of prayer. We talked last year in Detroit at this annual symposium about the importance of, the role, the responsibility, and in many ways the abrogation of its responsibility to Black America. Talking now about the Black church. It is without question one of the most abiding institutions in our community. And so we talked at last year's heated symposium, you'll recall, very– last year's honest symposium about the role and the responsibility of the African American church. And so there is no institution that has done more for us than the Black church. Always on the vanguard, on the cutting edge of the issues that matter to Black America. Always the conscience of our community, indeed, in many ways, the conscience of this country. But there would not be a Black church if there were no Black family. So in this important election year again, we decided that this year was the best time to have a critical conversation in the community about the importance of Black family. [TS]

When presented in juxtaposition with one another, these two stretches of speech beg the question of the extent to which many African American professionals are capable of alternating between more vernacular and more standard ways of speaking, in ways that might actually mask their true linguistic range and dexterity. John Baugh described his own struggles growing up in an environment where "mixed messages" about language ultimately led to a "sociolinguistic paradox."

I didn't want to sound "lame" (see Labov 1972a), and, as I had observed "on the corner," most of the "cool brothers" could "talk the talk" – and those who exhibited urban eloquence never did so in standard English. What, then, was I to do? Should I use standard English, to the exclusion of African American speech norms, and risk ridicule or social rejection from my black peers? Or, should I resist my parent's [*sic*] standard English advocacy and suffer the domestic consequences of open linguistic rebellion at home? (Baugh 2000a: 6)

Baugh's solution was to become a "linguistic chameleon," alternating between more vernacular and more mainstream ways of speaking depending on the context. His experience is not unique, however, but rather one that many African American professionals face as they learn to navigate the linguistic push-pull of mainstream America and the African American speech community.

Conclusion

Far from being "lames" who are removed from vernacular language and culture, the range of linguistic behaviors exhibited by the SOBU participants demonstrate how African Americans at higher levels of the socioeconomic spectrum can strategically draw on the vernacular while simultaneously demonstrating their familiarity with more mainstream norms of usage in ways that allow them to reap the benefits of both in-group and out-group membership. Key to accomplishing the task of "talking/sounding Black" (i.e., race-based identity construction), while appealing to the expectations of the mainstream establishment (i.e., class-based identity construction), is the strategic use of vernacular features, particularly at the level of phonology, as well as lexical and rhetorical features that are salient in terms of their racial/ethnic marking, but not highly stigmatized from a mainstream perspective. By contrast, saliently marked features such as *ain't* or the pronunciation of *ask* as [aeks] are typically reserved for more stylized performances, in which the intentionality of vernacular usage is made evident.

   While the SOBU participants varied considerably in the extent to which they drew on the vernacular and other elements of the African American repertoire for various purposes, the collective patterns of variability displayed by them suggest an awareness of not just the features themselves but of the rules that govern their linguistic and social constraints. While such skill and dexterity are particularly visible in public spaces such as the SOBU forum, where dual audiences are engaged, we are left to imagine how the personal motivations and histories of the participants informed the linguistic behaviors on display. As observed by Rickford (2001),

[S]ome verbal (and non-verbal) performances – especially those that involve radio broadcasts, large audiences, and public occasions *are* more stylized than others. And ... people in such situations *are* trying more consciously than most of us may do in everyday life, to project personas of various types. ... There are undoubtedly parallels to this kind of stylization in one-on-one conversation, but the oppportunities and possibilities for it seem to increase as audience size grows [emphasis in the original]. (Rickford 2001: 230)

In the next chapter, I attempt to capture some of these more personal dynamics through the lens of a self-study.

4 Language and Double-Consciousness
A Personal Account

It is a peculiar sensation, this double-consciousness, this sense of always looking at one's self through the eyes of others, of measuring one's soul by the tape of a world that looks on in amused contempt and pity. One ever feels his two-ness – an American, a Negro; two souls, two thoughts, two unreconciled strivings. . .

—W. E. B. Du Bois (1903)

Introduction: From "Babs" to "Biggie"

Papa, can you hear me? Papa, can you see me?
Papa, can you find me in the night?

—Barbra Streisand
"Papa Can You Hear Me"

I love it when you call me Big Poppa.
Throw ya hands in the air, if you's a true playa.

—Notorious B.I.G. (aka "Biggie Smalls")
"Big Poppa"

I begin this chapter with a confession of sorts. The soundtrack of my life ranges from Barbra Streisand to Biggie Smalls. My public persona, my "Babs" side, is primarily a mainstream-oriented one, through which I regularly assimilate to White cultural norms and expectations. My private persona, my "Biggie" side, is primarily an African American one that includes a predominately Black circle of friends, cultural practices, and ways of speaking. There are people in my life who know only the "Babs" side of me, and others who are primarily familiar with my "Biggie" side. While both sides reflect various aspects of my identity and experiences, I am most comfortable negotiating the two worlds separately. However, there are occasions when these worlds collide – when, for example, I drive to work blasting a song from Mary J. Blige and pass by a colleague before turning down my music, or I have a friend in the car from my "Biggie" circle when the song selection suddenly switches to Carrie Underwood. It is at these times that I am made especially aware of the dual worlds that define my daily existence.

In 1903, W. E. B. Du Bois famously articulated this experience, shared by many Americans of African descent, as one of "double consciousness." Over a century later, this reality still rings true for many African Americans, and perhaps especially for many middle-class African Americans, who find themselves having to negotiate multiple, and sometimes conflicting, norms and identities, given their more central positioning along the socioeconomic and sociocultural spectrum of American society. When it comes to language, this sense of double consciousness is often reflected through Geneva Smitherman's concept of "linguistic push-pull" (1977, 2006). To navigate this complicated terrain, I often shift between ways of speaking that are more mainstream and those that are more ethnically marked. Alternating my speech in this way has allowed me to satisfy mainstream expectations while still maintaining allegiance with the African American community. Nevertheless, the practice has at times felt like, as Du Bois puts it, "two unreconciled strivings" – to sound "Black enough" to be accepted by the African American community, while at the same time not sounding "so Black" that you get penalized by the norms and expectations of White America.

I became aware of the utility of "codeswitching"[1] early in life, as I observed many of the adults around me change the way that they talked when White people were present. The so-called White or Proper voice was a means of accommodating to White speaker sensibilities, but also a way of presenting oneself as someone who had achieved a certain level of education or sophistication. "Talking Black" was fine for the home and was often expected in certain predominately Black spaces, but it was also widely regarded as "bad English" – as something that was to be "corrected" in mainstream circles. As discussed in Chapter 2, such practices adhered to the notion of "respectability politics" – the idea that certain cultural practices and behaviors should be eschewed in favor of more mainstream behavioral norms (Higginbotham 1993).

By way of analogy, I often liken this phenomenon to the politics of Black hair. Like others of my generation, I got my hair straightened as a little girl, in compliance with White cultural norms of beauty. During the Civil Rights Movement of the 1960s and 1970s, the "Afro" gained popularity as a hairstyle that symbolized Black pride and, to some extent, a rejection of the "respectability politics" that had guided the aesthetic preferences of earlier

[1] While I maintain the working definition of African American English (AAE) presented in Chapter 1, as a continuum ranging from collections of standard varieties to collections of vernacular varieties, and acknowledge that such a model privileges a one-system approach to intraspeaker variation, I use the term "codeswitching" here, and elsewhere in this chapter, as it has been adopted by certain segments of the general public to refer to different ways of talking and behaving in different contexts and/or for different purposes or audiences (see, e.g., NPR's podcast series "Code Switch" [www.npr.org/sections/codeswitch/]).

Figure 4.1 Weldon (right) pictured at home with younger sister (circa 1979)

generations. However, it was a style that my younger sister and I (pictured in Figure 4.1) would only wear at home.

During most of my youth, it was not uncommon to hear people refer to courser hair textures as "nappy" or "kinky" – terms that had decidedly negative connotations themselves – or simply as "bad hair," while hair textures that were straighter or curlier were celebrated as "good hair." In recent years, the "natural hair" movement has made considerable strides in combatting the stigma associated with Black hair and has inspired many African American women (and men) to embrace their natural hair textures. When I made the decision, as a middle-aged adult, to stop straightening my own hair, I was struck by the fact that after decades of having done so, I was completely unfamiliar with my own natural hair texture.

While many today recognize the racist ideologies that have imbued prejudice against Black hair, there is still a general ignorance about the ways in which Black language has fallen prey to similarly biased perspectives. Despite decades of linguistic research demonstrating that all language varieties are systematic and rule-governed, many still believe that there is something inherently "bad" or "incorrect" about Black language varieties and something inherently "good" or "correct" about White varieties. The reality, however, is that such judgments are a reflection of the social evaluations of the speakers themselves and are in no way supported by linguistic evidence.

In this chapter, I offer an autoethnographic account (Adams et al. 2014; Choi 2016) of my experience as an AAE speaker. By turning the lens on myself, as a middle-class, middle-aged, African American female from the southern USA, who is a native speaker of AAE and a trained linguist, I offer here a glimpse into a segment of the African American speech community that has been underrepresented in sociolinguistic research. While it is not my intention to suggest that my particular experience is illustrative of *all* middle-class African American speakers or even *all* middle-class speakers of AAE, it is an experience that I believe will resonate with many African Americans of my generation with similar regional and socioeconomic backgrounds. In the next section, I provide some information about myself and my family of origin to help situate myself in this regard.

This Is My Story...

I was born in 1969 in Columbia, South Carolina – a southern, mid-sized town located in the central part of the state. Columbia is the state capital and home to the flagship campus of the University of South Carolina and the Fort Jackson military base – two major contributors to the local economy. I grew up in a nuclear family setting, with my mother, father, and younger sister (see Sound Files 4.1a and 4.1b for a glimpse into this early chapter of my life). Both of my parents were born and raised in the 1930s on small farms in rural South Carolina. My father received his bachelor's degree from a Historically Black College/ University (HBCU) in SC and his master's degree in Clinical Psychology from a Predominately White Institution (PWI) in Kansas. Over the course of his career, he worked in both education and counseling, but ultimately retired from state government administration. My mother received her bachelor's degree from an HBCU in Alabama and her master's degree in Counseling from the same school. She worked in education throughout her career and retired as a school guidance counselor. My sister and I were raised in an all-Black, upper working-class/ lower middle-class neighborhood, where the mean home value was slightly above the local median. We attended a racially integrated, but predominately

Sound File 4.1a Weldon at two years old ("Happy Birthday")

Sound File 4.1b Weldon at two years old ("Mary Had a Little Lamb")

Black, Catholic preschool and then matriculated through the K-12 public schools to which we were zoned, which, because of neighborhood zoning practices, were almost exclusively Black. This type of de facto school segregation was the norm in Columbia in the 1970s and 1980s and, to some extent, remains so today, as periodic waves of "White flight" (Woldoff 2011), school choice, and strategic school redistricting practices have served to maintain the status quo (cf. Kohn 2015; Rosiek and Kinslow 2016).

Like other Black middle-class families, we participated in activities that reflected a certain level of "social capital" in the African American community. We attended an all-Black church, whose membership included many community leaders, educators, and professionals. My father was a member of the local "Townsmen's Club" – a social/civic organization for African American men in the community. And my mother played cards with a Bridge club comprised of all African American women, many of whom were educators. Both of my parents were members of historically Black Greek organizations, whose origins date back to the early twentieth century on HBCU campuses. And as teenagers, my sister and I were presented as debutantes in a local cotillion that accepted participants by "invitation only" and was largely restricted to elite Black families in the area (cf. Graham 1999). While these and other such activities were largely reflective of Black professional life, and, to some extent, the privileges and practices of the Black elite, our network of family and friends, from the perspectives of both race and class, was broad and diverse. Thus, whether I was getting my hair done at the local beauty salon, playing with other kids in my neighborhood, working on choreography at the Governor's School for the Arts, or performing in the church hand bell choir, I became adept at blending into my environment, both socially and linguistically.

My circle of friends consisted primarily of school-oriented, college-bound kids for whom Standard English was both expected and accepted, at least in certain contexts (cf. "jocks" in Eckert 1989). During my senior year in high school, I was elected Senior Class president and voted "Most Likely to Succeed" by my classmates. My grade point average earned me the distinction of being named class Valedictorian and giving the commencement address at my high school graduation. Standard Language Ideology[2] (Milroy and Milroy 1991; Lippi-Green 1997, 2012) was reinforced both at school and at home. I was "corrected" for certain grammatical "errors" by my teachers, parents, and other family members, many of whom were educators themselves. Nevertheless, there was always an unspoken (and sometimes spoken) stigma associated with "sounding Proper" or "talking White." And erring too far in that direction could result in being labeled an "oreo" (i.e., a Black person who "acts White") (cf. Fordham and Ogbu 1986). While I did not have a name for it at the time, and indeed, no circulating label exists for it even today, Standard African American English (cf. Hoover 1975, 1978; Taylor 1983; Spears 1988, 2015; Rahman 2008) (i.e., the use of standard grammar, but with a rhythm, intonation, and pronunciation that is ethnically distinct) became a means of satisfying these seemingly conflicting in-group expectations.

After graduating from high school, I attended a private, predominately White, politically conservative university in the South, whose undergraduate student population numbered less than 3,000. I was able to attend this elite university, which was priced well out of reach for most middle-income families, including my own, thanks to a full academic scholarship, that was achievement-based but also likely tied to some Affirmative Action initiatives (cf. Chapter 1). Despite my exposure to diverse groups of people while growing up, this was a difficult transition for me socially, as I was pulled out of my predominately Black environment and thrust into a world of privilege (and, to some extent, prejudice) with which I was largely unfamiliar. One of the earliest memories of my transition to college is of a phone conversation that I had with my assigned roommate. Though I was not informed of her race, she "sounded White" to me on the phone, and perhaps I "sounded Black" to her. We chatted briefly and made some preliminary plans for decorating our dorm room. Shortly thereafter, the University notified me that there had been a

---

[2] Lippi-Green (1997) defines *Standard Language Ideology* as: "a bias toward an abstracted, idealized, homogenous spoken language which is imposed and maintained by dominant bloc institutions and which names as its model the written language, but which is drawn primarily from the spoken language of the upper middle class" (64).

change in plans, and that I had been assigned a different roommate. While the decision to reassign me might have had nothing, or everything, to do with language and race, it was the kind of experience that fed my self-conscious awareness of (and insecurities about) both. Over time, I made a more concerted effort to alter the way that I talked in such situations in order to reduce the risk of being "linguistically profiled" (Purnell et al. 1999; Baugh 2003).

As an additional "coping mechanism" (cf. Fordham and Ogbu 1986), that was as much about guarding myself against prejudice as it was about seeking familiarity and solidarity, I actively befriended other African American students on campus. My newly assigned roommate, who was African American, was the first of several students who ultimately comprised my predominately Black network of friends and associates in college. I sat at the "Black table" in the cafeteria (cf. Tatum 2017), sang on the all-Black Gospel Choir, was co-captain of the predominately Black Dance Team, and participated in the Student League for Black Culture, thus ensuring a significant amount of interaction and engagement with the fewer than 100 African American students who were enrolled at the university at the time. I was among a group of students who advocated for the school's first Black Student Affairs Office. And I was among a group of women who became the first members of a historically Black Greek organization on campus.

Despite these intentional acts of aligning myself with the African American community in college, I had frequent interactions with White students as well. Given the small percentage of African American students enrolled in the school, I was typically the only African American student or one of only two or three in most of my classes. There were often incidents relating to language and race that defined these interactions. I recall once having a conversation with a White classmate who mentioned to me that he was from Alabama. When I responded that he did not sound particularly southern to me, he took offense and, to my surprise, said that I did not sound particularly Black to him. I, too, took offense, though it was difficult, at the time, to pinpoint what offended me most – the implication that I *should* sound a certain way because I was Black or the suggestion that I was somehow "less Black" because I did not fit this stereotype. (In retrospect, I imagine that he likely felt similarly conflicted about my assessment of his speech.)

During my sophomore year, I participated in a three-month exchange to France, where I was the only African American student in the program. While there, I was complimented by my French family for having a "good French accent," but also told, while I read to their youngest son in English, that I spoke English well. The latter seemed like an odd "compliment" to me at first, given that English was my first language. But I later came to suspect that stereotypes about African Americans speaking "bad English" had likely informed their expectations of what I would (or should) sound like.

Following the completion of my BA, I enrolled in a PhD program in Linguistics at a large Midwestern university, where I was the only African American graduate student. There, I not only found myself removed from the African American support system that I had established in college, but for the first time in my life, I was living outside the South. While I attempted to connect with the African American community in town, for example through church and sorority affiliations, and with other African American graduate students on campus through various student organizations, my circle of friends was largely White and/or international. This experience also played a significant role in my socialization into adulthood, some of which I elaborate on in the next section.

Today, I am back in Columbia, SC – the hometown where I was raised – working as a Linguistics professor at the University of South Carolina. My husband is a West Indian Jamaican, who immigrated to the USA as a preteen. And together, we are raising our children in a racially integrated, suburban neighborhood on the outskirts of the city, where the mean home value is moderately above the local median. While my social network consists of friends, colleagues, and associates from a wide variety of backgrounds, my closest circle of friends remains predominately Black.

Hearing Myself through the Ears of Others

As a linguist, I am often made privy to observations about language from linguists and laypeople alike. And on some occasions, the commentary has been directed at my own speech, thereby granting me the opportunity to hear myself through the ears of others. Once, while living in the Midwest as a graduate student, I was the victim of a prank phone call. I responded to the caller by "sucking my teeth"[3] in frustration before hanging up the phone. The person immediately called back and threatened me with a racial slur before hanging up herself. When I shared this experience with my neighbors, a group of African American undergraduate women from Cleveland, Ohio, they expressed surprise that the caller would have used that particular racial slur with me, noting that, in their opinion, I did not "sound Black" on the phone. On another occasion some years later, I was told by two African American students in a course that I was teaching that they were surprised, on the first day of class, to learn that I was Black. They had assumed otherwise after having heard my voice on my office voicemail. While these comments, both from African Americans with whom I was only casually familiar and relatively

---

[3] The act of "sucking teeth" is used in the African American speech community to signal disgust or disapproval. Variations of this discursive act can be found throughout the African diaspora (see Rickford and Rickford 1976 [1999]).

formal, construct a particular narrative of my voice as "Proper" or "White sounding," the comments of some of my fellow linguists have told a different story.

I recall several instances in graduate school when comments regarding my speech had an "othering" effect. Once, a classmate who was a non-native speaker of English brought to my attention how unusual she thought my pronunciation of *umbrella* was, because I placed primary stress on the first syllable. While walking down the hall with a group of students, a professor expressed amazement at how "flat" (i.e., monophthongal) the vowel was in my pronunciation of the word *mail*. And, during an office hours visit, another professor offered an unsolicited assessment of my speech as "mostly Standard," though he did not elaborate on the qualified nature of his assessment. I also have a particularly vivid memory, as a young faculty member, of attending a linguistics conference where I had volunteered to read a colleague's paper for a plenary that she was unable to attend. After the event, a colleague from the audience noted, with surprise, how pronounced my *pin/pen* merger was, even though she knew that I was from the South. Another approached me to ask how I would describe my speech. When I responded that I had assumed that it was some version of Standard English, she paused with deep reflection before walking off. I, too, stood there in deep reflection, wondering if anyone had actually heard the content of my colleague's paper that evening or if it was, instead, my language that had inadvertently become the focus of the keynote address.

While observations such as these could be as much about my regional background[4] as they are about my racialized identity, they seem to run counter to the narrative of "Proper" and "White sounding" alluded to in earlier anecdotes. I would contend, however, that these seemingly conflicting assessments of my speech are, in fact, characteristic of the linguistic "no man's land" that is Standard African American English (SAAE) (cf. Young 2007). While studies have shown that many middle-class African Americans view SAAE as a way of satisfying the often competing demands of mainstream America and the African American speech community (see, e.g., Hoover 1975, 1978; Rahman 2008), I have found that the soulful rhythm of SAAE, the voice through which I have largely constructed my own "Black academic" identity, elicits different responses from different audiences. From the perspective of more vernacular-speaking African Americans, I can be perceived as "sounding White/Proper," while for my predominately White, and primarily standard-speaking, academic colleagues, I am often perceived as "mostly standard" but not fully assimilated. And, indeed, while I have made some effort, particularly

---

[4] Incidentally, I have also been told on a number of occasions that I do not sound like I am from the South.

in my professional life, to adjust certain aspects of my voice accordingly (e.g., attempting to pronounce words like *pen* with an [ɛ] rather than an [ɪ], trying to round out the diphthong in words like *mail*, or even altering the pitch and intonation of my voice in certain contexts [cf. Holliday 2016]), I have found that such adjustments have been challenging both in terms of the level of awareness and control that I have over these aspects of my voice (cf. Babel 2016), as well as my lack of motivation to fully assimilate to White middle-class norms (cf. LePage and Tabouret-Keller 1985). My goal, after all, is not to "sound White" but to be accepted in my professional sphere as an educated speaker and writer.

When it comes to the observations of linguists, perhaps even more surprising to me have been comments made by those who have assumed that I do not adjust my speech at all in less formal contexts. I recall once having a conversation with a White colleague about a project that I was working on involving the grammatical environments affecting copula absence. He chuckled when I pronounced *going to* as *gon* [go:n], briefly shifting into the accent that I would normally use when speaking African American Vernacular English (AAVE), but in the context of the more mainstream style that he was accustomed to hearing me use. My pronunciation of the word apparently sounded inauthentic to him, prompting him to ask whether I had been ridiculed by other African Americans for not "sounding Black" when I talk. I responded by saying that, on the contrary, my use of AAVE, which I reserve mostly for my closest friends and relatives, is not typically commented on at all and, in fact, appears to be viewed as largely unremarkable in my more intimate spaces. On another occasion, when I shared with a colleague my plans for doing this self-study, she expressed grave doubt that I was capable of shifting into more vernacular styles of speaking and suggested that I instead direct my ethnographic attentions to other speakers who were more fluent in the vernacular. Another colleague predicted that this study would reveal to me that, in fact, my language really did *not* shift that much from one context to another. I have been particularly struck by comments such as these from people who have only been exposed to my more public persona. Indeed, this is the double-edged sword of "codeswitching." In order to "fit in" in the workplace, I have strategically masked my racial and cultural identity by assimilating to mainstream norms. But in doing so, I have masked a part of my identity that is central to who and what I perceive myself to be.

Once, at a conference where I presented some of the results of this self-study, I was asked by someone in the "Question & Answer" session how I knew that I was "doing blackness" when I switched into AAVE. I was initially puzzled by this question, because it seemed obvious to me that my use of AAVE was linked to my African American identity. But I ultimately interpreted the question as stemming from a social constructionist perspective, which acknowledges that linguistic forms can and do, in fact, index multiple meanings (Eckert 2008, 2012). I engaged that perspective in my response, by acknowledging that my vernacular usage was not *just* about blackness, as that was only one aspect of my identity, but that it was primarily in familiar Black spaces that I used AAVE. What I did not say at the time was that it is my blackness that I attempt to minimize when I switch into less vernacular ways of speaking. To put it in Labovian terms, AAVE is the style that I use when my guard is down and I am paying the least amount of attention to my speech – in other words, the vernacular is my "vernacular" (cf. Labov 1972b). And while it is true that I also use AAVE at times to "perform" other aspects of my identity (cf. Chapter 3), in most instances, speaking in a more vernacular style is simply about being me, my whole uninhibited self (cf. Sharma 2018), not hiding or minimizing my blackness to appease a world that "gazes" upon it with "amused contempt and pity" (Du Bois 1903) or even just benign curiosity and ignorance.

A Self-Study

In this section, I share the results of a self-study that I conducted, in which I recorded myself in a variety of settings in order to document my language use and explore the range of features that I employ along the standard-vernacular continuum. While intuitive accounts of language are not uncommon in linguistic research, sociolinguists have typically relied on empirical observation as their primary method of analysis (Labov 1972b). Labov (1972a), in fact, cautioned against African American linguists using their own intuitions to study the vernacular.

The position of the black graduate student in linguistics is no different from that of any linguist in his removal from the vernacular. If a black student should take seriously [Noam] Chomsky's claim that the primary data of linguistics is the intuition of the theorist and begin to write an introspective BEV [Black English Vernacular] grammar, the results would be bad ... The problem we are dealing with here is one of the greatest generality, for it must be realized that most linguists are lames. (Labov 1972a: 290)

Heeding this advice, John Baugh, in his 1983 study of *Black Street Speech*, explicitly acknowledged his decision *not* to develop an intuitive account of the variety, for fear that the standardized nature of his own speech would cloud his intuitions of the vernacular (38–39). While such concerns are certainly legitimate and speak to the importance of empirical observation as a primary means of sociolinguistic analysis, particularly if "tapping into the vernacular" (i.e., observing one's most relaxed style of speaking) is the goal (Labov 1972b), there is also much to be gained from mining the insights and perspectives of middle-class African American speakers, and perhaps African American linguists, in particular.

While the concept of "autoethnography" dates back to at least the 1970s, its currency as an accepted method of analysis in various fields is largely a twenty-first-century phenomenon (Choi 2016: 2). As the name suggests, auto-ethnography aims to combine the literary genre of autobiography with the anthropological method of ethnography, thus yielding a "systematic analysis of the actions, thoughts, reasons, and situations of a particular individual operating in a particular culture that aims to understand his/her way of life" (Choi 2016: 2). By reflecting on his own styleshifting patterns while conduct-ing fieldwork for his dissertation, Samy Alim (2004) provided an effective model for this type of analysis within the field of linguistics.

Being a sociolinguist who studies the variable nature of speech, with a focus on BL [Black Language], I am particularly attuned to the variation in that language variety. Beyond most speakers' intuitions, I can list the syntactic features that exhibit variation and the ones that don't. In other words, while I may share the consciousness of my stylistic adjustments with most speakers, I also have access to sociolinguistic language and theory to engage in a more precise metalinguistic analysis of my speech. (Alim 2004: 61)

While Alim's primary aim was to observe the effects of his own interactional style on the speech of his study participants (cf. Trudgill 1986), the goal of my self-study is to explore the range of my own stylistic repertoire and, in so doing, to provide an analytic perspective that is, at once, both inductive and deductive in its approach (cf. Baugh 1983).

For the purposes of this self-study, I recorded myself in a variety of settings to get a sense of the extent to which my language shifts from one context to another. In 2009 and then again in 2011, I periodically recorded myself talking to family, friends, co-workers, and other acquaintances. Because of the risk to privacy associated with capturing other speakers' voices in more intimate settings, I found that recordings of myself talking to family members and one-sided recordings of myself on the phone were best for capturing my more informal speech styles.[5] And given the compromised quality of recordings done in public settings with lots of background noise, I found that public lectures or presentations where I was the primary speaker, and audience participation and other background noise were minimized, were ideal for capturing my more formal or careful styles.[6] Another benefit to these types

[5] In order to ensure that speakers on the other end of the phone talked to me as they normally would, I did not typically inform my interlocutors of the self-recordings while they were in progress, though many of them knew in advance that I was doing a self-study and that I would be periodically recording myself.
[6] Participants at these public events were made aware of the recording. But because they were not given the opportunity to individually opt out of the recording, I do not include their voices in any of the audio excerpts that I share.

of recordings was that the interlocutors and audience members provided a built-in "pressure" for me to speak as "naturally" as possible under the circumstances, thus minimizing, though certainly not eliminating, the effects of the Observer's Paradox[7] on my speech (Labov 1972b). Thus, for the purposes of this self-study, these two contexts became my primary focus, not only because of the quality and relative naturalness of the recording contexts, but also because they represented opposing ends of the formality spectrum. While it has been demonstrated that styleshifting or codeswitching can be triggered by a variety of factors, including setting, topic, and addressee, as well as more "micro-level" considerations such as stance-taking and identity construction (see, e.g., Eckert and Rickford 2001), an examination of how my language shifts along the formality dimension seemed ideal for observing the extent to which it varies along the standard-vernacular continuum.

For this study, I analyzed approximately five hours of recorded speech – consisting of roughly two and a half hours of lecture and two and a half hours of conversation with my immediate family. In order to protect the privacy of my family, I transcribed and coded the conversations myself. The public lectures were first transcribed and coded by my research assistants and then checked and verified by me. As in Chapter 3, the recordings were transcribed using standard orthography, with certain nonmainstream pronunciations represented by alternative spellings (e.g., *runnin'*, *'fore*, *git*). A coding system was then used to indicate where phonological, grammatical, lexical, and rhetorical features typically associated with AAE appeared. Of primary interest were (1) the range of my stylistic repertoire along the formality continuum, (2) the social factors that seemed to motivate my use of vernacular features along the continuum, and (3) the role of salience and stigma in the quantitative distribution of certain vernacular features. To facilitate this analysis, I introduce here a **risk/reward** framework that interprets **risk** from the perspective of Mainstream American English listeners (i.e., overt prestige) and **reward** from the perspective of the African American speech community (i.e., covert prestige). I begin with a discussion of my public lectures, which represented my more formal style.

Public Lectures

For my formal style, I recorded myself giving two public lectures, each lasting approximately one hour and fifteen minutes.[8] The first was a lecture given to a

___

[7] As described in Labov (1972b), "to obtain the data most important for linguistic theory, we have to observe how people speak when they are not being observed" (113). This is known as the Observer's Paradox.

[8] Both of the public lectures from which the sound files and excerpts were drawn depended heavily on secondary source materials, which were cited within the context of the lectures themselves. I would especially like to acknowledge here the contributions of Wolfram (1998),

graduate sociolinguistics class in 2009. With their permission, I recorded myself during one class period near the end of the semester, after we had developed a relatively comfortable rapport with one another. The recording was done using a Sony IC digital recorder (ICD-MX20) and a Sony electret condenser microphone (ECM-MS907), which was placed on the table in front of me. The students were aware that I was recording the lecture and knew that it was for the purpose of a self-study. Nevertheless, there was a certain degree of guardedness in their participation that day, particularly at the beginning of the class period, perhaps because they were aware of their own voices being captured on the recorder.[9] Of the nine students in the class, one was Black and eight were White. There were three men and six women, all roughly between twenty-five and thirty-five years of age, and from a variety of regional backgrounds. The topic was philosophical and methodological approaches to teaching Standard English to vernacular speakers. Sound File 4.2 was drawn from the beginning of the lecture.

Sound File 4.2 Excerpt from class lecture

As this excerpt illustrates, my class lecture, though conversational in tone, reflected a relatively formal speaking style, largely devoid of overtly stigmatized grammatical features. The formality of my style was likely influenced by a variety of factors, including the class setting itself, an awareness of my status as a university professor, my role as instructor of the course, the formality of the students' speech, and, of course, the presence of the recorder. However, I was also consciously aware of being one of only two African Americans in the room – an awareness that was only heightened by the focus of the discussion that day on approaches to nonstandard dialects in the classroom. Upon reviewing the transcript, I was also struck by the fact that most of the students in the class (including the one African American student) made comments that day that were largely sympathetic to Standard Language

Wolfram and Schilling-Estes (1998), Pullum (1999), and Rickford (1999a) to the content of these lectures.
[9] Because I was only capturing the students' voices for the purpose of context (not for analysis), I did not request that they sign consent forms to do the recording.

Ideology, thus positioning me as the sole "defender" of the vernacular during much of the class discussion. My self-conscious awareness of these factors might have triggered the following shift from a casual, lax vowel, [ə], to a more formal, tense vowel, [u], in Excerpt 4.1:

Excerpt 4.1

*I would think the Dialect Rights would be the most cumbersome one **tuh** [tə]– **to** [tu] um institute– because uh it sort of wipes out the standard in that respect.*

However, there were also instances in which I shifted into more *casual* pronunciations (cf. "Context A" in Labov 1972c). For example, at the very beginning of the recording, before I started the lecture, my pronunciation of *it's on* in reference to the recorder reflected an ethnically and regionally marked pronunciation (Excerpt 4.2).

Excerpt 4.2

*An' I think it's recording. Okay, alright, so **i's on** [ɪs o:n].*

And in Excerpt 4.3, I pronounced *pen* with an [ɪ], as I moved out of lecture mode to talk about writing something on the board.

Excerpt 4.3

*So this goes back to um– I can pull out a **pen** [pɪn] and write again. It goes back to um the observation that this Eradicationism method alone is not entirely effective in gettin' everyone to speak Standard English. Right?*

A few minutes later, after having written the text on the board, I also deleted the second syllable in *probably*, as shown in Excerpt 4.4.

Excerpt 4.4

*We **prob'ly** [pɹabli] won't need this anymore now that I put it up, but I put it up.*

There were also instances in which I *intentionally* used vernacular constructions for performative effect (cf. Chapter 3). For example, in responding to a student who made the claim that parents and peers of college students "will argue with you to bring you down a notch to back to where you were" when you use Standard Academic English around them, I said the following (Excerpt 4.5):

Excerpt 4.5

But even s– even some of those parents while they wouldn't expect you to use that college talk with them [student: uh-huh] are really proud of you, you know, [student: uh-huh] in certain settings where– "Look at my college educated kid. **Ain't he smart.***" Right? Um, so you do sort of get that double message.*

There was also an observable clustering of vernacular phonological features, including nasal fronting and unstressed syllable reduction, as I described (and voiced) myself as a child becoming aware of my mother's codeswitching tendencies (Excerpt 4.6):

Excerpt 4.6

Yeah, yeah, 'cause my– my norm at home was codeswitching. Right? I think I've talked about that before. I would know, you know, if my mom was **talkin'** *to somebody White or Black by the way she answered the phone [student: the phone, yep.] "She's* **talkin'** *to somebody White now." So there I saw the* **codeswitchin'***. That was my model. It wasn't that I had one model at home and one at school. I had codeswitching at home.*

I also used nasal fronting to hedge a claim that I was making about double modals not being as stigmatized as multiple negation or *ain't* (Excerpt 4.7):

Excerpt 4.7

And you don't lose a lot in– in using it, right, in terms of your own social status. I'm **makin'** *this up as I'm* **goin'** *along. But it sounds good. Right? I don't know.*

And my vernacular usage also extended to metalinguistic commentary, as in my response to a student who questioned the authenticity of the language excerpted from a *Bridge* dialect reader (Simpkins et al. 1977) that we were examining in class. Here, I suggested that it was her reading of the text, rather than the text itself, that was problematic and suggested that the *they* in *they wheels* be read with an initial stop rather than a fricative (Excerpt 4.8).

Excerpt 4.8

*So you wouldn't say "**they wheels**" [ðe wɪlz]. You'd say "**dey wheels**" [de wɪlz].*

Notably, both the student and I produced the vowel in *wheels* as [ɪ] rather than [i], reflecting a regionally and ethnically marked vowel merger that was not overtly commented on by anyone during this exchange, and only became apparent to me as I reviewed the recording.

These excerpts from the class lecture demonstrate fairly minimal use of vernacular features that were relatively low in salience and stigma, being confined primarily to phonological features that were either shared with southern regional varieties (e.g., vowel shifts and mergers) and/or more casual registers (e.g., unstressed syllable reduction and nasal fronting). The use of grammatical features (e.g., *ain't*) or more overtly marked phonological features (e.g., fricative stopping) were largely reserved for purposes of intentional voicing or stylization.

The second lecture was presented in the summer of 2011 to a local African American Studies (AAS) council, as part of an annual guest lecture and luncheon series. The title of the talk was "Language, Literacy, and African American Students." There were approximately 25–30 audience members, consisting largely of African American women working in the field of education. To my knowledge, none of the participants had received any formal training in linguistics. And with one or two exceptions, most were people I had never met before. While I informed the audience at the start of my lecture that I was recording myself for a self-study, I only sought express permission from the event organizers to do the recording. As with the class lecture, I placed the Sony recorder and microphone on the podium in front of me for the duration of the lecture. An excerpt from an early portion of this lecture is provided in Sound File 4.3.

Sound File 4.3 African American Studies lecture

As with the class lecture, the formality of this speech event was dictated by the academic setting and topic, the relative formality of the participants' speaking styles, my lack of familiarity with most of the addressees, my status as a university professor, and my role as the keynote speaker of the event. Unlike the class lecture, however, where I was one of only two African Americans in the room, my recollection is that all of the participants at this event were African American, with the exception of two White audience members. Furthermore, in my role as an African American scholar, trying to appeal to an audience of African American educators about the value and legitimacy of AAVE, I found myself having to adopt a more nuanced linguistic approach than that employed for the class lecture. Thus, while the AAS lecture was delivered in Standard English, again largely free of overtly stigmatized grammatical features, there were several ways in which I adjusted my speech to appeal to the sensibilities of the audience and to the task at hand.

As with the class lecture, there were instances in which I exhibited a self-conscious monitoring of my speech, as in Excerpt 4.9, where I pronounced *been* with an [ɛ] rather than an [ɪ] when referring to it metalinguistically, even though I merged the vowel in the word *when* that preceded it and shortly thereafter in a nonmetalinguistic production of *been* in the same stretch of speech, as shown in Excerpt 4.9.

Excerpt 4.9

Another type of marking, grammatical marking, of aspect, **when "been"** *[wɪn bɛn] is stressed—* **when "been"** *[wɪn bɛn] is stressed, it indicates that something either happened a long time ago or has* **been** *[bɪn] in effect for a long time.*

There were also some seemingly unintentional lapses into casual speech when I was not in official "lecture mode," as observed at the start of the recording, when I deleted the [t] in *it's* (Excerpt 4.10).

Excerpt 4.10

And I'll try to forget that i's [ɪs]— that it's there.

Other examples could be described as fast-speech reductions, perhaps attributed to nervousness, as in my pronunciation of *little* in Excerpt 4.11:

Excerpt 4.11

Um one of the unfortunate things that came— and I'll talk a little bit about that a **li'l** *[lɪl] bit later today— but one of the unfortunate uh things that came out of that particular controversy was that it opened the door for a lot of uh what we call Ebonics humor.*

However, there were also instances in which I drew on the vernacular more intentionally, for example, to *demonstrate* the features that I was describing, as in the following discussion of remote past *BEEN* in Excerpt 4.12.

Excerpt 4.12

So *"I BEEN called them"* [Audience: knowing laughter] means "I called them a long time ago." *"I BEEN married."* Am I married now? *"I BEEN married."* Am I married now? I've been married for a long time.

Other performative uses of the vernacular were intended to build solidarity with the audience and with one audience member in particular from whom I sensed a palpable resistance to the premise of my lecture. This particular audience member became visibly upset when I asked the group to work through an exercise on habitual "be" in order to identify the rules that govern its usage. In the following excerpt, I attempted to acknowledge and voice her frustration, using nasal fronting and [ay] monophthongization in an effort to lighten the mood, as shown in Excerpt 4.13.

Excerpt 4.13

What I'd like you to do is look at the options. Does everyone have a sheet? Okay, so you'll have these pairs. Right? One through five. Uh, read them to yourselves. Read them out loud, if you need to. And pick one in each pair that sounds better with the "be." Okay, if you're not sure, just guess, u– use your best guess. And then we'll talk as a group about what our answers are. Um once you've answered those five if you would think about what you think the pattern is, right, for "be" usage, okay, and then at the very end— She said, *"No, Ah'm not playin'."* And at the very end, uh once you think you've discovered the pattern, if you would, determine whether or not those five sentences at the bottom are good use of "be" based on the pattern you've observed. So take a few minutes to do that, and then we'll talk about it together.

I later acknowledged her frustration again, using nasal fronting and fast-speech reduction in an attempt to present myself as more casual and less threatening, as illustrated in Excerpt 4.14.

Excerpt 4.14

I already see I'm um **frustratin'** at least one person, and I **wanna** give you the chance to say whatever it is that you want to say because I really do want this to be a dialogue. There's a lot I don't know, and I always welcome the opportunity to talk to educators in particular. So uh any thoughts, questions, comments?

There were also occasions when I used nasal fronting and fast-speech reduction to construct a humble, even self-effacing, persona, again as a way to build solidarity with the audience (Excerpt 4.15).

> **Excerpt 4.15**
>
> *This is where I'm really just **tellin'** you what other people have said because I don't know what I'm **talkin'** about, and some of you may have, you know, more recent information that you **wanna** share here, but these are some of the approaches.*

I also used the combination of nasal fronting and fast-speech reduction to prepare the audience for the use of linguistic jargon when I talked about more technical aspects of language (Excerpt 4.16).

> **Excerpt 4.16**
>
> *So I keep **talkin'** about rules, rules, rules. So I **wanna** talk about some of the rules. And I'm **gonna** be **watchin'** your eyes very closely. When they start to glaze over I'm **gon** stop, okay? 'Cause I know that there's a– a limit to how much of this you can take. Alright? So what I **wanna** do here is just show you a little bit of what we're **talkin'** about when we talk about rules governing African American English. And I picked a couple of pronunciation rules and a coup– couple of grammar rules. This is not an exhaustive list. Not even close. Right? But I tried to pick some features that are easy enough to communicate without– not **usin'** a lot of jargon um and that illustrate, you know, the fact that all of this is rule-governed. Right?*

My reliance on features like nasal fronting[10] and fast-speech reductions, in other words phonological phenomena shared by AAVE and other American English varieties, including more casual styles of Standard English, seemed to be a "low risk" way of building solidarity with the audience without resorting to overtly stigmatized vernacular features that, in this context, would likely have come across as marked and possibly patronizing to the audience. The use of these features also helped reduce the likelihood of my speech coming across as too formal or "Proper," which would also have had an alienating effect.

Nevertheless, there were instances in which I drew on certain grammatical constructions to deliver the technical material in a way that came across as

---

[10] It is perhaps significant to note that impressionistically, I found the vowel in the *–ing* suffix more difficult to discern in this particular recording, where it often tended to hover between [i] and [ɪ], compared to the class lecture and my more casual speech styles, where the vowels were more clearly discernable.

more conversational and less threatening. For example, in Excerpt 4.17, I used the expression *you got to have*, as opposed to the more mainstream *you've got to have* or *you have to have* in order to explain the rules of copula absence in AAVE. Note that there was also an instance of unstressed syllable deletion (i.e., *'cause* for *because*) near the end of this excerpt that contributed to the conversational tone that I was trying to convey.

Excerpt 4.17

*On the mainland, African American English, you can't say "I the teacher." **You got to have** "I'm" or "I am." Right? So it's not absent there. And it's not absent in past tense. Right? "We were working." You can't get rid of the "were" **'cause** where's the past tense there?*

I also used a null subject, omitting the dummy subject *it*, in my explanation of metathesis in Excerpt 4.18.

Excerpt 4.18

Ø happens in Standard English too. People say "perscription" instead of "prescription" all the time.

However, unlike in the class lecture, there were also occasions when I intentionally drew on more ethnically marked features to build solidarity with the immediate audience and to align myself with the African American speech community and with vernacular-speaking students, in particular. For example, in Excerpt 4.19, as I talked about the significant ways in which the African American speech community, and the hip-hop community, in particular, have contributed to the slang lexicon, I produced *tomorrow* with perseverative nasal assimilation of the initial [t] and laxing of the final vowel, yielding a more ethnically marked pronunciation.

Excerpt 4.19

*I guess we know what those are. Some of them stick around. Uh, but others are here today gone **tomorrow** [nəmarə]. And guess where a lot of them end up coming from? The hip-hop community. Right? And so a lot of times they begin in the African American speech community, and they get adopted by the mainstream through vehicles like music.*

There were also several occasions when I tried to construct an *us/them* dichotomy, by using more ethnically marked features to defend vernacular-speaking children and distance myself from those who label them as linguistically deprived. For example, in Excerpts 4.20 and 4.21, I used /ay/ monophthongization to speak frankly to the audience, as I mocked the flawed logic of those who disparage the vernacular.

Excerpt 4.20

"Well, these poor deprived children can't produce the 'sk' sound, so they have to reverse it." **I** *[a:] don't know* **why** *[wa:] "ks" is easier than "sk." But people say that. Right?*

Excerpt 4.21

"Oh this poor **child** *[tʃa:ld] does not have a copula. What will we do?" But the* **child** *[tʃa:ld] does have a copula.*

In another part of the lecture, I described the media's mishandling of the Oakland Ebonics controversy and explained how the misinformation led to further denigration of AAVE. Here, I exhibited a notable uptick in *th*-stopping[11] and nasal fronting, as well as [t] deletion in the contraction **what's**, as shown in Excerpt 4.22.

Excerpt 4.22

Dis *is what they meant. But what* **dey** *said is what* **de** *media publicized. What* **dey** *said's what* **de** *media publicized. And what the message was that got communicated was that* **dey** *wanted to teach Ebonics in* **'e** *classroom. Right? So they were* **usin'** *the term Ebonics for what we're* **callin'** *African American English. But* **wha's** *wrong with that?* **Dose** *students already spoke Ebonics. Fluently.*

There were also a few instances in which I used copula absence, accompanied by phonological phenomena such as nasal fronting, fricative stopping, and consonant cluster reduction, to construct an indignant stance against the

---

[11] Included under *th*-stopping were instances in which the word-initial *th* underwent perseverative assimilation in the context of a preceding nasal stop (e.g., *in the* pronounced as [ɪn nə]).

misrepresentation of AAVE and the academic plight of AAVE speakers (see Excerpt 4.23).

Excerpt 4.23

*And **den** 'e third myth is African American Vernacular English is Standard English with mistakes. Right? This is the idea that African American Vernacular English speakers are really trying to speak Standard English. **They Ø just making mistakes** in gettin' there. Right? These are the **readin'** and **writin'** scores of Ravenswood, which was a primarily African American and Hispanic school district, and Palo Alto, which was predominantly white **an'** affluent. **Those numbers Ø not even close.***

Finally, I engaged in several instances of call-response with the audience. In at least one instance, shown in Excerpt 4.24, I invited the response myself, using the expression *Isn't that fascinating?* with fricative stopping in *isn't*, to encourage the audience to share in my enthusiasm about a particular rule in AAVE. There were also times when the audience offered such feedback with minimal prompting on my part, as in Excerpt 4.25, when they responded affirmatively to my discussion of what it means to be labeled as "talking Proper" or "talking White" in the African American speech community.

Excerpt 4.24

***Idn 'at fascinating?** [audience laughs] I think it is. Uh, and so there're others there. I won't go through them. But AAVE/AAE is rich in that.*

Excerpt 4.25

*So this is a nice option. [Audience member: **Right**.] Uh, but even speakers who have full access to Mainstream American English, Standard English, will often choose– CHOOSE to maintain either African American English or African Vernac– African American Vernacular English, because they don't wanna be ostracized by their peer group. **Right?** So this idea of talkin' White or talkin' Proper, that's fightin' words. **Right?** [Audience responds in agreement.] I mean that's serious. It doesn't seem like it's serious. But most people don't want to be labeled in that way. And so this is one way– I think in particular **goin'** back to African American Standard English– it's one way to identify as part of the African American community while still, you know, **reapin'** all the benefits that **speakin'** a standard grammar brings you, yes?*

And in Excerpt 4.26, some audience members provided unprompted back-channeling support that seemed more characteristic of a church service than an academic talk (cf. Chapter 3).

Excerpt 4.26

We would never say that. Right? That German sounds like really bad French. That doesn't make any sense. And that's because we recognize that German and French are two distinct systems. [Audience back channels]

While the features described above might not have been perceived as particularly marked in this context, they undoubtedly helped guard against impressions of my speech as sounding too "Proper." In this regard, my AAS lecture style, perhaps even more than my class lecture style, drew on the resources of "Standard African American English" (Hoover 1978; Taylor 1983). In this context, the use of standard grammatical constructions was essential to listeners' acceptance of my professional credentials, especially given that most of the audience members not only endorsed, but *enforced* Standard Language Ideology in their own professions. If I had used more marked grammatical constructions like multiple negation or subject-verb nonagreement or even phonological features such as [sk] metathesis (i.e., "ask" as [aeks]), my bona fides as a PhD recipient, college professor, language expert, etc. would likely have been called into question or I would have been perceived as acting disingenuous and/or patronizing to the audience.[12] Nevertheless, the particular dynamics of this setting allowed for (and perhaps even necessitated) some strategic use of ethnically marked features to establish a comfortable rapport with the audience. Of course, it is important to acknowledge that not everyone hears my voice in the same way or shares the same ideologies about language and race that I bring to my interpretation of a given speech event. But these are the kinds of linguistic expectations (real or imagined) that I regularly strive to satisfy in my professional career. Earlier in this chapter, I described SAAE as a "linguistic no man's land." However, the linguistic nuances employed in the AAS lecture demonstrate the ways in which SAAE can also provide the kind of linguistic "middle ground" needed to navigate the complex terrain of "talking/sounding Black" in academic and other professional settings.

---

[12] Gender may have been a factor here as well, however, as it has been suggested to me that female academics are afforded a lot less leniency in these kinds of stylized demonstrations than male academics. (Conversely, it could be argued that men feel greater pressure to demonstrate fluency in the vernacular even in more formal settings.) Regardless of gender, the conditions for such demonstrations have to be carefully negotiated to ensure that one is not perceived as "coonin'" or "shuckin' and jivin'," terms used colloquially to refer to minstrel-like performances.

Private Conversations

For my casual style, I analyzed one recording of myself talking to my children, one conversation with my husband, and two conversations with my mother. Each lasted a little over thirty minutes. All of the recordings were conducted in 2011, using a Sony IC digital recorder (ICD-MX20) and a Sony tie-tac lavalier microphone (ECM-T115). Sound Files 4.4 and 4.5 were drawn from a recording of me talking to my children in the car, after picking them up from school. They were ages four and six at the time.

Sound File 4.4 Excerpt from conversation between Weldon and four-year-old

Sound File 4.5 Excerpt from conversation between Weldon and six-year-old

The next excerpt, presented in Sound File 4.6, was drawn from a recording of me talking to my husband while building a storage shed in our backyard.

Sound File 4.6 Excerpt of conversation between Weldon and husband

Sound File 4.7 was drawn from one of two one-sided recordings of phone conversations with my mother.

Sound File 4.7 Excerpt of conversation between Weldon and mom

Compared to my lecture style, these recordings reflected a more casual style of speaking that drew on the vernacular in terms of both phonology and grammar. Table 4.1 lists some of the phonological features that were observed in these recordings. Because these were casual conversations that took place in private settings with familiar acquaintances, my phonology included features like consonant cluster reduction, nasal fronting, and unstressed syllable

Table 4.1 *Phonological features in casual style*

Vowels	
/ay/ monophthongization	fine [faːn], ride [ɹaːd]
Diphthongization	dog [daʊg]
Vowel laxing in unstressed syllables	tomorrow [təmɑɹə]
	memory [mɪmɹɪ]
	to [tə]
Vowel laxing /_[l]	feel [fɪl], email [imɛl]
Vowel mergers	Clemson [klɪmsn̩];
	get [gɪt], pretty [pɹɪri]
Vowel shifts	want [wont], long [loŋ], on [on];
	thing [θeŋ], think [θeŋk];
	can't [kent]

Consonants	
Consonant cluster reduction	just *jus'*, find *fin'*
Loss of [t] in contractions	it's [ɪs], that's [ðæs], what's [wʌs], let's [lɛs]
Deletion of initial [d] or [g] in auxiliaries	I don't *I 'on(t);* I'm going to *I'ma/I'mo*
Fricative stopping/assimilation	these *dese*; with *wit*
	all that *all lat*; and that *an nat*
[l] vocalization/deletion	alright *a'right*
Nasal fronting	working *workin'*
Post-vocalic [r]-lessness	sister *sista*, for *fuh*
Word-final deletion of [v]	of [ə]

Other Phonological Features	
a + vowel-initial word	*He sent me **a** email*
Unstressed syllable deletion	because *'cause*, probably *prob'ly*

deletion, all of which are commonly found in more casual registers in American English. However, there was also a denser distribution of regionally and/or ethnically marked phonological features, such as /ay/ monopthongization, diphthongization, post-vocalic [r]-lessness, and fricative stopping.

In my casual style, I also used a variety of AAE grammatical features, illustrated by sentences 1–42 below.

Absence of –ed suffix

1. *No, I as' you if you had a good day, a great day, or an amazin' day.*
2. *De holes are not line' up.*
3. *She call' me yesterday w– when we were at soccer practice.*
4. *An– an over-price' like crazy.*

Absence of relative pronoun

5. *Useta be Ø you could git a sample or two.*
6. *Where you grow up Ø you don't know 'bout hags?*

Absence of third-singular –s marking

7. *Dis one look_ like it's higher.*
8. *He find_ out I'm goin', he Ø not gon' go prob'ly .*
9. *'Cause you git in nere an' everythang smell_ good.*
10. *It don't take but a coupla days.*

Absence of do-support

11. *Ø you trick Mommy?*
12. *Ø dey ask 'bout de kids?*
13. *What Ø you have in your mouth?*
14. *Where Ø you grow up you don't know 'bout hags?*

Ain't

15. *Dat ain't it.*
16. *Dey ain't got time da put de stuff out on 'e shelves.*
17. *Dey ain't gon heal up by tomorrow.*
18. *I ain't never heard dat, Mama, in a hundred years.*
19. *He ain't bin in 'e position what, but two days.*
20. *Ø ain't no need duh spen' money on sompm like dat.*

Aspectual done

21. *Lord ha' mercy, dis chile done broke sompm else.*
22. *Next thing you know you done spent all dis money on some junk.*
23. *I done missed dat.*

Copula absence

24. *He Ø averagin' like twen'y da twen'y five stores.*
25. *What Ø you talkin' 'bout, baby?*
26. *You Ø such a smart boy.*

Demonstrative *them*
27. *It ain't on none o' **dem** roads.*
28. ***Dem** li'l scratches on his face have all scabbed up.*

Existential *it*
29. *Dey don't even know **it's** a recession.*

***Got = has/have* (or absence of *has/have_ got*)**
30. *What you **got** goin' on today?*
31. *Dey **got** mine?*
32. *Dey **got** like three- and four-year-olds.*

Multiple negation
33. *I **don't** even have **no** doctors dat'll even give me samples **no** more **hardly**.*
34. *I'm **not** puttin' **nothin'** on it.*
35. *I **ain't** got **nothin'** ta wear.*

Object pronoun as personal dative
36. *I gotta git **me** some clothes.*

Possessive *they*
37. *De people who own de stores should put **dey** products out.*
38. *Dey jus' call' **dey** own li'l special practice.*

Subject absence
39. *Ø turns out there are no more.*
40. *Ø thought you were gonna take Clifford.*
41. *Ø useta be Ø you could git a sample or two.*
42. *Ø don't make no sense.*

As with the phonological features, some grammatical constructions, like subject absence and *got = have/has*, reflected a more casual style of speaking. But most of the grammatical features observed in my conversational style were features found in both Southern and African American vernacular varieties.

In addition to the phonological and grammatical features listed above, examples 43–48 illustrate some of the lexical, discursive, and rhetorical features that I used in my conversational style, all of which might also be seen as indicative of my southern African American identity.

Lexical/rhetorical/discursive features
43. *Great Day! [gre:d de]*
44. *Oh Glory! [o: glorɪ]*
45. *Come on [o:n], baby [bebɪ]!*
46. *(sucks teeth) Lemme see de thang!*
47. *Mm mm mm (= disgust, disappointment, disapproval)*
48. *Mama or Ma (= mother)*

While the collection of features observed in my more casual style demonstrated a clear shift in the direction of vernacularity, there were still ways in which I "policed" my vernacular usage in terms of the salience and stigma of certain features. For example, I sometimes avoided the use of highly stigmatized features, replacing them, instead, with features that were ethnically marked, but less overtly stigmatized. Instead of pronouncing "ask" with metathesis (i.e., [æks]), I sometimes pronounced it with consonant cluster reduction (i.e., [æs]). Instead of using subject-verb nonagreement (e.g., "she don't"), I would sometimes use the standard grammatical construction (e.g., "she doesn't") but with fricative stopping (i.e., [dʌʔn̩t]). I tended to delete the -ed suffix primarily in environments that were candidates for consonant cluster reduction (e.g., called as call), thus begging the question of whether the absence represented a phonological process or a true shift in grammatical structure (or both). And there was a tendency for me to "standardize" constructions if asked to repeat myself, in other words in ways that were reflective of Labov's (1972c) attention-to-speech model.

While there was a more salient clustering of vernacular features in my casual style compared to my lecture style, an impressionistic assessment of the casual recordings pointed to a higher density of vernacular feature usage in the conversations with my mother compared to the conversations with my children and with my husband. While it is difficult to assess why this might have been the case, and there were likely many factors at work, I suspect that my shifts in and out of more standard usage with my children likely reflected the "motherese" register that I employed with them, particularly when they were younger. In the recording with my husband, my periodic shifts into more standard usage might have been triggered, in part, by our focus (and commentary) on the technical aspects of building the shed. However, with my mother, the conversations were not linked to any particular activity, but instead represented "talk for the sake of talk." And, perhaps, in my role as "daughter" I tend to revert to a style that is more reminiscent of my formative years, and my language of "home."

To get a sense of whether these impressionistic judgments reflected actual quantitative differences in my vernacular feature usage, and to gauge the extent to which such usage differed from the formal speaking styles described earlier, I conducted a quantitative analysis of three select features, representing differing levels of salience and stigma. The results of this analysis are presented below.

Intraspeaker Variation: A Quantitative Analysis

In order to observe the extent to which my vernacular feature usage varied along the formality continuum, I conducted a quantitative analysis of three features – *nasal fronting*, *th-stopping*, and *copula absence* – which I perceived as representing three different levels of salience and stigma.

Nasal Fronting From a mainstream perspective, nasal fronting (e.g., *working* [wɨkɪn]) represents the lowest level of salience and stigma because it is a feature that is found in other vernacular varieties of American English, as well as more casual styles of Mainstream American English. It, therefore, garners less overt attention (and commentary) by listeners and, as such, seems to get used largely below the level of conscious awareness. It is, however, a feature whose "prestige" variant (i.e., *working* [wɨkiŋ]) is perceived by many in the African American speech community as indicative of "sounding White/Proper." From this perspective, the use of nasal fronting represents a **low risk/high reward** option, in other words one through which I am able to align myself with the African American speech community without being perceived as particularly low status or uneducated.

A quantitative analysis of this feature showed a shift from 28.2% [ɪn] usage in my lecture style to 88.7% usage in my conversation style, which a Two-proportions test found to be a statistically significant difference (p = 0.000) (Table 4.2).[13] The fact that nasal fronting showed up with moderate frequency in my lecture style supports my perception of it as a "low risk" vernacular feature. And, as noted earlier, there was perhaps even some benefit to using it moderately in my formal style for purposes of solidarity-building or otherwise minimizing distance for performative effect. In more relaxed settings, however, the use of nasal fronting became much higher, signaling a shift to a norm in which the use of [iŋ] became marked.

When broken down by audience/addressee, there was a steady increase in the use of the [ɪn] variant along the hierarchy shown in Table 4.2, revealing a gradient stratification of the variable within each respective speech style and a sharp stratification across styles (see shaded rows). Note that there was a statistically significant increase at each point along this hierarchy, with the exception of the *w/Children<w/Husband* comparison, which showed a non-significant increase in [ɪn] usage.

The greater use of [ɪn] in my AAS lecture, compared to my class lecture, likely reflected the racial as well as interpersonal dynamics described earlier in this chapter, which required a more strategic use of vernacular features than that required (or perhaps even permitted) in the class lecture. And while my use of this feature increased considerably in conversations with my children and husband, they became near-categorical in conversations with my mother, thus signaling a shift to a more vernacular norm.

---

[13] The coding of this variable was done impressionistically and attended more to vowel quality (i.e., [ɪ] vs. [i]) than nasal quality (i.e., [n] vs. [ŋ]), the latter of which was difficult to perceive without the aid of acoustic measurement. As in Chapter 3, the Two-proportions test results are reported as a Chi-square statistic.

Table 4.2 (ing) variation across speech styles

(ing)	Lecture			Conversation				
	Class		AAS	w/Children		w/Husband		w/Mom
N =	254		263	34		28		115
[iŋ]	76%		67.7%	23.5%		21.4%		5.2%
[in]	24%	<	32.3%	76.5%	<* (ns)	78.6%	<	94.8%
X²(1) =		4.396	25.075		.039		7.698	
p =		0.036	0.000		0.844		0.006	

	Lecture	Conversation
N =	517	177
[iŋ]	71.8%	11.3%
[in]	28.2%	88.7%

$X^2(1) = 195.952, p = 0.000$

Note: *Results marked by (ns) did not meet the $p \leq 0.05$ threshold for significance.

130

Th-stopping Compared to nasal fronting, *th*-stopping (e.g., *this* [dɪs]) represents a higher level of salience and stigma from a mainstream perspective. While it is a feature that is found in other vernacular varieties, including southern White varieties of American English, it is not a feature that goes undetected in mainstream circles. Rather, it is a feature that gets perceived by mainstream listeners as indicative of lower social status, even if listeners are not able to overtly articulate what they are attending to linguistically. In the African American speech community, however, this feature can be perceived as a marker of ethnic/racial solidarity, in other words as a way of "sounding Black." As such, it might be described as a **high risk/high reward** feature.

Compared to the (ing) variable, a comparison of (th) across speech styles revealed a sharper styleshift for *th*-stopping, from 0.9% frequency in lecture style to 81.5% frequency in conversation style.[14] However, a breakdown of the variable by audience/addressee in Table 4.3 reveals the same hierarchy within and across speech styles that was observed in Table 4.2 for (ing).

The wider range of variation observed for this feature supports my assessment of it as a **high risk/high reward** feature. In my class lecture, there were no instances of *th*-stopping at all. And while a few instances were observed in the AAS lecture (N = 17), they still represented less than 2% overall frequency, thus suggesting a strategic use of this feature, perhaps in response to the racial and interpersonal dynamics described earlier. In conversation style, the use of this feature ranged from 63.2% with my children to 86.5% with my mother, reflecting a much more vernacular norm than that observed in my lecture style, but with slightly lower frequencies than those observed with the (ing) variable. Each point along this hierarchy showed a statistically significant increase, both within and across speech styles.

Copula Absence As a final consideration, I did a quantitative analysis of the copula. As noted in Chapter 3, the copula is a hallmark feature of sociolinguistic research on AAE, in large part because of its implications for the debate over the origins and development of the variety. While *are* absence occurs in a number of vernacular varieties of American English, and may be compounded by the process of post-vocalic [r]-lessness (Labov 1972a), *is* absence appears to be largely restricted to African American varieties. And as a nonstandard *grammatical* feature, copula absence is highly salient in comparison to the two phonological features described above. However, the level of markedness or stigma associated with *is* absence may be even greater than that

---

[14] This variable included the production of [ð]/[θ] as stops (e.g., *this* [dɪs] or with [wɪt]), as well as the assimilation of word-initial weak fricatives in the context of preceding nasals/liquids, resulting in consonant gemination and/or fricative deletion (e.g., *in the* [ɪn ðə] as *in 'e* [ɪn nə] or [ɪnə]; *all these* [ɑl ðiz] as all '*ese* [ɑl liz] or [ɑliz]).

Table 4.3 *(th) variation across speech styles*

(th)	Lecture			Conversation				
	Class		AAS		w/Children		w/Husband		w/Mom
N =	808		1,109		68		171		414
fricative	100%		98.5%		36.8%		23.4%		13.5%
"stop"	0%	<	1.5%	<	63.2%	<	76.6%	<	86.5%
$X^2(1) =$		12.497		504.216		4.394		8.586	
p =		0.000		0.000		0.036		0.003	

	Lecture	Conversation
N =	1917	653
fricative	99.1%	18.5%
"stop"	0.9%	81.5%

$X^2(1) = 1882.870$, p = 0.000

Table 4.4 *(is) variation across speech styles*

is	Lecture		Conversation		
	Class	AAS	w/Children	w/Husband	w/Mom
N =	42	98	18	15	35
full	98%	97%	72.2%	66.7%	74.3%
contracted	2%	3%	27.8%	33.3%	17.1%
zero	0%	0%	0%	0%	8.6%
	Lecture		Conversation		
N =	140		68		
full	97.1%		72.1%		
contracted	2.9%		23.5%		
zero	0%		4.4%		

associated with *are* absence, given its limited social distribution and high racial/ethnic association. Given the greater stigma associated with nonstandard grammatical constructions in American English (cf. Wolfram and Schilling-Estes 1998), copula absence would likely be described as a **high risk/low reward** feature, perhaps especially for speakers positioned at more intermediate levels of the socioeconomic spectrum, where grammatical stigma has the potential to carry a higher penalty for upward social mobility (cf. Labov 1966). Nevertheless, there are undoubtedly ways in which copula absence, when placed in its proper context, can have the effect of signaling membership in the African American speech community, in other words, as a means of "talking Black."

A comparison of *is* absence across speech styles revealed an extremely low rate of overall usage, from 0% frequency in lecture style to only 4.4% frequency in conversation style (Table 4.4), compared to *are* absence, which ranged from 2.2% to 44.6% usage across speech styles (Table 4.5).[15] And a breakdown of the *is* variable by audience/addressee showed a heavy "policing" of *is* absence, which was only used in conversations with my mother, at a rate of 8.6% (N = 3).

---

[15] Consistent with other quantitative analyses of the copula, the coding of this variable excluded categorical environments and other "don't count" cases such as negated constructions, tokens occurring in sentence-final, inverted, exposed, and emphatic positions, past tense realizations, tokens occurring with first-person singular subjects, *what/it/that* (WIT) and *there* subjects, and tokens occurring in phonological environments where the presence or absence of the copula could not be clearly discerned (cf. Blake 1997).

Table 4.5 *(are)* variation across speech styles

are	Lecture				Conversation				
	Class		AAS		w/Children		w/Husband		w/Mom
N =	53		85		25		11		38
full	36%		51%		60%		27.3%		26.3%
contracted	64%		46%		16%		27.3%		15.8%
zero	0%	<*(ns)	3%	<	24%	<*(ns)	45.4%	<*(ns)	57.9%
$X^2(1)$ =		1.912		**10.776**		1.657		0.534	
p =		0.167		**0.001**		0.198		0.465	

	Lecture	Conversation
N =	138	74
full/contr.	97.8%	55.4%
zero	2.2%	44.6%

$$X^2(1) = \mathbf{61.487},\ \mathbf{p = 0.000}$$

Note: *Results marked by (ns) did not meet the $p \leq 0.05$ threshold for significance.

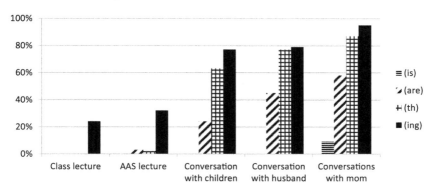

Figure 4.2 Summary of vernacular variant distribution across speech styles

The three tokens of *is* absence are shown in sentences 49–51.

49. *So he Ø averagin' like twen'y da twen'y five stores.*

50. *I thank she Ø jus' tired.*

51. *Oh yeah, I don't know why she Ø doin' nat.*

By contrast, *are* absence was distributed along the same hierarchy observed for the other two variables. Like fricative stopping, it did not occur at all in the class lecture. However, in contrast to (ing) and (th), which peaked at 94.8% and 86.5%, respectively, in conversations with my mother, the highest rate of *are* absence was only 57.9% frequency, reinforcing the assessment of this variable as a **low reward** feature, even in casual, familiar exchanges.

As shown in Table 4.5, the only significant increase observed in the (are) hierarchy was across speech styles, again suggesting a more controlled use of this vernacular variant in comparison to the phonological features observed.

Figure 4.2 summarizes the distribution of the vernacular variants across speech styles. The (ing) variable, which I described as a **low risk/high reward** feature, displayed the widest stylistic distribution, with the vernacular variant occurring in every speech style observed and reaching near-categorical frequency in conversations with my mother, which I identified as the most vernacular style observed for the self-study. By contrast, *is* absence, which I described as a **high risk/low reward** feature, with an even higher ethnic marking than *are* absence, only occurred in my most vernacular style. The vernacular variants for (are) and (th) were distributed across all of the speech styles observed, except the class lecture, where I was my most conservative (i.e., standard). However, there was a sharper shift between my lecture and conversation styles for (th), which had the potential to garner some positive reward in casual settings for "sounding Black," in contrast to *are* absence, which displayed a more measured shift across styles, as the risk of sounding uneducated

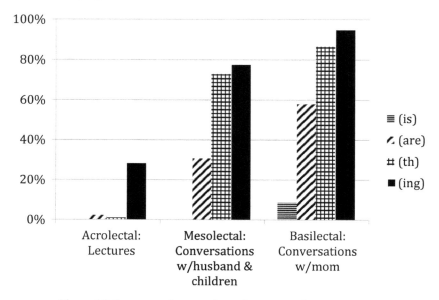

Figure 4.3 Summary of vernacular variants across lects

or lower status likely competed with the possible reward of being perceived as "talking Black."

Given the observed patterns of distribution, Figure 4.2 might also be reorganized into a three-way lectal cline, in which my lectures represent the acrolectal (i.e., standard) end of my stylistic continuum, the conversations with my husband and children represent more mesolectal (i.e., intermediate) speech styles, and the conversations with my mother represent the basilectal (i.e., vernacular) end of my stylistic continuum (see Figure 4.3).

As shown in Table 4.6, this three-way distinction is supported by the statistical evidence, which points to a significant shift at each of the three junctures for every variable tested. Arranging the data in this way also facilitates a comparison of my styleshifting with patterns of social stratification that have been observed in community-based studies. For example, Figure 4.4 compares my rates of *is* absence with those reported in Wolfram's 1969 Detroit study. While my rates of *is* absence, at 0% in both acrolectal and mesolectal styles, fall just below the frequencies exhibited by Wolfram's Upper Middle Class (UMC) speakers, the rates that I used in conversations with my mom (i.e., my basilectal style) fall between those exhibited by Wolfram's Lower Middle Class (LMC) and Upper Working Class (UWC) speakers. However, my rates of *are* absence, shown in Figure 4.5, span the full socioeconomic continuum observed by

Table 4.6 *Chi-square results for three-way lectal cline*

	Acrolectal (Class and AAS lectures)		Mesolectal (Conversations w/Children and Husband)		Basilectal (Conversations w/Mom)
(ing)					
N =	517		62		115
[iŋ]	71.8%		22.6%		5.2%
[ɪn]	28.2%	<	77.4%	<	94.8%
$X^2(1) =$		60.099		12.117	
p =		0.000		0.000	
(th)					
N =	1,917		239		414
fricative	99.1%		27.2%		13.5%
"stop"	0.9%	<	72.8%	<	86.5%
$X^2(1) =$		1361.227		18.757	
p =		0.000		0.000	
are					
N =	138		36		38
full/contr.	97.8%		69.4%		42.1%
zero	2.2%	<	30.6%	<	57.9%
$X^2(1) =$		31.086		5.592	
p =		0.000		0.018	

Wolfram, positioning me at the upper end of the continuum for my acrolectal style, between Wolfram's LMC and UWC speakers for my mesolectal style, and between his UWC and lower working-class (LWC) speakers for my basilectal style.

As noted in earlier chapters, the data for Wolfram's Detroit study were drawn from sociolinguistic interviews, which presumably would have elicited a fairly formal style of speaking. However, the comparison of these data to the patterns of styleshifting exhibited in my own speech suggests that these participants might also have been capable of producing a much wider range of variation if other styles had been captured.

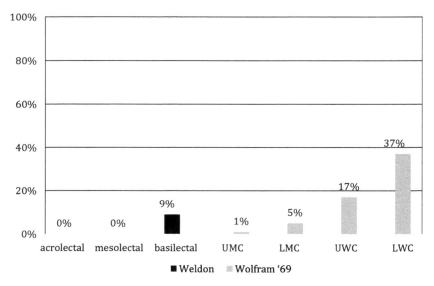

Figure 4.4 Comparison of Weldon's *is* absence across lects to Wolfram's 1969 Detroit study

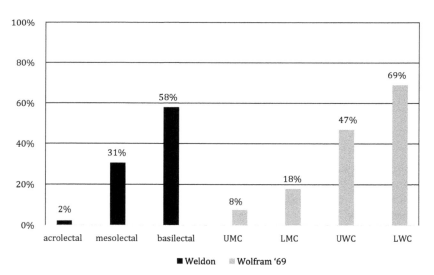

Figure 4.5 Comparison of Weldon's *are* absence across lects to Wolfram's 1969 Detroit study

Conclusion

The findings of this self-study detail a linguistic profile that at once reinforces and complicates traditional assumptions about middle-class AAE. Having spent my formative years immersed in a southern, middle-class, African American environment, where the overt prestige of Mainstream American English held sway but competed with the covert prestige of African American Vernacular English, I felt the tensions of competing linguistic norms from very early on. As observed by Marcyliena Morgan, such tensions present a linguistic quandary for many middle-class African American speakers.

Though exclusive use of GE [General English] is disparaged, it is considered odd if one cannot speak it as a young adult. And those who are suspected of having little or no facility in GE are routinely teased. Yet it is also odd if one cannot speak AAE to some extent and without error too. Whether a person has access to the code-switching skills expected depends on the relationship between education, social class and community of language socialization. Thus, William Labov's description of linguistic insecurity . . . is only partially shared with members of the African American speech community. (Morgan 2002: 68)

Over time, I have honed the skill of negotiating multiple identities through language, by carefully assessing the risks and rewards associated with the use of certain vernacular features. Key to achieving this balance has been finding ways to "sound Black" (or avoid "sounding White") through the manipulation of racially marked, but less overtly stigmatized phonological features, while minimizing the use of highly salient and overtly stigmatized grammatical features, for which I run the risk of mainstream censure. Thus, while my racial orientation has remained one of "intentional blackness" (Dyson 2005), my ability to survive (and thrive) in mainstream America has necessitated a type of "strategic assimilation" (Lacy 2007) that often masks this orientation in more public or formal contexts. Dyson (2005) explains:

These strategies of blackness are used in varying ways and degrees in different contexts at different times, so that a person who is intentional in one setting – say, on the front lines of a protest before the Supreme Court to preserve affirmative action – may be incidental at the company picnic. Circumstances, and, of course, political and ideological factors, and one's take on the stages, struggles, and status of black identity, determine what strategy one employs to survive. (Dyson 2005: 43)

As linguists continue to extend definitions of the African American speech community beyond the working classes, there should be room in this growing body of research for autoethnographic approaches such as this, which go beyond the limits of our traditional observational methods. And while all of the caveats about self-study should be acknowledged and carefully vetted, linguists whose repertoires include vernacular usage should be especially encouraged to reflect on their own experiences and perspectives as they navigate the complex norms and expectations that define their daily existence.

5   Race, Class, and Camouflaged Divergence*

We here. We BEEN here. We gon be here.

—Mos Def (2004)
"Def Jam Poetry" (Season 3, Episode 7)

Introduction: The Divergence Hypothesis

The nature of the relationship between African American and European American varieties of English has been a topic of debate among sociolinguists for several decades (see Chapter 1). For much of the early twentieth century, this debate was inextricably linked to the question of AAE's origins. Supporters of the Dialectologist (aka Anglicist) Hypothesis argued that AAE derived from British English sources, like other varieties of American English, and that African Americans spoke the same varieties as European Americans with whom they shared comparable socioeconomic and regional backgrounds. Supporters of the Creolist Hypothesis argued that AAE derived from an earlier plantation Creole and that its deep structure differed from that of other English dialects because of this unique history. By the latter half of the twentieth century, the nature of this debate had shifted to allow for synchronic and diachronic perspectives to be held separately. Along these lines, Wolfram (1974) observed that, regardless of whether one posits a Creole origin for AAVE, contemporary patterns of convergence or divergence could alter the nature of their synchronic relationship:

it may appear that one's viewpoint on Black-White speech relations on a synchronic level must invariably be linked with the question of historical origin . . . Theoretically, however, this is not necessarily the case. It may be possible, for example, to maintain that Black speech was originally derived from British dialects, but that social and geographical segregation patterns allowed it to develop in a direction slightly different from the varieties spoken by Whites. Or it may be possible to maintain that Black

---

* An abridged version of this chapter appeared in *The Routledge Companion to the Work of John Rickford* (Blake and Buchstaller 2019). My thanks to the anonymous referees for comments on the abridged version.

140

speech was derived from a creole, but that it decreolized to the extent that it is nearly indistinguishable from White varieties. And, of course, it may be maintained that Black speech has not fully decreolized, but that White speech has assimilated features of the not-fully decreolized form of Black speech so as to become quite similar. (Wolfram 1974: 501)

This new approach to the debate cleared the way in the 1980s for a consensus between Dialectologists and Creolists, with supporters of the Dialectologist Hypothesis conceding the likelihood of a Creole origin for AAE, but maintaining that the process of decreolization had made contemporary varieties of AAE more or less indistinguishable from comparable European American varieties.[1] This consensus was short-lived, however, as a new debate ensued over the question of whether African American and European American varieties were, in fact, converging, as the theory of decreolization would suggest, or instead diverging as a result of increased social and economic segregation.[2]

This "Divergence Hypothesis," as it was called in the 1980s, was readopted in the late twentieth and early twenty-first centuries by some earlier supporters of the Dialectologist Hypothesis, to account for certain distinctive African American Vernacular English (AAVE) features, particularly in the tense/ mood/aspect (TMA) system, that had not been attested in other varieties of American English. Labov (1998) explained:

The general conclusion that is emerging from studies of the history of AAVE is that many important features of the modern dialect are creations of the twentieth century and not an inheritance of the nineteenth. The creole affinities of AAVE and the creole-like structural properties that we do observe are not to be accounted for by direct transmission, but by the more subtle process of substrate influence and by parallel drift or development. This view of the situation is presented as the best working hypothesis to date, certainly not one that is established beyond challenge. If we accept for the moment that AAVE has diverged in many respects from OAD [Other American Dialects] in recent decades, and is continuing to diverge, we tend to draw different conclusions about the structure of the dialect. (Labov 1998: 119)

---

[1] As discussed in Chapter 1, consensus over the Creole origins of AAE was later challenged by researchers citing a lack of sociodemographic evidence to support the theory that home-grown creolization took place anywhere other than in South Carolina and Georgia, where Gullah developed. Mufwene (1997) proposed instead that some early variety of African American English likely *preceded* Creole formation on the North American plantations. (See also Winford 1997.) However, Winford (1997) and Rickford (1999c) maintained that Creole influence was likely present during the formative years of AAE's development, either through language contact or language shift between English-speaking and Creole-speaking enslaved persons who were imported into the North American colonies from various parts of the Caribbean.

[2] For more on the "Divergence Hypothesis," see Labov and Harris (1986), Rickford ([1987] 1999), Bailey and Maynor (1987), Fasold et al. (1987), Butters (1989), and Rickford (1992).

This position was also challenged, however, by those who questioned whether the features were actually twentieth-century innovations or simply features that had not been elicited in the early data (see, e.g., Singler 1998).[3]

At the heart of this "Neo-Anglicist Hypothesis," as it has been called (Wolfram and Thomas 2002), is the assumption that segregation and isolation are directly tied to linguistic divergence, and that integration of AAVE speakers into the American mainstream would likely threaten the variety's vitality and distinctiveness. Labov (2010) suggested that such a loss might be an unfortunate, but necessary, by-product of the mainstreaming of vernacular speakers.

> The primary correlates of such divergence are residential segregation and poverty, which are part of a developing transgenerational cycle that includes also crime, shorter life spans, and low educational achievement ... In confronting residential segregation, we must be aware that its reduction will lead to greater contact between speakers of AAVE and speakers of other dialects. Recent research implies that, if residential integration increases significantly, AAVE as a whole may be in danger of losing its distinctiveness as a linguistic resource. (Labov 2010: 15)

Rickford (2010) challenged this premise, however, noting that there are many African Americans who aspire to integrate but not assimilate.

> Many African Americans want integration in the sense of access to middle-class jobs and housing and schools and other institutions. But others are also seeking housing in Black neighborhoods ... within large urban centers like Los Angeles; Washington, DC; and Atlanta, determined to retain some of their distinctive cultural traditions. Perhaps, in a Jesse Jackson conception of race mixing in a salad bowl rather than a melting pot, there will be room for distinctive linguistic traditions as well. (Rickford 2010: 32)

Unfortunately, middle-class African American speakers have been largely excluded from this debate because of the long-time assumption that most are mainstream-oriented "lames" for whom integration and assimilation are the presumed norm (see, e.g., Labov 1972a). However, understanding how or whether linguistic divergence is realized among groups of speakers who are

---

[3] Using data from modern-day Liberian Settler English (LSE), an African American diaspora variety dating back to the first half of the nineteenth century, Singler (1998) contested the assertion made in Myhill (1995) that the absence of nine features from the Ex-Slave Recordings (ESR) corpus (Bailey et al. 1991) should be taken as evidence that the features are recent innovations in AAVE. Singler found all but two of these features in his LSE data, as well as in the speech of at least one ESR interviewee who was excluded from Myhill's analysis. On that basis, Singler argued that most of the features were not new, but rather features that were not elicited in the ESR data, perhaps in part because the interview conditions were not amenable to the production of more vernacular constructions. It is worth noting that the two features that Singler could *not* rule out as innovations were the increased use of habitual *be* as a preverbal auxiliary (i.e., *be* + Ving) and the use of remote past *been*, which is one of the features that is the focus of the current analysis.

less socially isolated and marginalized vis-à-vis the American mainstream could inform this debate in important ways and provide a more complete picture of the diachronic trajectory of AAE.

Linguistic Camouflage

Camouflaged features offer a unique perspective on the Divergence Hypothesis, as the distinctiveness of such features tends to go undetected, even among the speakers who use them. Arthur Spears introduced the concept of linguistic camouflage in a 1982 paper on semi-auxiliary *come*, a mood marker used in AAE to express speaker indignation (e.g., *He come walking in here like he owned the damn place* [Spears 1982: 852]).[4] Table 5.1 provides examples of some other camouflaged features that have been discussed in the sociolinguistic literature, with sample sentences drawn from my own intuitions.

According to Spears, the specialized meanings of camouflaged features tend to go undetected because of their superficial resemblance to grammatical constructions found in mainstream varieties. And yet, there appears to be a persistent racial divide in the use and interpretation of these forms. Importantly, because these features are not overtly stigmatized, they are often used by African American speakers across the socioeconomic spectrum to index racial/ethnic identity, but without the negative judgments typically associated with use of more overtly stigmatized forms. As such, they provide a useful means of exploring patterns of racial/ethnic divergence at higher ends

Table 5.1 *Camouflaged features in AAE*

Camouflaged Features	Sample Sentences
Continuous *Steady* (cf. Baugh 1984)	*She steady whispering* "She is whispering in an intense, continuous, and determined manner"
Counterfactual *Call Oneself* (cf. Wolfram 1994)	*I call(ed) myself fixing things* "I thought I was fixing things, but I wasn't" or "I pretended to be fixing things, but I really wasn't"
Indignant *Gon* (cf. Spears 1982, 2006, 2009; Collins et al. 2008, Moody 2011)	*He gon tell me how to raise my kids* "He had the nerve to tell me how to raise my kids"
Habitual Frequentative *Stay* (cf. Spears 2000, 2017)	*They stay arguing about something* "They are always arguing about something"

[4] See Spears (2009, 2017) for more recent accounts of camouflaged features.

of the socioeconomic spectrum. In this chapter, I focus on the use and interpretation of two camouflaged features – *BEEN* and *read* – and consider the implications of my findings for our current understanding of the relationship between African American and European American varieties of English. These features are discussed in more detail in the next two sections.

BEEN

This April 2015 headline, shown in Figure 5.1, illustrating the use of remote past *BEEN*, appeared in *Ebony* magazine, a historically African American owned and operated publication with a predominately African American readership. In the article, *BEEN* was used to make the claim that the widely publicized protests following the death of Freddie Gray while in police custody should come as no surprise to anyone, as tensions leading up to the incident had been simmering in Baltimore *for a long time*.

Remote past *BEEN* (also known as stressed *BEEN* because it is typically produced in spoken form with primary stress[5]) is an aspectual marker used in AAE to mark events that happened *a long time ago* or to describe states that have been in existence *for a long time*. The marker is typically written in the

Figure 5.1 Remote past *BEEN* in print

[5] As observed in Spears (2017), remote past *BEEN* can also occur without primary stress, though such realizations are less frequent and less well-documented in the linguistic literature. It remains distinct from other forms of *been*, however, due to the high-pitch contour that accompanies it (see Spears 2004).

linguistic literature in all capital letters to distinguish it from unstressed realizations of *been* that do not carry the remote past meaning (e.g., We['ve] been there before). As illustrated by Sound File 5.1 and accompanying Figures 5.2 and by Sound File 5.2 and accompanying Figure 5.3, respectively, remote past *BEEN* is marked by a high-pitch intonational contour, which signals the remote past meaning.

The pitch contour on *BEEN* is a variation of that which might accompany the word "long" in adverbial expressions like "a long time ago" (Sound File 5.3; Figure 5.4) and "for a long time" (Sound File 5.4; Figure 5.5).

Sound File 5.1 *She BEEN told me that*

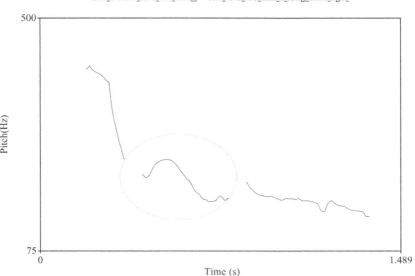

Figure 5.2 Remote past *BEEN* + action

Sound File 5.2 *She BEEN married*

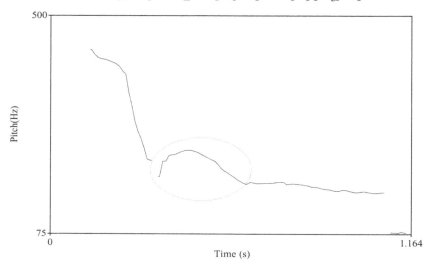

Figure 5.3 Remote past *BEEN* + state

Whereas mainstream varieties require the use of adverbial expressions to communicate the remote past meaning, AAE shifts the prosodic information that would accompany these expressions onto the aspectual marker itself.[6]

---

[6] Because they communicate the same information, adverbial expressions like *for a long time* and *a long time ago* are blocked from co-occurrence with stressed *BEEN* within the same Intonational Phrase (IP), as shown in (a). They can, however, co-occur, in separate IPs, in order to emphasize or reiterate the remote past meaning, as shown in (b), where the ellipsis represents a pause marking the IP boundary.
(a) **She BEEN married for a long time!*
(b) *She BEEN married ... for a long time!*

Sound File 5.3 *a LONG time ago*

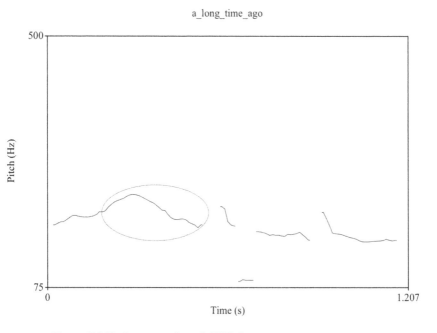

Figure 5.4 Pitch contour for *a LONG time ago*

As explained in Spears (2017), the use of "phonemic stress" is one of the ways in which the African American auxiliary system distinguishes itself from that of other American English dialects. "AAE … has basically the same auxiliaries as non-AAE dialects of English as well as a set of African American Auxiliaries (Labov 1998), a set unique to AAE that gives the variety a remarkably higher level of expressive efficiency" (Spears 2017: 165). Furthermore, as observed by Labov (1998), the specialized use of these aspectual markers facilitates a type of "semantic efflorescence" not found in the General English (GE) grammar. (See also Dayton 1996; Green 2002.)

Sound File 5.4 *for a LONG time*

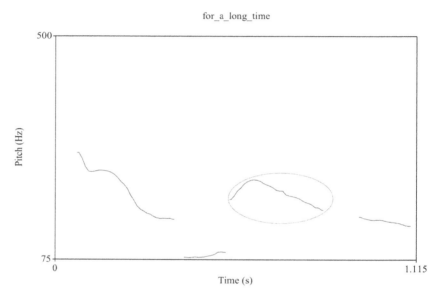

Figure 5.5 Pitch contour for *for a LONG time*

The assignment and realization of tense is almost entirely handled by the GE system. This is also true of the main constituents of the aspect system: the progressive and the perfect. The optional AA [African American] component can then be said to be freed from the drudgery of every-day grammatical work, and can be specialized to develop the highly colored semantics of social interaction that we have reviewed. This process is the opposite of the semantic bleaching that is typical of grammaticalization: it may be thought of as grammatical colorization. (Labov 1998: 147)

While the use of *BEEN* to mark the remoteness of an action like *told* (as in *She BEEN told me that*) stands out as distinct from Mainstream Standard English (MSE), the use of this feature to mark the extended duration of a state like *married* (as in *She BEEN married*) is camouflaged by its resemblance to

Sound File 5.5 *She BEEN married* (nonremote past)

She_BEEN_married_ = She_has_been_married_before_but_she_is_not_married_now_

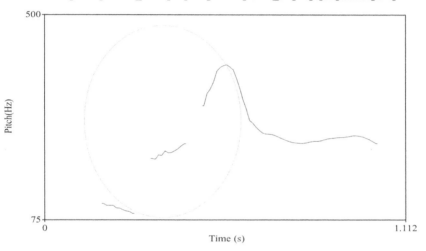

Figure 5.6 Nonremote past *BEEN*

more mainstream constructions like *She('s) been married*, where *been* is unstressed and lacks the high-pitch contour characteristic of remote past *BEEN*, or *She('s) BEEN married* (Sound File 5.5) where the stress on *been* is accompanied by a rising intonational contour (Figure 5.6) that indicates that she has been married before, but is not married now. Note that this rising contour is a variation on that which might accompany "used to" in expressions like "used to be" (Sound File 5.6; Figure 5.7).

According to Spears (2017), stressed *BEEN* might have originated through the merging of past participle *been* in present perfect constructions, as illustrated in (1), which occurs variably with or without the *have* auxiliary in both AAE and non-AAE varieties, and an unstressed past tense marker, illustrated in (2), which has been attested in some varieties of AAE,

Sound File 5.6 *USED TO be*

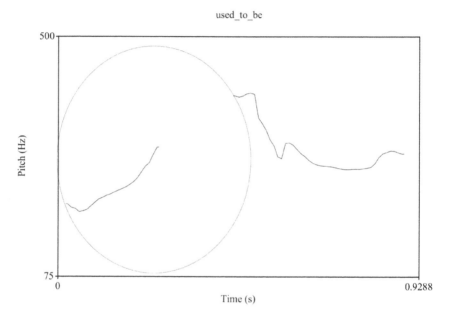

Figure 5.7 Pitch contour for *USED TO be*

including Gullah, as well as a number of Caribbean English Creoles (CECs) (see, e.g., Dayton 1996; Weldon 1998; Moody 2011; Weldon and Moody 2015; Spears 2017).[7]

---

[7] Winford (1992b) posited a similar scenario, by which the remote phase interpretation of *BEEN* resulted from "the partial reanalysis of an earlier creole anterior *bin* under the influence of continuative perfect *bin*" and represented "a type of partial semantic shift, with transfer of semantic features from a creole substrate, and incorporation of features derived via *bin* from English dialects, the 'target of the shift'" (346). (See also Winford 1998). As noted in Singler (1998), such a scenario would necessitate a much earlier emergence for remote past *BEEN* than that proposed by those who identify *BEEN* as a twentieth-century innovation.

1. *She bin*[8] *married a long time now* (Spears 2017: 161)
   "She's/has been married a long time now"
2. *She bin married when I met* her (Spears 2017: 161)
   "She was married when I met her"

Spears explains,

Unstressed *bin* then may have been used variably with stress, or high pitch, or high tone. This high tone would be used if there existed then the minimal tone system we find in some varieties of AAE today (Spears 2004). These prosodic features would have signaled various kinds of emphasis, including that related to length of time/ remoteness, and eventually would have done so invariably, thus connecting stress (or pitch or tone) to the notion of remoteness, that is, "for a long time"/"a long time ago." (Spears 2017: 166)[9]

By Spears's account, non-AAE varieties, which do not use phonemic stress in this way, would not have developed stressed *BEEN* through such a process.

In a 1975 study of *BEEN*, John Rickford interviewed twenty-five Black participants and twenty-five White participants from a variety of regional backgrounds to determine the extent to which speakers across racial lines were familiar with its remote past meaning. The results showed a clear racial divide, with 87 percent of the responses from Black participants, but only 37 percent of the responses from White participants reflecting familiarity with the remote past meaning of *BEEN* (1975 [1999]: 25). While social class was not a primary focus of his study, Rickford observed that "BÍN[10] is understood by a range of black subjects considerably wider than is normally associated with the Black English vernacular" (1975 [1999]: 27). By way of illustration, he recalled once attending a dinner party where the lone African American in the group, a Philadelphia judge, was surprised to learn that he was the only one who could correctly identify the meaning of remote past *BEEN*. Rickford observed,

From his normal level of speech, one would hardly have classed him as a speaker of "Black English." But his ability to interpret BÍN in the same way that other BE speakers do indicates the deep-seated sensitivity and exposure to this form that exists among black Americans, of all levels, and suggests a possible creole history. It also raises the

---

[8] The spelling *bin* is often used in the linguistic literature to reflect the [ɪ]/[ɛ] vowel merger typical of pronunciations in AAE and CECs. It is also sometimes used to distinguish the Creole anterior/past marker *bin* from the English past participle *been*.
[9] A similar scenario is posited by Winford (1998), except that the past participle *been* is described as having undergone a reanalysis (rather than a merger) "under the influence of an earlier creole past marker *bin*" (128). In Spears's analysis, unstressed *bin* is recognized as an AAE feature itself.
[10] In Rickford (1975 [1999]) the "remote phase" marker, as it was called, was written as BÍN to reflect the [ɪ]/[ɛ] merger of the vowel, and primary stress, which was indicated by an acute accent on the vowel, and an all-caps spelling.

question of whether linguistic grammars should be written on the basis of "productive" or "receptive" competence. (Rickford (1975 [1999]: 27)

To determine the extent to which this racial divide has persisted since Rickford's study and to explore more fully the level of familiarity that middle-class speakers have with the remote past meaning of *BEEN*, I replicated some aspects of Rickford's study, using my own online survey. As an extension of Rickford's study, I presented the participants with both written and spoken stimuli in order to tease out the effects of intonational contour on interpretations of *BEEN*.[11] These results are presented later in the chapter.

Read

"Reading" is a term used in the African American speech community to refer to the discursive act of chastising or "verbally unmasking" someone – the loose equivalent of what might be described in mainstream circles as "telling someone off." As described in Morgan (2002), the term *read* is traditionally understood to refer to a type of *directed discourse*, which I will call *Read* 1, by which a speaker calls out another "in an unsubtle and unambiguous manner" (53). However, a second, and seemingly newer, use of the term *read*, which I will call *Read* 2, has become popular particularly among African American women and members of the (Black) LGBTQIA+ community. Unlike *Read* 1, *Read* 2 refers to a more subtle act, by which a speaker criticizes or insults someone in an indirect manner. Also referred to in the African American speech community as *throwin' shade* (a term that has been appropriated by the American mainstream) or *crackin'* (a term that remains relatively in-group, though dated), this newer use of *read* represents a form of *signifying* or *indirect discourse*.[12] Importantly, both uses of *read* are camouflaged by their resemblance to the more mainstream interpretation of *read* meaning "to figure someone out" (e.g., *I find it difficult to read her* "I find it difficult to figure her out").

To illustrate these camouflaged uses of *read*, I provide below Excerpt 5.1 from "Fashion Queens" – a show that aired on the Bravo television network from 2013 to 2015, and featured three hosts, Bevy Smith, Miss Lawrence, and

---

[11] The data in the Rickford (1975 [1999]) study were elicited via interviews. So it is presumed that the interviewers presented participants with the prototypical intonational contour associated with the remote past meaning in their elicitations. However, the current study adds more controlled measures to this elicitation technique in order to tease out the effects of both written and spoken stimuli on levels of familiarity with this construction.

[12] To be clear, it is this particular use of the term "read" that appears to be a more recent development. The act itself has been around for decades.

Excerpt 5.1 "Fashion Queens" (Bravo Television Network)[13]

BEVY SMITH:	Now it's time for this week's Reading Room, where we like to tell it like it t-i-is. Ms. Lawrence, who are you reading this week?
MISS LAWRENCE:	Well, I am going to have to read, um Keyshia Cole ...
STUDIO AUDIENCE & DEREK J:	(*snickering*)
MISS LAWRENCE:	... for slandering ...
STUDIO AUDIENCE & DEREK J:	(*more snickering*)
MISS LAWRENCE:	... no, for slandering Beyoncé on Twitter about Beyoncé's new single "Bow Down." And in the song, she says "Bow down, bitches."
BEVY SMITH:	Yaasss.
MISS LAWRENCE:	Now, some people, like Keyshia Cole, has taken it so literal – someone who's working on their litera*cy* level –
STUDIO AUDIENCE & DEREK J:	(*laughing*)
MISS LAWRENCE:	– is taking this so – has taken it so literal ...
BEVY SMITH:	Okaaay.
MISS LAWRENCE:	... that she has completely twisted it. And she has come for Beyoncé. I don't like how she tried to come for her. Anybody came for Beyoncé. That girl is at the top of her game.
BEVY SMITH:	She's such a role model. And so now children are gonna be saying "Bow down, bitches," which is not appropriate. I think we can all agree. You know, Sasha and Malia, and will they be in the White House now saying that? And, now, will they be evicted? These are things that we're very concerned about?
STUDIO AUDIENCE & HOSTS:	(*laughing and applauding*)
BEVY SMITH:	We're concerned about this. You know=
MISS LAWRENCE:	=Well, I don't think– I mean, come on. It's not like Keyshia Cole has been the perfect role model either.
BEVY SMITH:	Keyshia Cole lives in her truth.
MISS LAWRENCE:	She does ... Oh, that was a =read ... too.
BEVY SMITH:	=And now– No, it wasn't.
MISS LAWRENCE:	Oh, that was a read, Bevy.
BEVY SMITH:	She lives in her truth.
MISS LAWRENCE:	She does ... And it ain't much to it.

---

[13] Source: https://youtu.be/_DpzjDiSskU.

(cont.)	
STUDIO AUDIENCE:	Oooh!
BEVY SMITH:	Now that was a =read, sir.
DEREK J:	=read *(laughing)*
MISS LAWRENCE:	I'm just going off of you.
BEVY SMITH:	No, you not, 'cause Keyshia Cole is my girl.
	Don't start none, there won't be none.
MISS LAWRENCE:	I live for Keyshia Cole!

Derek J, who used the show's platform to dish celebrity gossip and critique fashion. As a regular segment of the show, the hosts would enter what they called "The Reading Room," where each person was given the opportunity to *read* a celebrity or other public figure for some poor fashion choice or other social violation. In Excerpt 5.1, Bevy Smith invites Miss Lawrence to launch into a *Read* 1, "where we tell it like it t-i-is." However, Miss Lawrence's *Read* 1 is quickly derailed by Bevy Smith herself, who challenges the *read*, leading to a seemingly playful[14] back and forth exchange that includes several subtler *reads* in the sense of *Read* 2.

While such discursive uses of *read* are probably still largely camouflaged from the perspective of speakers who have no significant ties to either the African American or LGBTQIA+ speech communities, the term has undergone some degree of crossover into the American mainstream, having been infused into popular culture through television shows like "Fashion Queens." As with *BEEN*, I examine the extent to which such uses of *read* are familiar to middle-class speakers both within and outside the African American speech community and consider the implications of these findings for the divergence debate discussed earlier.

Participants

In the fall of 2013, I distributed an online survey, entitled "Change and Variation in American English," to test participants' familiarity with a variety of camouflaged features, including, but not limited to, the two that are the

---

[14] The discursive practice of "reading" in AAE need not constitute an actual argument. Rather, as demonstrated by the excerpt from "Fashion Queens," it is often the case that speakers will playfully engage in such practices as a way of demonstrating their verbal prowess, a talent that is highly valued in the African American speech community (see, e.g., Smitherman 1977). Because such exchanges are not commonly observed in more mainstream circles, however, they can be easily misinterpreted and judged as signs of verbal aggression and anger even when they are not intended as such (see, e.g., Kochman 1981).

focus of this chapter. Participation in the survey was restricted to those who claimed to be native speakers of American English with limited or no familiarity with linguistics. No one claiming to have had an advanced degree in linguistics (earned or in progress) was allowed to participate. Using email and social media, I initially distributed the survey to members of my own social network, including family members, friends, colleagues, and other professional contacts. Participants were then asked to share the survey link with members of their own social networks in an effort to trigger a snowball sampling effect (Goodman 1961). After about three months of targeted solicitation, I had received a total of 360 completed responses, 63% (or 228) of which were from European American participants and 28% (or 102) of which were from African American participants. For the purposes of this chapter, I will focus on the results from these two groups (N = 330), as they not only represent the majority of those who participated in the study, but they are also the two groups whose responses are most pertinent to the divergence debate described at the start of this chapter.[15]

To get a sense of the group's socioeconomic makeup, I asked participants to provide information about their highest level of *education*, their *occupation* at the time that the study was conducted, and their *annual household income*. As discussed in Chapter 1, one of the goals of this research was to determine the extent to which speakers with sufficient access to Standard English, which is typically associated with access to (higher) education, employ and evaluate vernacular features. It was, thus, useful for my purposes to prioritize education in my consideration of middle-class status. Accordingly, some form of higher education (either completed or in progress) was used as a baseline for middle-class status in this study.

Figure 5.8 shows the distribution of participants according to their highest level of education. As illustrated in Figure 5.8, roughly 65 percent of those with less than a BA reported having at least "some college." Among those with a BA or higher, the largest percentage of participants had either a Bachelor's or a Master's Degree. The participants for this study, thus, comprised a fairly well-educated group, likely reflecting a more middle-class perspective overall. However, the results to follow will be sorted by level of education, in order to examine possible class differences among them.

As shown in Figure 5.9, there was a positive correlation between education levels and annual household income, as those with less than a BA (i.e., black

---

[15] Of the remaining participants, four identified as Asian American (1%), sixteen as Biracial/Multiracial (4%), five as Latina/Latino/Hispanic American (1%), three as "Other" (1%), and two chose not to answer the question (1%). (Note: percentages do not add up to 100% due to rounding.)

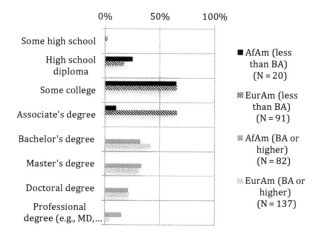

Figure 5.8 Participants by education

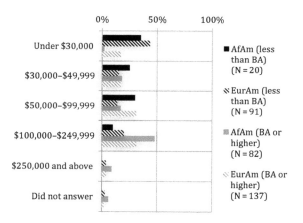

Figure 5.9 Participants by annual household income

bars) tended to fall lower on the income scale than those with a BA or higher (i.e., gray bars).

It is perhaps noteworthy here that nearly half (48 percent) of the African American participants in the BA or higher group reported annual household incomes between $100,000 and $250,000, thus representing a particularly high-status group, at least from the perspective of income (cf. Pattillo-McCoy 1999; Lacy 2007).[16]

Figure 5.10 shows the distribution of participants according to occupation. Of those with less than a BA, the highest percentages of participants were students, and the highest percentages of those with a BA or higher worked in education. Given the breakdown of the participant group by occupation, it seems likely that most of the participants in this study had some command of (or at least some familiarity with) Standard English.

In addition to race/ethnicity and socioeconomic status, participants were asked to report information about their *age*, *regional background*, *gender*, and *sexual orientation*. Among those with less than a BA, the majority of European American participants (72%) were between the ages of fourteen and twenty-four, and the largest percentage of African American participants (35%) were between the ages of thirty-five and forty-four, though the second-largest percentage (30%) were between the ages of fourteen and twenty-four. Among those with a BA or higher, the largest percentage of European Americans (46%) were between twenty-five and thirty-four, and the largest percentage of African American participants (54%) were between thirty-five and forty-four. These figures are displayed in Figure 5.11.

In order to track regional distribution, I asked the participants to indicate where they were born, where they currently lived, and to list places where they had lived for five or more years. As shown in Figure 5.12, most of the participants had either spent their entire lives in the South or had lived in multiple regions.

Finally, as shown in Figure 5.13, among those with less than a BA, 75% of African Americans and 70% of European Americans identified as female. Among those with a BA or higher, 56% of African Americans identified as male, and 65% of European Americans identified as female. Over 90% of all participants identified as heterosexual.

Results

BEEN *Results*

To test levels of familiarity with the remote past interpretation of *BEEN*, the online survey asked participants a series of questions that included both written

---

[16] Recall from Chapter 1 that the median household income among Black families in 2010 was $32,068 (adjusted dollars). Source: Table H-5 "Race and Hispanic Origin of Householder – Households by Median and Mean Income 1967–2010" (www.census.gov).

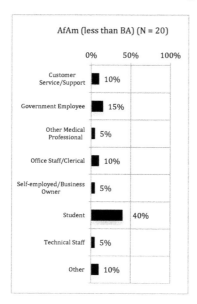
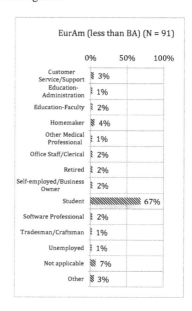

Figure 5.10 Participants by occupation[17]

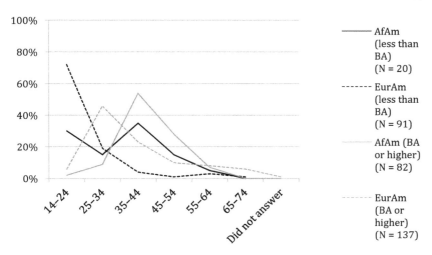

Figure 5.11 Participants by age

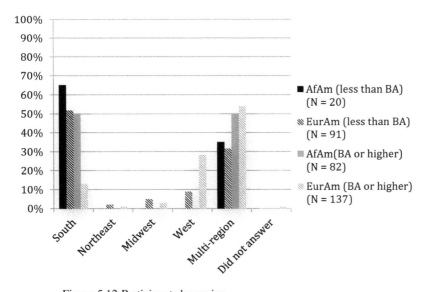

Figure 5.12 Participants by region

and spoken stimuli. The first *BEEN* stimulus, drawn from Rickford (1975 [1999]), was written (Figure 5.14).[18] This stimulus represented a more

---

[18] In Rickford (1975 [1999]), the subject pronoun was feminine – *She BEEN married*. To reduce the potential for gender stereotyping in the online survey, I changed the pronoun to masculine. Note, however, that for purposes of gender balance, I used *she* in the intonational contour discussion at the start of this chapter.

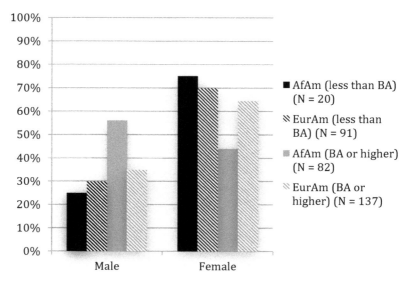

Figure 5.13 Participants by gender

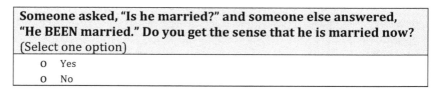

Figure 5.14 *BEEN* stimulus 1 (written) *He BEEN married.*
Source: adopted from Rickford (1975 [1999])

camouflaged use of *BEEN*, which, from a mainstream perspective, might have been interpreted as *He has been married, but he is not married now.* However, for the remote past interpretation (i.e., *He has been married for a long time*), the correct response was *yes*.

The second stimulus, *I BEEN paid for it*, also adopted from Rickford (1975 [1999]), represented a less camouflaged use of *BEEN* (Figure 5.15). The correct interpretation of this stimulus was *I paid for it long ago.*[19]

---

[19] In Rickford (1975 [1999]), the same response options were given, but the scenario described the purchase of a "new stereo," updated in the current study to a "new home theater system." In the online survey, I inadvertently made a typo in response option #4 (i.e., *I've been playing* [sic] *for it for a long time, and haven't finished yet*). In Rickford's 1975 study, this option read *I've been paying for it for a long time, and haven't finished yet.*

Frank asked his friend if he had paid off the bill on his new home theater system, and got the answer, "I BEEN paid for it." What does he mean? (Select one option)
o   I paid for it long ago
o   I was paying for a long time, but I'm finished now
o   I've already paid for it
o   I've been playing (sic) for it for a long time, and haven't finished yet
o   Other (please specify) _____

Figure 5.15 *BEEN* stimulus 2 (written) *I BEEN paid for it.*
Source: adopted from Rickford (1975 [1999])

To examine the role that intonational contour played in the interpretation of remote past *BEEN*, participants were then presented with a spoken stimulus that featured the high pitch, remote past contour described at the start of this chapter (Figure 5.16; Sound File 5.7).[20] As with *BEEN* stimulus 1, the correct response to the question was "yes."

Listen to the audio clip below. Based on what you hear in the clip, does "He BEEN married" mean that he is married now? (Select one option)
o   Yes
o   No

Figure 5.16 *BEEN* stimulus 3 (spoken) *He BEEN married* (remote past meaning)

Sound File 5.7 *BEEN* stimulus 3 (spoken) *He BEEN married* (remote past meaning)

---

[20] The spoken stimuli were all produced by a southern African American female in her early forties, who was employed as a secondary school teacher at the time that the recordings were done. Beyond some basic information about the goals of the recordings, she did not receive any coaching in advance, as the constructions produced were all part of her native dialect.

Next, participants heard a spoken stimulus that featured the nonremote past, rising intonational contour, also illustrated earlier, for which the correct meaning was "No, he is not married now" (Figure 5.17; Sound File 5.8).

Finally, to determine whether a richer linguistic context might also lead to a keener understanding of the remote past interpretation of *BEEN*, I presented the participants with one last spoken stimulus, *They BEEN finna get a divorce*, which combined remote past *BEEN* with the immediate future marker *finna* meaning "about to," variations of which are also found in Southern White varieties of American English.[21] Here, the correct answer was "They have been on the brink of a divorce for a long time" (see Figure 5.18 and Sound File 5.9).

Listen to the audio clip below. Based on what you hear in the clip, does "He BEEN married" mean that he is married now? (Select one option)
o   Yes
o   No

Figure 5.17 *BEEN* stimulus 4 (spoken) *He BEEN married* (nonremote past meaning)

Sound File 5.8 *BEEN* stimulus 4 (spoken) *He BEEN married* (nonremote past meaning)

---

[21] *Finna*, variably pronounced as *fixing to*, *fixin' ta*, *finta*, etc., is a preverbal marker in AAE that marks an event as imminent (see, e.g., DeBose and Faraclas 1993; Rickford and Rickford 2000). It is typically pronounced as *fixing to* or *fixin' to/ta* in Southern White varieties (see, e.g., Bailey et al. 1991). Green (2002: 70–71) describes some of the ways in which *finna* combines with other verbal markers in AAE.

Listen to the audio clip below. Which of the following best describes the meaning of what you hear? (Select one option)
o   They were about to get a divorce, but now they are not
o   They have been on the brink of a divorce for a long time
o   They have been divorced for a long time
o   They got a divorce a long time ago
o   Other (please specify) _____

Figure 5.18 *BEEN stimulus 5 (spoken) They BEEN finna get a divorce*

Sound File 5.9 *BEEN* stimulus 5 (spoken) *They BEEN finna get a divorce*

Figure 5.19 displays the racial distribution of correct responses to these five stimuli, followed by Table 5.2, which displays the results of a series of Pearson Chi-square tests for independence, conducted using the statistics software

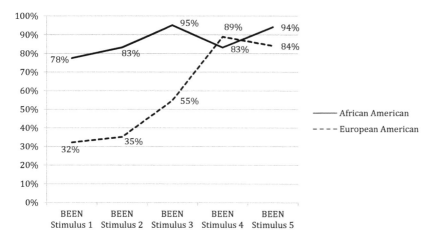

Figure 5.19 Correct responses to *BEEN* stimuli by race

Table 5.2 *Pearson Chi-square results: Correct responses to* BEEN *stimuli by race*

Order	*BEEN* stimuli	Pearson Chi-square results
1	*He BEEN married* (written)	$X^2(1) = 58.084$, p = 0.000
2	*I BEEN paid for it* (written)	$X^2(1) = 65.614$, p = 0.000
3	*He BEEN married* (spoken, remote)	$X^2(1) = 51.917$, p = 0.000
4	*He BEEN married* (spoken, nonremote)	$X^2(1) = 2.063$, p = 0.151 (ns)
5	*He BEEN finna get a divorce* (spoken)	$X^2(1) = 6.227$, p = 0.013

Note: *Results marked by (ns) did not meet the $p \leq 0.05$ threshold for significance.

package SPSS. Note that with the exception of *BEEN* stimulus 4, which featured the nonremote intonational contour, the responses identified as "correct" were those that signaled a remote past interpretation of *BEEN*.

The Chi-square tests identified a strong association between race and recognition of the remote past meaning of *BEEN*. With the exception of *BEEN* stimulus 4, the nonremote intonational contour, which showed no significant difference by race, African American participants chose the remote past meaning of *BEEN* at a significantly higher rate than European American participants for every stimulus. Furthermore, *BEEN* stimulus 4 notwithstanding, there was a steady increase in recognition of the remote past interpretation of *BEEN* from stimulus 1 to stimulus 5, indicating that participants were also attuned to the effects of intonational contour and linguistic context.

For *BEEN* stimulus 1, "*He BEEN married*" (written), 78% of African American participants identified the remote past meaning, compared to just 32% of European American participants (p = 0.000). This difference was comparable to that observed in Rickford 1975 [1999]), where 92% of Black respondents but only 32% of White respondents answered this question correctly.[22] When the camouflage effect was reduced in *BEEN* stimulus 2, "*I BEEN paid for it*" (written), recognition of the remote past interpretation increased slightly for both groups, but remained low among European Americans at 35%, compared to 83% of African American participants (p = 0.000). It was only with the introduction of the remote past intonational contour in *BEEN* stimulus 3, "*He BEEN married*" (spoken, remote contour), that more than half of the European American participants (55%) identified the

---

[22] These percentages were calculated using the figures shown in Table 2.2 of Rickford (1975 [1999]), page 25. Because of how Rickford's results were displayed, I was not able to extract other percentages from this table for purposes of comparison with those in the current study.

remote past interpretation. However, African American participants were nearly unanimous in their identification of the remote past meaning of this stimulus, with a 95% correct response rate, yielding another statistically significant racial difference (p = 0.000). The racial gap did narrow for *BEEN* stimulus 5, "*He BEEN finna get a divorce*" (spoken), where 84% of European American participants chose the remote past meaning, compared to 94% of African American participants. Presumably, participants who were not familiar with the remote past interpretation of *BEEN* were able to glean it from the richer linguistic context provided in *BEEN* stimulus 5.[23] It is also likely, however, that the preceding stimuli helped participants who were not familiar with remote past *BEEN* to arrive at this interpretation. Nevertheless, the racial gap for this stimulus was also deemed to be statistically significant (p = 0.013).

While these results point to divergent interpretations of stressed *BEEN* across racial lines, the differences between African American and European American responses actually leveled out for *BEEN* stimulus 4, "*He BEEN married*" (spoken, nonremote contour). In fact, there was no statistically significant difference between the European American participants, 89% of whom chose the correct response to this stimulus, and African American participants, 83% of whom chose the correct response (p = 0.151). Thus, African American participants in this study were familiar with both the mainstream and more racially marked uses of *BEEN*, while European American speakers were largely unfamiliar with the AAE uses, though many were able to glean their intended meanings when given sufficient contextual cues.

To determine whether education informed these results in any significant way, I also considered the distribution of responses by education within each racial group, as shown in Figure 5.20.

---

[23] Regional background was also a likely factor in how accurately participants were able to interpret this stimulus. Among those who chose the response "other" for this question, several participants, all of them nonsouthern European Americans, offered comments that revealed a lack of familiarity either with *BEEN*, *finna*, or the combination of the two.

M: *I have no clue.*

F: *I couldn't even understand the word said before "been"!*

M: *Could not hear the phrase well enough to determine the meaning.*

F: *They are going to get a divorce (no inference for how long that option has been on the table).*

F: *They are in the process of getting a divorce.*

M: *I seriously cannot understand what the lady is stating.*

M: *I cannot understand the clip "They BEEN ... to get a divorce" Fitting? Fixing? The former would imply situational buildup, the latter would imply intent without action.*

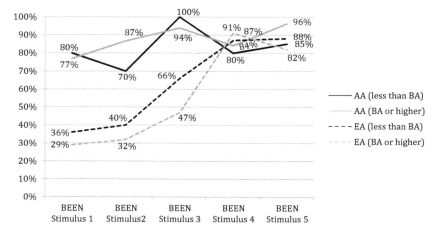

Figure 5.20 Correct responses to *BEEN* stimuli by race and education

Among the African American participants, there was no significant correlation between levels of education and remote past interpretations of *BEEN*.[24] Accuracy rates ranged from 70% to 100% among those with less than a BA, and from 77% to 96% among those with a BA or higher. While the differences were not statistically significant, it is interesting to note that for *BEEN* stimulus 2, "*I BEEN paid for it*," the more marked (i.e., less camouflaged) written stimulus, 87% of African American participants with a BA or higher identified the remote interpretation, compared to only 70% of those with less than a BA (p = 0.095). If we accept education as a proxy for social class status, these results challenge the assumption that those higher on the socioeconomic scale are further removed from the linguistic norms and practices of the African American speech community (i.e., more "lame" à la Labov 1972a), a point that I will return to later.

Among European American participants, there was a significant correlation observed for *BEEN* stimulus 3, "*He BEEN married*" (spoken, remote past contour), where 66% of European Americans with less than a BA identified the remote past interpretation, compared to 47% of those with a BA or higher (p = 0.006). If we, again, take education as a proxy for class, one might conclude from these results that those lower on the socioeconomic scale were more

---

[24] Given the small number of African American participants with less than a BA (N = 20), all of the Chi-square tests for independence violated the assumption that no more than 20% of expected frequencies be less than 5. For African American participants, therefore, p-values for Fisher's Exact Test were consulted instead.

familiar with the remote past intonational contour. One cautionary note in how we interpret these results, however, regards the age interaction in this study. Recall that more than 70% of European Americans with less than a BA were between the ages of fourteen and twenty-four. And 67% of them were students. So while the largest percentage of European American participants with less than a BA (43%) reported annual household incomes below $30,000, it is likely that most were on a higher income trajectory, pending completion of their degrees, economic uncertainties notwithstanding. Another possible explanation for these results is that younger European American participants were more familiar with the remote past contour because of their exposure to AAE through music, film, social media, sports, and other forms of popular culture, which often serve as vehicles for the "crossover" of AAE features into the American mainstream (see, e.g., Smitherman 1998; Cutler 1999). A more rigorous examination of the independent effects of age and class is needed to determine whether these results are, in fact, reflective of class differences or instead point to some change in progress with regard to European American recognition of the remote past intonational contour.

Read *Results*

The first stimulus for *Read* 1 was a written stimulus, for which participants were asked to interpret the meaning of the expression "*I will READ*[25] *you*," by selecting all that applied from a list of options that included both AAE and more mainstream interpretations (see Figure 5.21).

Among the options provided, "I will tell you a story" was included as a **distractor**. "I will tell you off" represented the **AAE** response. And "I will figure out what you're about" represented the more **mainstream** response. The fourth option, "I will tell you about yourself," was an **ambiguous** response (i.e., a camouflage construction itself) with at least two possible interpretations – one, the rough equivalent of "I will tell you off" (i.e., the AAE response), the other, the rough equivalent of "I will tell you what you're about" (i.e., the more mainstream response).

For *Read* 1 stimulus 2, participants were presented "I will READ[26] you" in *spoken* form (Figure 5.22; Sound File 5.10) and instructed to interpret its meaning by selecting all that applied from the same list of options presented for *Read* 1 stimulus 1.

---

[25] As noted in the instructions to *Read* stimulus 1, *READ* was written in all capital letters in the stimulus in order to place emphasis on the word *read*. However, stress and pitch do not serve a specific *semantic* function for *read* in AAE as they do for remote past *BEEN*.

[26] Here, again, the use of all capital letters indicates that emphasis was placed on the word *read*, but not with the intention of marking any particular aspectual meaning, as in the case of *BEEN*.

Which of the following matches your interpretation of the sentence "I will READ you" (Note: All caps represents emphasis on the word "read"). If more than one interpretation seems possible, please select all that apply.
o   "I will figure out what you're about"   o   "I will tell you off"   o   "I will tell you a story"   o   "I will tell you about yourself"   o   Other (Please specify) _____

Figure 5.21 *Read* 1 stimulus 1 (written) *I will READ you*

Please listen to the audio clip below and then indicate which sentence matches your interpretation of what you've heard. If more than one interpretation seems possible, please select all that apply.
o   I will figure out what you're about   o   I will tell you off   o   I will tell you a story   o   I will tell you about yourself   o   Other (Please specify) _____

Figure 5.22 *Read* 1 stimulus 2 (spoken) *I will READ you*

Sound File 5.10 *Read* 1 stimulus 2 (spoken) *I will READ you*

Next, participants were presented with the spoken stimulus "I will read, write, and erase you" (Figure 5.23; Sound File 5.11), an expression that circulated in the African American speech community many years ago, but is used much less frequently today. In addition to the acoustic cues, this stimulus added a richer linguistic context that was more consistent with the AAE response, "I will tell you off." Note, importantly, that for this stimulus,

Please listen to the audio clip below and then indicate which sentence matches your interpretation of what you've heard. If more than one interpretation seems possible, please select all that apply.
o   I will figure out what you're about
o   I will tell you off
o   I will tell you a story
o   I will tell you about yourself
o   Other (Please specify) _____

Figure 5.23 *Read* 1 stimulus 3 (spoken) *I will read, write, and erase you*

Sound File 5.11 *Read* 1 stimulus 3 (spoken) *I will read, write, and erase you*

the mainstream response, "I will figure out what you're about," as well as the mainstream interpretation of the ambiguous response, "I will tell you about yourself," were less likely to be perceived as viable options. The expectation, therefore, was that participants would choose the AAE response "I will tell you off" for *Read* 1 stimulus 3, even if it was not a meaning with which they were familiar.

Finally, participants were presented with one last spoken stimulus *Don't make me read you* – a long-standing expression in the African American speech community that continues to circulate today (see Figure 5.24 and Sound File 5.12). Depending on which meaning of *read* one assumes, this stimulus could be interpreted as a threat, "Don't make me tell you off" (i.e., the AAE response), or as a plea, "Don't make me figure out what you're about" (i.e., the mainstream response). The ambiguous response, "Don't make me tell you about yourself" would again have two possible interpretations, (i.e., "Don't make me tell you off" [the AAE response] or "Don't make me tell you what you're about" [the mainstream response]).

Figure 5.25 shows the percentages of African American and European American participants who chose the AAE response (i.e., "... tell you off"). Pearson Chi-square results are provided in Table 5.3.

Please listen to the audio clip below and then indicate which sentence matches your interpretation of what you've heard. If more than one interpretation seems possible, please select all that apply.

- ○ Don't make me figure out what you're about
- ○ Don't make me tell you off
- ○ Don't make me tell you a story
- ○ Don't make me tell you about yourself
- ○ Other (please specify)_____

Figure 5.24 *Read* 1 stimulus 4 (spoken) *Don't make me read you*

Sound File 5.12 *Read* 1 stimulus 4 (spoken) *Don't make me read you*

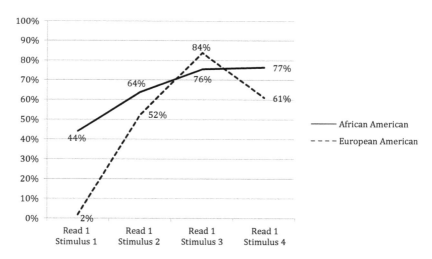

Figure 5.25 AAE response ("... tell you off") to *Read* 1 stimuli by race

Table 5.3 *Pearson Chi-square results: AAE response ("... tell you off") to* Read *1 stimuli by race*

Order	Read 1 stimuli	Pearson Chi-square results
1	*I will READ you* (written)	$X^2(1) = 100.029$, p = 0.000
2	*I will READ you* (spoken)	$X^2(1) = 3.799$, p = 0.051 (ns)
3	*I will read, write, and erase you* (spoken)	$X^2(1) = 3.168$, p = 0.075 (ns)
4	*Don't make me read you* (spoken)	$X^2(1) = 7.525$, p = 0.006

Note: *Results marked by (ns) did not meet the $p \leq 0.05$ threshold for significance.

The results for *Read* 1 stimulus 1, *I will READ you* (written), were statistically significant, with 44% of African American participants, but only 2% of European American participants choosing the AAE response (p = 0.000). When this same stimulus was presented in spoken form (i.e., *Read* 1 stimulus 2), the racial differences leveled out considerably, with 52% of European American participants choosing the AAE option, compared to 64% of African American participants (p = 0.051)[27]. This jump in the percentage of European American participants selecting the AAE response was surprising, given how few chose this option for *Read* 1 stimulus 1. To the extent that participants who were not familiar with the AAE interpretation of *read* perceived the voice for stimulus 2 to be that of an African American woman, one possible explanation is that the spoken stimulus triggered circulating stereotypes of the "angry Black woman," thus prompting them to select "I will tell you off" as a possible interpretation of *I will READ you*.

Less surprising was the nonsignificant difference in response rates for *Read* 1 stimulus 3, *I will read, write, and erase you* (spoken), where 76% of African American participants and 84% of European American participants chose the AAE option "I will tell you off" (p = 0.075). As noted earlier, the content of this particular stimulus likely blocked the mainstream responses, as well as the distractor, from being viable options, thus making "I will tell you off" the most likely interpretation. However, when the mainstream options were once again made viable with *Read* 1 stimulus 4, *Don't make me read you*, the racial gap returned, with 77% of African American participants choosing the AAE option, compared to 61% of European Americans, a difference that was statistically significant (p = 0.006).

To determine whether education played a role in the patterns of response for *Read* 1, I also examined the distribution of AAE responses by education within

---

[27] Because this result falls just outside of the 0.05 threshold for statistical significance, the racial difference for this stimulus might be better described as "marginally significant" rather than "insignificant."

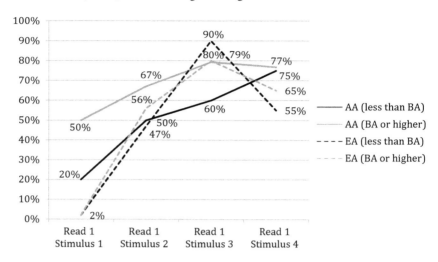

Figure 5.26 AAE response ("... tell you off") to *Read* 1 stimuli by race and education

each racial group (Figure 5.26). Here, the data revealed two significant correlations.[28] For *Read* 1 stimulus 1, *I will READ you* (written), 50% of African American participants with a BA or higher chose the AAE option "I will tell you off" compared to just 20% of those with less than a BA (p = 0.015). In fact, for *Read* 1, African American participants with a BA or higher consistently chose the AAE response with greater frequency than those with less than a BA, though the gap narrowed to a nonsignificant margin for stimuli 2–4. Among European American participants, there was a significant correlation (p = 0.034) for *Read* 1 stimulus 3, *I will read, write, and erase you* (spoken), where 90% of participants with less than a BA chose the AAE option, compared to 80% of those with a BA or higher.

Before moving to the results for *Read* 2, I would like to reflect briefly on the ambiguous response option, "... tell you about yourself." Recall that there were at least two different interpretations of this option – an AAE interpretation ("... tell you off") and a more mainstream interpretation ("... tell you what you're about"). While participants were not asked explicitly which interpretation of the ambiguous response they had in mind when selecting it, the results shown in Figure 5.27 suggest that African American participants

---

[28] Where Chi-square tests violated the assumption that no more than 20% of expected frequencies be less than 5, the p-values for Fisher's Exact Test were consulted instead.

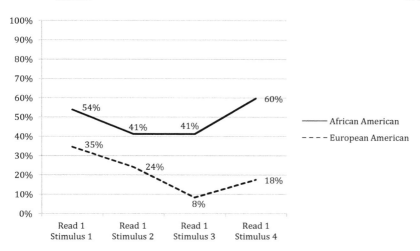

Figure 5.27 Ambiguous response ("... tell you about yourself") to *Read* 1 stimuli by race

and European American participants interpreted the ambiguous option differently.

As shown in Table 5.4, African American participants chose "... tell you about yourself" as a possible interpretation of *Read* 1 at a significantly higher rate than European American participants for *every* stimulus. For *Read* 1 stimulus 1, *I will READ you* (written), 35% of European American participants chose the ambiguous option, compared to 54% of African American participants (p = 0.001). With the introduction of the acoustic cues, in *Read* 1 stimulus 2, *I will READ you* (spoken), the percentage of European American participants choosing the ambiguous option dropped to 24%, compared to 41% of African American participants. However, the racial gap was still statistically significant (p = 0.002). For African American participants, the highest rate of selection of the ambiguous option was for *Read* 1 stimulus 4 *Don't make me read you* (spoken), where "Don't make me tell you about yourself" was chosen by 60% of African American participants, compared to only 18% of European American participants (p = 0.000).

However, the stimulus that provided the greatest insight into how participants interpreted the ambiguous option was *Read* 1 stimulus 3, *I will read, write, and erase you*, where the linguistic context blocked the mainstream interpretation, "I will figure out what you're about." The compatibility of "I will tell you about yourself" with *Read* 1 stimulus 3, *I will read, write, and erase you*, can only be explained by activating the AAE interpretation, "I will tell you off," for both. This interpretation was only viable for 8% of European

Table 5.4 *Pearson Chi-square results: Ambiguous response ("... tell you about yourself") to* Read *1 stimuli by race*

Order	Read 1 stimuli	Pearson Chi-square results
1	*I will READ you* (written)	$X^2(1) = 10.853, p = 0.001$
2	*I will READ you* (spoken)	$X^2(1) = 9.875, p = 0.002$
3	*I will read, write, and erase you* (spoken)	$X^2(1) = 50.449, p = 0.000$
4	*Don't make me read you* (spoken)	$X^2(1) = 59.259, p = 0.000$

Note: *Results marked by (ns) did not meet the $p \leq 0.05$ threshold for significance.

American participants, but was a viable option for 41% of the African American participants, pointing to yet another statistically significant difference along racial lines ($p = 0.000$). A breakdown in the selection of the ambiguous option by education levels revealed no significant differences within either group.

In order to test familiarity with *Read* 2, I presented participants with the scenario shown in Figure 5.28, which was inspired by an episode of Bravo's "Fashion Queens," discussed earlier. Here, participants were asked to select the closest synonym to *read*, which was "crack."[29] For this question, 84% of African American participants chose the correct response, compared to 49% of European American participants, a result that was statistically significant ($X^2(1) = 37.184$, $p = 0.000$). While there was no significant difference by education level within each racial group, African American participants with a BA or higher chose the correct option at a higher rate (88%) than those with less than a BA (70%) ($p = 0.080$), thus challenging the theory proposed earlier that *Read* 2 was gaining currency among younger speakers. Among European Americans, however, the pattern was reversed, with 51% of those with less than a BA choosing the correct response, compared to 47% of those with a BA or higher ($p = 0.646$).

Finally, participants were asked to self-report their level of familiarity with *Read* 2, as shown in Figure 5.29. When viewed as a binary choice between those who had heard or used *Read* 2 and those who had never heard it before, the Pearson Chi-square results revealed another statistically significant

---

[29] The term *crackin'* represents one of several ways of referring to what linguists have called *signifying* or *sounding* in AAE. Other terms include *joanin'*, *cappin'*, and, more recently, *bakin'*, *roastin'*, or *burnin'*. The perpetual process of lexicalizing this verbal act from one generation to the next speaks to its cultural and linguistic significance in the African American speech community (see, e.g., Smitherman 1998; Green 2002).

Please read the following exchange and then answer the question that follows:
Pat: That hairstyle made her look so youthful, I barely recognized her. Ali: Ah! Is that a read? Are you tryin' to read?
In the exchange above, which of the following seems like the closest equivalent to Ali's use of *read*? (Select one option)
o   bite o   snip o   crack o   tag o   Other (please specify) _____

Figure 5.28 *Read* 2 question 1

Which of the following best describes your level of familiarity with Ali's use of *read* in the exchange above? (Select one option)
o   This is an expression that I have used myself o   This is an expression that I have heard, but have not used myself o   I have never heard this expression before

Figure 5.29 *Read* 2 question 2

difference between African American participants, 53% of whom had reportedly heard or used it before and European participants, only 7% of whom had reportedly heard or used it before ($X^2(1) = 91.598$, p = 0.000). When the results were broken down by education levels within each racial group, no significant differences were found. However, the results in Figure 5.30 show that European American participants were overwhelmingly unfamiliar with this newer use of *read* compared to African American participants, whose responses were more mixed.

Interestingly, 60% of African American participants with less than a BA reported never having heard this use of *read* before, compared to just 44% of those with a BA or higher. Thus, even for this newer use of *read*, which was relatively popular within the African American speech community at the time that the study was conducted, African American participants higher on the socioeconomic spectrum appeared to be more connected to the trend, at least according to this self-report mechanism. The implications of these findings are discussed in the section below.

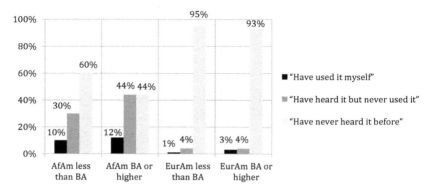

Figure 5.30 Responses to *Read* 2 question 2 by race and education

Conclusion

The results of this study show that divergent patterns of linguistic behavior between African Americans and European Americans can be observed even at higher levels of the socioeconomic spectrum. The divergent patterns observed in Rickford (1975 [1999]) for remote past *BEEN* have persisted in the decades since he conducted his research. European Americans remain largely unfamiliar with the remote past interpretation of *BEEN*, though they are able to glean its meaning if given sufficient acoustic and contextual cues. African Americans, on the other hand, appear to be familiar with both its AAE and more mainstream interpretations. Similarly, for *read*, African American participants exhibited greater familiarity with both *Read* 1 and *Read* 2, compared to European American participants, who depended heavily on contextual information to arrive at the AAE interpretations. Consistent with Rickford (2010), results such as these support the claim that middle-class African Americans are able to maintain a certain degree of linguistic distinctiveness, even if they are less marginalized vis-à-vis the American mainstream.

Somewhat surprising here were the patterns observed *within* the African American participant group, where those with a BA or higher often demonstrated greater familiarity with the AAE uses of *BEEN* and *read* than those with less than a BA. While most of these differences were not statistically significant, the results beg the question of whether *BEEN* and *read* patterned this way because they were not part of the vernacular "core" and were thus considered "lame" among younger speakers who fell lower on the socioeconomic spectrum. However, the distribution of the results by race suggests that these forms have maintained a significant amount of in-group marking, making them less likely to be perceived as "lame" within the African American speech community, though the gradual appropriation of *Read* 2 into mainstream discourse perhaps makes it vulnerable to this interpretation over time.[30]

Another possible explanation is that African American participants with less than a BA took a more conservative approach to this study and were, thus, less inclined to demonstrate familiarity with constructions that they deemed to be "racially marked" or "nonmainstream"– a phenomenon that was described in the early sociolinguistic literature as the "linguistic insecurity" of the lower middle class (cf. Labov 1972c). By contrast, those with a BA or higher (48% of whom reported annual household incomes between \$100,000 and \$250,000) might have felt pressure to tout their "street credibility" or "Blackness" by demonstrating familiarity with these more racially marked expressions. This pressure might have been further compounded by a gender bias in the sample, given that 56% of the African American participants in the BA or higher category were male. As discussed in earlier chapters, there is evidence to suggest that African American men, particularly at higher levels of the socioeconomic spectrum, experience greater pressure than their female counterparts to adhere to vernacular norms (see, e.g., Garner and Rubin 1986). Importantly, this would be a different type of "linguistic insecurity" than that observed in the early sociolinguistic literature, which was predominately focused on European American speech communities. Delving further into the complexities of class (and age) differences *within* the African American speech community may help to illuminate some of these more subtle linguistic differences.

So what are the implications of these findings for the divergence debate? And what do they suggest about the diachronic trajectory of AAE? In a statement reminiscent of W. E. B. Du Bois' 1908 concept of "double consciousness," William Labov attributed the kind of racial divide observed in this study to the "dual worlds" that many African Americans find themselves having to navigate.

The social matrix in which this development has taken place is the asymmetric position of African Americans in American society. White speakers live in one linguistic world, continually illuminated and informed by borrowings and partial glimpses of African-American lexicon and idiom, but with almost no input from the AA [African American] system of AAVE. African Americans live in two worlds. . . . Even among core members of the AAVE community who have the least contact with OAD, there is the continual contact with African Americans who have been influenced by OAD grammar. Though this may not reduce the further divergence of the AA element, it reinforces those parts of the GE system of AAVE that are held in common with OAD. (Labov 1998: 147)

---

[30] See Smitherman (1998) for a discussion of the linguistic effects of mainstream appropriation on the African American lexicon.

By Labov's account, middle-class African Americans, presumably included among those perceived to "have been influenced by OAD grammar," play an important role in bridging the divide between "core members of the AAVE community" and other speakers of American English, perhaps especially speakers of Mainstream Standard English. The results of this study would support such an hypothesis, at least to the extent that they demonstrate the degree of familiarity that many African Americans have with both AAE and more mainstream linguistic norms. However, the results of this study also suggest that middle-class African Americans play an important role in *maintaining* a certain degree of linguistic distinctiveness, perhaps particularly through the use of camouflaged features, where the salience and stigma typically associated with more vernacular African American features is minimized and the work of racial/ethnic identity and affiliation can be performed largely "under the radar" of mainstream detection.

Thus, contrary to the claims made in Labov (1998), the results of this study challenge the view that mainstream integration is necessarily a barrier to linguistic distinctiveness or a threat to the continuation of linguistic divergence along racial lines. Instead, these findings provide a poignant illustration of the ways in which convergence and divergence can occur simultaneously (cf. Rickford [1987] 1999). Spears (2017) uses the term *mainstreaming* to describe "instances where a language variety, as a result of sociopolitical pressures, converges toward a socio-politically dominant language variety or group of them" (164). Unlike traditional conceptions of decreolization, however, *mainstreaming* "avoids any claim or suggestion that change toward the lexifier or a dominant language is desirable, inevitable, linear, unceasing, and/or necessary for mass education and economic development" (164). Rickford ([1987] 1999), drawing on a distinction made in Whinnom (1971), makes a similar claim, when he urges linguists to consider not only the "ecological factors" of language contact, for example "how many Blacks, how many Whites, where are the neighborhoods located, what is the nature of their interrelations" but also the "ethological factors, including emotional and attitudinal factors" ([1987] 1999: 257). For many middle-class African Americans, integration into the mainstream is not about abandoning African American norms and practices, but about acquiring the linguistic tools needed to move fluidly through both African American and more mainstream circles. Results such as those presented in this chapter should caution us against making predictions about the linguistic consequences of mainstreaming, without also taking into account the intersecting dynamics of racial identity and social consciousness that influence these phenomena.

6   Sounding Black[*]

> ... Try to think bigger than you ever have
> or had courage enough to do:
> that blackness is not where whiteness
> wanders off to die: but that it is
> like the dark matter
> between stars and galaxies in
> the Universe
> that ultimately
> holds it all
> together.

—Alice Walker (2016)
Excerpt from "Here It Is"

Introduction

Social commentary on "sounding Black" circulates widely within (and, to some extent, outside) the African American speech community. Studies such as Baugh (1996), Purnell et al. (1999) and others have observed that listeners are able to identify the racial and/or ethnic background of speakers, often with only minimal acoustic cues (see also Buck 1968; Abrams 1973; Lass et al. 1979; Foreman 2000; Wolfram 2001a; Thomas and Reaser 2004) and are even sensitive to the variable patterns of constraint that govern them (Labov et al. 2011). Beyond racial and ethnic identification, however, the concept of sounding Black also speaks to perceptions of racial and ethnic identities (cf. Holliday 2016). Consistent with Smitherman's (1977, 2006) concept of linguistic push-pull, there are often conflicting attitudes associated with sounding Black. Though linguistically unfounded, references to "sounding Black" often connote a lack of education or sophistication (cf. "bad English") and can even

---

[*] An earlier version of this chapter, entitled "Sounding Black: Labeling and Perceptions of African American Voices on Southern College Campuses," appears in *Language Variety in the New South: Contemporary Perspectives on Change and Variation* (Reaser et al. 2018). Thanks to the anonymous reviewers for comments on the earlier version of this chapter.

allude to minstrel-like behavior and other negative racial stereotyping. Yet there remains a keen sense of the importance of "sounding Black" as a means of constructing an African American identity and demonstrating one's loyalty to and solidarity with the African American speech community (see Hoover 1978). This concept stands in opposition to that of "sounding White" (also known as "sounding Proper"), which, while also linguistically unfounded, tends to connote a certain level of education, sophistication, or "correctness" (cf. "good English"). And yet, African American speakers who are perceived as "sounding White" are often ridiculed and ostracized by members of the African American speech community (see, e.g., Mitchell-Kernan 1971). There are many circulating labels (cf. Mitchell-Kernan's 1971 "folk categories") that describe the more nuanced distinctions that listeners make in their perceptions of African American voices. Labels such as "Ghetto" and "Proper," for example, speak to the salience of certain African American voices (and identities) to elicit social and linguistic commentary. From a linguistic perspective, however, little is known about how listeners assign such labels to speakers' voices and what social characteristics get indexed through those assignments.

College campuses provide an interesting context for examining such dynamics, given the "linguistic tightrope" that many college-educated African Americans find themselves having to navigate. Because "sounding Black" plays such an important role in the construction of African American identity, but is often perceived as being incompatible with sounding educated, many African American college students tend to develop a heightened awareness of the reactions to their linguistic choices and practices. In a study of the attitudes of African American college students, staff, and administrators at a California university, Rahman (2008) found that Standard African American English (SAAE)[1] (i.e., the use of standard grammar, in combination with ethnically marked phonological and prosodic features) was deemed by many African Americans to be the best way to meet "establishment requirements" while also allowing speakers to express their racial or ethnic identities (170). (See also Buck 1968; Tucker and Lambert 1975; Hoover 1978). However, listener perceptions of African American voices are likely to vary according to regional context. And the South adds an additional layer of complexity to these issues, given the marked and often stigmatized nature of both Southern and African American language varieties in the United States (see, e.g., Lippi-Green 1997, 2012). In this chapter, I present the results of a study conducted in South Carolina that examined the attitudes and perceptions of college students toward various African American voices.

---

[1] In her study, Rahman used the label Black Standard English (BSE) to refer to what I call in the text Standard African American English.

Speakers

To collect the stimuli for this study, I recorded ten African American college students from South Carolina (six female and four male), with the goal of identifying a variety of African American voices among speakers who were social and regional peers of my targeted participant group (i.e., college students in the Southeastern region of the United States). I set out to recruit African American speakers representing a range of salient varieties. To this end, I recorded speakers whose voices sounded "Proper" – a label that circulates widely within the African American speech community, typically to refer to African American speakers whose voices do not "sound Black" from a prototypical (or even stereotypical) perspective and who are often ostracized by community members because of the perception that they do not embrace their African American heritage and culture. While I identified these speakers myself, I discussed this label with the speakers, each of whom acknowledged that their voices had been described by others as "Proper." I also recorded speakers of SAAE (i.e., speakers whose voices might be perceived as ethnically marked [or as "sounding Black"], but without any overtly stigmatized phonological or grammatical features). Because SAAE is not a label that circulates within the general public, I did not discuss this label with the speakers, but instead identified them myself, based on my own judgments as a linguist and as a member of the African American speech community. Finally, I recorded speakers of Gullah (also known as Geechee) – an African American Creole variety spoken along the coasts of South Carolina and Georgia. I chose this variety because of its salience (and often stigma) in the region, as well as its distinctiveness vis-à-vis the other two varieties described above. All of the Gullah speakers whom I recorded identified Gullah as part of their own linguistic repertoires, though they were fluent in other varieties as well. And while they acknowledged the stigma that too often accompanies Gullah, they also spoke of its significance as a marker of culture and identity, consistent with Smitherman's "push-pull" concept, described throughout this volume.[2]

The stimuli for the study were ultimately drawn from six of the ten recorded speakers – one female and one male representing each of the three varieties described above. The six speakers were chosen based on the quality of their recordings, the distinctiveness of their voices vis-à-vis others of the same

---

[2] While anecdotal in nature, it may be relevant to note the gender divide that I observed among those whom I recorded for this study. While one of the male speakers talked about his own voice as having been described by others as "sexy," one of the female speakers said that she tried very hard *not* to sound "Geechee" on campus. Another female speaker was so uncomfortable switching to Gullah for the purposes of the recording that she ultimately backed out and asked not to participate in the study.

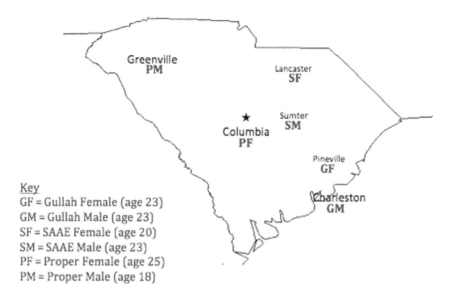

Figure 6.1 Distribution of speakers by age, gender, and hometown

gender, and the extent to which their voices seemed exemplary of the above-mentioned varieties. With the exception of the "Proper" male, who self-identified as Black-White biracial, all of the speakers identified as African American.[3] The "Proper" female was a native of Columbia, South Carolina, who had moved around as a military dependent. All of the other speakers were born and raised in South Carolina, with the exception of the "Proper" male, who was born in Pasadena, California, but raised in Greenville, South Carolina. Figure 6.1 shows the distribution of the speakers by age, gender, and hometown.

Participants

To solicit participation for this study, I emailed faculty members and student leaders at several colleges and universities in South Carolina and Georgia and asked them to help distribute the survey link to students at their respective schools. I restricted the solicitation to these two states in an effort to increase the likelihood of listeners having at least some familiarity with Gullah. The

[3] Holliday (2016) provides a detailed examination of the ways in which some Black-White biracial speakers draw on both Mainstream US English and African American Language as ethnolinguistic repertoires in identity construction.

anonymous survey, which was designed to take approximately ten to fifteen minutes to complete, was conducted online. Participants were informed at the outset that the focus of the study was on the labeling and perception of African American voices and the concept of "sounding Black." After about three months of periodic solicitation, over the fall 2014 and spring 2015 semesters, a total of fifty students had responded to the survey, the results of which are presented in an earlier version of this chapter (see Weldon 2018). To increase the size of the participant pool and provide a more robust set of data for purposes of statistical analysis, I collected a second set of responses over a period of about five months in the summer and fall of 2016. In this chapter, I present the results from this expanded data set, focusing specifically on African American (AA) participants (N = 54) and European American (EA) participants (N = 42), who represented the majority of those who responded to the survey.

Ultimately, all but one of the study participants who shared their university affiliation reported being enrolled in a South Carolina school. One student was enrolled at a university in North Carolina. And one participant chose not to share their university affiliation. With the exception of one EA student who was attending a Historically Black College or University (HBCU), all of the EA participants were enrolled in Predominately White Institutions (PWIs). Of the AA participants, 52% attended HBCUs; 46% attended PWIs; and, as noted above, one participant chose not to report their university affiliation. In terms of gender, 83% of AA participants and 57% of EA participants identified as female. One EA participant identified as agender. All remaining participants identified as male. The AA participants ranged in age from eighteen to fifty-five, with an average age of twenty-five, and the EA participants ranged in age from seventeen to fifty-five, with an average age of twenty-four. Among the AA participants, 85% were enrolled as undergraduate students at the time of the study, 13% as graduate students, and one participant provided no response. Among the EA participants, 93% were enrolled as undergraduate students and 7% as graduate students. Among AA respondents, 81% had never taken a linguistics class before, 17% had taken a small number of linguistics classes, and one participant was majoring/minoring in linguistics. Among the EA respondents, 67% had never taken a linguistics class, 28% had taken a small number of linguistics classes, and two were majoring/minoring in linguistics.

To get a sense of the participants' perceptions of their own linguistic backgrounds, I asked them to select, among a list of options, which of the given varieties they spoke, if any (Figure 6.2). They were asked to select all that applied. Given the focus in this study on "sounding Black," the list of options that participants were provided heavily favored African American language varieties (i.e., African American English, Ebonics, Gullah, Geechee). Other labels provided were either specific to the South (i.e.,

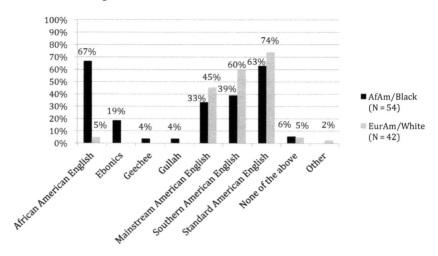

Figure 6.2 Participants by linguistic variety

Southern American English) or labels that described varieties that were distributed across regional and ethnic boundaries in the USA (i.e., Mainstream American English, Standard American English).

Among the AA participants, African American English was the most popular response selected, at 67%, followed by Standard American English, which was selected by 63% of AA participants. The most popular variety selected among EA respondents was Standard American English, which was chosen by 74% of participants, followed by Southern American English at 60%. No other variety was selected by more than 50% of either participant group. It is perhaps noteworthy that Ebonics, which is arguably a much more familiar term than African American English for most members of the general public, was only selected by 19% of participants, perhaps because of the more negative connotations associated with the term since the Oakland School Board controversy that erupted in the late 1990s.

Participants were also asked to choose from among a list of options, which, if any, of the given labels they would use to describe their own speech and which, if any, of the given labels others had used to describe their speech. Again, they were instructed to select all that applied (see Figures 6.3 and 6.4). The labels that they were presented with were either labels that circulate widely in the South (i.e., Country) or labels that circulate widely in the African American speech community (i.e., Ghetto, Geechee, Proper). These same labels were ultimately used in the perception study itself for participants to rate the voices that they heard.

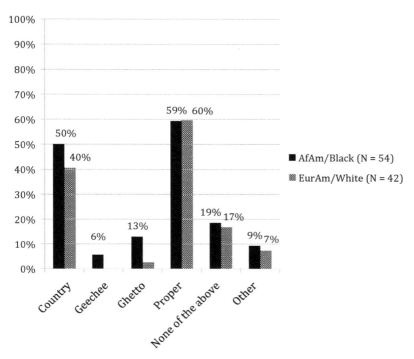

Figure 6.3 Participant response to the question "Which, if any, of the following labels would you use to describe your own speech?"

Perhaps not surprisingly, given the focus of this study on college-educated students, the most popular label for both groups was "Proper," which was selected by 59% of AA participants and 60% of EA participants as a self-description and by 65% of AA participants and 52% of EA participants as a label that others had used to describe their speech. The only other label selected by at least 50% of participants was "Country," which was selected by 50% of AA participants as a self-description and by 59% as a label that others had used to describe their speech. Country was also the second most popular label chosen among EA participants, but by just 40% as a self-description and 45% as a label used by others.

One final observation before turning to the results regards the label "Geechee," which, like many circulating labels for African American language varieties, was once perceived as a highly stigmatized term in the Gullah community. Note that 6% of AA participants selected this label as one that they would use as a self-description and that others had used to describe their speech. However, no EA participants selected this label. Despite the low rate

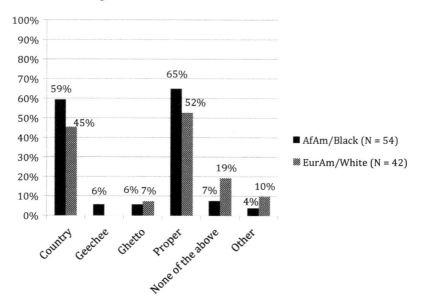

Figure 6.4 Participant response to the question "Which, if any, of the following labels have others used to describe your speech?"

of selection within this participant group, there is at least anecdotal evidence that Geechee is being reappropriated, particularly among younger members of the Gullah community.[4] What is noteworthy in the current study is that roughly 30% of EA participants reported having had *no* familiarity with the Geechee label at all, in contrast to the AA participants, almost all of whom were familiar with it. The connection between Gullah/Geechee language and culture and African American identity is one that I will return to later in the chapter.

---

[4] I base this claim on observations of commentary made particularly by younger community members, who seem to embrace the term "Geechee" while often distancing themselves from "Gullah" as something that their parents and/or grandparents speak or spoke. Once, following a lecture that I had given in Georgetown, SC, I was approached by a young woman who showed me her "Geechee girl" tattoo and expressed her preference for the label "Geechee" over "Gullah." It is, perhaps, also significant to note that the label "Geechee" is used in the name chosen for the federally commissioned Gullah/Geechee Cultural Heritage Corridor (www .gullahgeecheecorridor.org/) as well as the Gullah/Geechee Nation website (https:// gullahgeecheenation.com/) operated by Gullah Chieftess Queen Quet. And it is used, sans Gullah, in the name of the "Geechee Experience" website (https://geecheexperience.com/), which has recently gained popularity on social media. Such examples suggest that the "Geechee" label might be undergoing a shift in referential meaning as well as evaluation.

Results

In order to create the stimuli for the perception study, I asked each speaker to read several word lists and reading passages. Grammatical variables and other linguistic phenomena were controlled for through the use of these texts, thus facilitating comparison across speakers.[5] For the purposes of the perception study, I presented listeners with three different stimuli from each speaker – (1) the greeting "hello," (2) the act of "sucking teeth" followed by the expression "whatever," and (3) the first stanza of "Mary had a little lamb."[6] For the first two stimuli, participants were asked to rate the voices on four circulating labels – "Country," "Ghetto," "Geechee," and "Proper." Based on observed patterns of usage, I predicted that the Gullah voices would be rated highest on "Geechee," while the Proper voices would be rated highest on "Proper." In the absence of any circulating labels for SAAE, I had less clear expectations about how listeners might perceive and label these voices, though I expected them to pattern closer to Proper than to Gullah. The labels "Country" and "Ghetto" were included as additional circulating labels – the former typically used to refer to rural speakers, the latter to refer to urban speakers, both connoting a certain lack of "class" or sophistication. For the third stimulus, "Mary had a little lamb," participants were asked to rate the voices on a variety of social characteristics, such as friendliness, sexiness, nerdiness, etc. The responses to these stimuli are discussed in detail below.

Hello

Using the greeting "hello" as a stimulus to test listener perceptions, Purnell et al. (1999) found that listeners were able to accurately assess the race/ethnicity of speakers using only minimal acoustic cues. I presented "hello" as the first stimulus in this study to determine whether listeners could make more nuanced distinctions – in this case, across a variety of African American voices – using the same minimal stimulus.[7] Unlike Purnell et al., who employed a true "matched guise" technique, by which a single speaker represented multiple guises (cf. Lambert et al. 1960), I presented listeners with stimuli from multiple speakers in order to create a more naturalistic, though

---

[5] All recordings were done in my office, using Audacity 1.3.13-beta (Unicode) and the internal microphone on my MacBook Pro.

[6] As noted earlier, the speakers were initially asked to read several word lists and reading passages, which were designed to elicit a variety of phonological and prosodic cues. In the text, I discuss the reasoning behind each of the selections that was ultimately made for the purposes of the perception study.

[7] Participants were told in advance that the voices that they would be asked to rate were those of African American speakers.

less controlled, listening experience.[8] The audio samples for this stimulus are presented in Sound Files 6.1a–f.

a. Gullah Female	b. Gullah Male
c. SAAE Female	d. SAAE Male
e. Proper Female	f. Proper Male

Sound Files 6.1a-f "Hello"

For this stimulus, the female voices were played first, followed by the male voices.[9] Then, for each of the circulating labels, participants were asked to rate

---

[8] Other speakers in the Purnell et al. study were used as distractors, but were not included in the presentation of results.

[9] For each of the three stimuli, the voices were presented in a different order to keep participants attentive and prevent them from answering by rote.

Table 6.1 *Mean ratings of overall responses to "hello" (N = 96)*

	African American Responses (N = 54)					
	Female Voices			Male Voices		
Labels	Gullah	SAAE	Proper	Gullah	SAAE	Proper
"Country"	1.71	1.8	1.26	1.9	1.92	2.17
"Geechee"	3.58	1.17	1.19	2.6	1.29	1.29
"Ghetto"	2.26	1.33	1.05	2.39	1.24	1.55
"Proper"	1.9	3.81	4.72	2.44	3.3	3.17
	European American Responses (N = 42)					
	Female Voices			Male Voices		
Labels	Gullah	SAAE	Proper	Gullah	SAAE	Proper
"Country"	1.28	1.91	1.49	1.49	2.03	2
"Geechee"	3.65	1.19	1.1	1.95	1.50	1.32
"Ghetto"	2.42	1.46	1.24	3.31	1.89	1.51
"Proper"	2.31	3.38	4.55	2.33	3.4	3.18

Note: Order of presentation: GF→PF→SF→PM→SM→GM.

the voices on a scale of 1–5, where a rating of "1" meant that the voice did not exemplify the given label at all, a rating of "3" meant that the voice "kind of" exemplified the given label, and a rating of "5" meant that the voice "really" exemplified the given label. Any rating above "3," shaded in dark gray in Table 6.1, was interpreted as a positive rating, meaning that participants associated the voice with the given label.

As shown in Table 6.1, none of the voices received ratings above "3" for "Country," indicating that none of the voices was strongly associated with this label for this particular stimulus. Both AA and EA participants associated the female Gullah speaker's voice with the "Geechee" label and each of the SAAE and Proper speakers' voices with the label "Proper." Predictably, among the female voices, the Proper speaker's voice received the highest mean rating for "Proper." However, among the male voices, the SAAE speaker actually received the highest mean rating for "Proper." Among AA participants, the male Gullah speaker did not receive any mean ratings above "3," although the highest mean rating, at 2.6, was for "Geechee." Among EA participants, the Gullah male speaker received a meaning rating of 3.31 for "Ghetto."

To test these data for statistical significance, I used a repeated measures analysis of variance (ANOVA) (SPSS). As noted earlier, many of the EA

Table 6.2 *ANOVA results of significant main effects and interactions for "hello"*

label: f (3,39) = 32.490, p = 0.000		
voice: f (2,40) = 9.106, p = 0.001		
label*gender: f (3,39) = 12.176, p = 0.000		
label*voice: f (6,36) = 21.250, p = 0.000		**label*voice*gender**: f (6,36) = 10.029, p = 0.000
Country	*no significant differences*	*no significant differences*
Geechee	**Gullah** > SAAE (p = 0.000), Proper (p = 0.000)	**Female/Male:** **Gullah** > SAAE (p = 0.000), Proper (p = 0.000)
Ghetto	**Gullah** > SAAE (p = 0.000), Proper (p = 0.000)	**Female:** **Gullah** > SAAE (p = 0.021), Proper (p = 0.001) **Male:** **Gullah** > SAAE (p = 0.000), Proper (p = 0.001)
Proper	**SAAE** > Gullah (p = 0.000) **Proper** > Gullah (p = 0.000)	**Female:** **Proper** > Gullah (p = 0.000), SAAE (p = 0.001) **SAAE** > Gullah (p = 0.000) **Male:** **SAAE** > Gullah (p = 0.002)

Note: These results are based on **African American (N = 28)** and **European American (N = 15)** *completed responses only*. Participants with missing data were removed from the ANOVA. In a test of between-subjects effects, race/ethnicity was *not* found to be significant.

participants were unfamiliar with the "Geechee" label and, therefore, chose not to rate the voices that they heard on this particular label, thus resulting in many empty cells in the data. While the AA participants did not express a general lack of familiarity with any of the given labels, many of them chose not to answer certain questions in the survey as well.[10] Because the repeated measures ANOVA removes participants from the analysis when data are missing, the number of completed responses for the "hello" stimulus was reduced to fifteen

---

[10] One of the faculty members who assisted me with the solicitation process shared with me a concern expressed by one of her African American students that the process of rating the voices felt "racist" to him. While there was no mechanism for participants to share this kind of feedback with me through the survey itself, one might assume that several of the gaps in the AA data reflected similar sentiments.

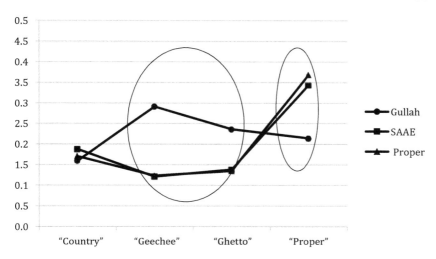

Figure 6.5 Estimated marginal means of label*voice ratings for responses to "hello"

EA participants and twenty-eight AA participants for the statistical analysis. Table 6.2 displays the significant main effects and interactions identified for this stimulus, with post-hoc comparisons reported for label*voice and label*voice*-gender interactions, which were of particular interest to the goals of this study.

While a test of between-subjects effects did not reveal any significant differences between the AA and EA responses, several significant main effects and interactions were identified. With regard to the label*voice and label*voi-ce*gender interactions, a comparison of the estimated marginal means for "Country" revealed no significant differences. However, for both the "Geechee" and "Ghetto" labels, the Gullah voice was rated significantly higher than both the SAAE and Proper voices. And the "Proper" label displayed a mirror-image effect by which both the SAAE and Proper voices were rated significantly higher than the Gullah voice, as illustrated in Figure 6.5.

The results for label*voice*gender, displayed in Figure 6.6, revealed the same basic pattern across male and female voices as those identified for the label*voice interaction. Both the male and female Gullah voices were rated significantly higher than their SAAE and Proper counterparts for "Ghetto" and "Geechee." For the "Proper" label, there was a well-defined Proper > SAAE > Gullah hierarchy among the female voices, which is marked in gray on Figure 6.6. Among the male voices, the only significant difference for "Proper" was between the SAAE and Gullah voices, with the SAAE voice rated as significantly more "Proper" than the Gullah voice.

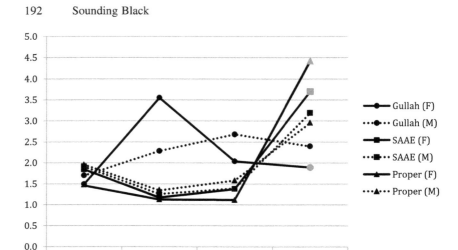

Figure 6.6 Estimated marginal means of label*voice*gender ratings for responses to "hello"

(Sucking Teeth) "Whatever!"

The second stimulus that participants heard was that of each speaker sucking their teeth, followed by "whatever," an expression that is typically used by speakers to signal dismissiveness or a lack of concern for something or someone (Sound Files 6.2a–f).

Unlike "hello," which is racially neutral, the act of "sucking teeth" is a racially marked gesture, used in the African American speech community to signal disgust or disapproval. According to Rickford and Rickford (1976 [1999]), the act of "sucking teeth" represents an African continuity, which, at least at the time of their study, was more or less restricted to African American speech communities in the United States. In fact, for most European American participants in their study, the distinctive meaning of this gesture vis-à-vis more mainstream gestures, such as the act of "cleaning one's teeth," was linguistically "camouflaged" (cf. Spears 1982, 2009, 2017). Before recording this stimulus for my own study, I asked each speaker if they understood what was meant by the expression "sucking teeth." Each one answered affirmatively, and then proceeded to demonstrate the gesture correctly, with the exception of the "Proper" male who said that he was familiar with the gesture, but then demonstrated something more akin to cleaning his teeth. The waveform images shown in Figure 6.7, which were captured using Praat (version 5.3.80), illustrate how his production of "sucking teeth" differed in length and amplitude from those of the other speakers. Because

a. Gullah Female	b. Gullah Male
c. SAAE Female	d. SAAE Male
e. Proper Female	f. Proper Male

Sound Files 6.2a-f (sucking teeth) "Whatever!"

I wanted to capture the speakers' natural tendencies for producing the given stimuli, I did not "correct" his interpretation of "sucking teeth," but instead used it for the perception study as he produced it. I presented (sucking teeth) "Whatever!" as the second stimulus in the study in order to determine whether a brief verbal cue that was racially marked and more semantically loaded would yield a different set of ratings than those observed for the more semantically neutral "hello." The order of presentation for this stimulus was male voices followed by female voices, as shown at the bottom of Table 6.3.

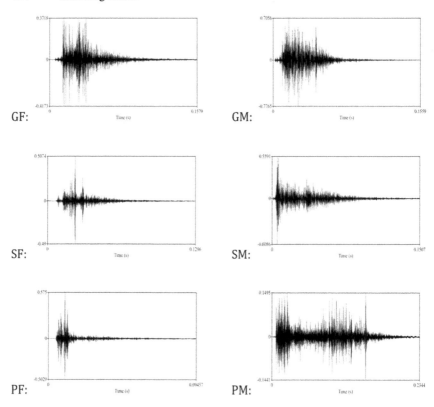

GF:

GM:

SF:

SM:

PF:

PM:

Figure 6.7 Waveforms for "sucking teeth"

As with "hello" (Table 6.1), the Proper female speaker received mean ratings above "3" for "Proper" by both AA and EA participants. AA participants rated the Proper male above "3" for "Proper" for both stimuli as well. However, EA participants did not mark him above "3" for any label in response to the second stimulus, though "Proper" received the highest rating at 2.71. Similarly, whereas AA and EA participants marked the SAAE female speaker above "3" for "Proper" in response to "hello," neither group marked her voice above "3" for any label in response to (sucking teeth) "Whatever!," though she received the highest ratings for "Proper," at 2.81 and 2.92, respectively. The SAAE male, on the other hand, went from ratings above "3" for "Proper" in response to "hello" to ratings above "3" for "Ghetto" in response to (sucking teeth) "Whatever!" This is a remarkable shift, given that these two labels typically denote opposing characteristics. The Gullah voices also exhibited dramatic shifts in ratings from the first to second stimulus. The Gullah female, whom both AA and EA participants rated above "3" for

Table 6.3 *Mean ratings of overall responses to (sucking teeth) "Whatever!"* *(N = 96)*

	African American Responses (N = 54)					
	Female Voices			Male Voices		
Labels	Gullah	SAAE	Proper	Gullah	SAAE	Proper
"Country"	3.23	1.71	1.7	2.88	1.86	1.87
"Geechee"	2.58	1.57	1.37	2.18	1.22	1.11
"Ghetto"	3.95	2.6	1.63	3.77	3.14	1.74
"Proper"	1.34	2.81	3.65	1.45	2.11	3.46
	European American Responses (N = 42)					
	Female Voices			Male Voices		
Labels	Gullah	SAAE	Proper	Gullah	SAAE	Proper
"Country"	2.44	1.79	2.28	1.79	1.4	1.5
"Geechee"	2.26	1.79	1.1	2	1.35	1.79
"Ghetto"	4.25	2.63	1.53	4.2	3.73	1.83
"Proper"	1.44	2.92	3.58	1.56	2	2.71

Note: Order of presentation: SM→PM→GM→PF→SF→GF.

"Geechee" in response to the "hello" stimulus, received ratings above "3" for "Country" and "Ghetto" by AA participants and for "Ghetto" by EA participants in response to the (sucking teeth) "Whatever!" stimulus. And the Gullah male received ratings above "3" for "Ghetto" by both groups on the second stimulus, whereas just the EA group rated his voice as "Ghetto" for the first stimulus.

Several factors might have contributed to these shifts in ratings. To the extent that "sucking teeth," as a racially marked and dismissive gesture, indexes a certain type of stereotypical "Blackness" (e.g., the trope of the "angry Black male/female") this act alone might have prompted the higher "Ghetto" ratings shown in Table 6.3. Secondly, given the strong association of post-vocalic [r]-lessness with both urban and rural working class speech, the [r]-less pronunciation of "whatever" might have prompted both the "Country" and "Ghetto" ratings that were activated by the second stimulus. A comparison of the F3 values in Figure 6.8 points to a continuum of rhoticity, ranging from the nonrhotic production of the Gullah speakers, to the more intermediate (but impressionistically rhotic) production of the SAAE speakers, to the acutely rhotic production of the Proper speakers, whose F3 values were more dramatically lowered. This rhotic effect might also have played a role in the relatively high ratings for "Proper"

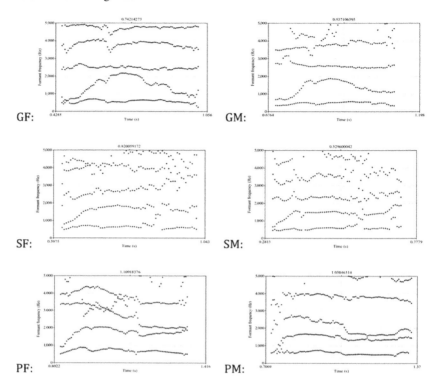

Figure 6.8 Formant contours for "Whatever!"

assigned to the Proper female, Proper male, and SAAE female voices, even in the context of this more racially marked stimulus. As observed in Labov (1966), [r] constriction serves as an important indicator of "formal, educated speech" in the African American speech community (264). Among AA respondents, the Proper male's rating for "Proper" actually went *up* on the second stimulus (from 3.17 to 3.46), perhaps due to his "r-ful" pronunciation of "whatever" in combination with the marked difference in "sucking teeth" described earlier.

With the empty cells removed, an ANOVA test was conducted on the responses of twenty-nine AA participants and eighteen EA participants for the (sucking teeth) "Whatever" stimulus. As with "hello," a test of between-subjects effects showed no significant difference between AA and EA responses to this stimulus. Table 6.4 displays the significant main effects and interactions that were identified, with additional results shown from post-hoc comparisons of the estimated marginal means for label*voice and label*voice*gender.

For the label*voice interaction, the Gullah voices were rated significantly higher on "Country" than the SAAE and Proper voices. Gullah was also rated

Table 6.4 *ANOVA results of significant main effects and interactions for (sucking teeth) "Whatever!"*

label: f (3,43) = 37.276, p = 0.000		
voice: f (2,44) = 30.862, p = 0.000		
gender: f (1,45) = 12.314, p = 0.001		
voice*race/ethnicity: f (2,44) = 4.269, p = 0.020		
label*gender: f (3,43) = 6.651, p = 0.001		
label*voice: f (6,40) = 27.904, p = 0.000		**label*voice*gender**: f (6,40) = 8.443, p = 0.000
Country	**Gullah** > SAAE (p = 0.000), Proper (p = 0.002)	**Female:** **Gullah** > SAAE (p = 0.000), Proper (p = 0.006) **Male:** **Gullah** > SAAE (p = 0.002), Proper (p = 0.032)
Geechee	**Gullah** > SAAE (p = 0.000), Proper (p = 0.000) **SAAE** > Proper (p = 0.050)	**Female:** **Gullah** > SAAE (p = 0.005), Proper (p = 0.000) **Male:** **Gullah** > SAAE (p = 0.000), Proper (p = 0.000)
Ghetto	**Gullah** > SAAE (p = 0.000), Proper (p = 0.000) **SAAE** > Proper (p = 0.000)	**Female:** **Gullah** > SAAE (p = 0.000), Proper (p = 0.000) **SAAE** > Proper (p = 0.008) **Male:** **Gullah** > SAAE (p = 0.033), Proper (p = 0.000) **SAAE** > Proper (p = 0.000)
Proper	**Proper** > Gullah (p = 0.000), SAAE (p = 0.000) **SAAE** > Gullah (p = 0.000)	**Female/Male:** **Proper** > Gullah (p = 0.000), SAAE (p = 0.001) **SAAE** > Gullah (p = 0.000)

Note: These results are based on **African American (N = 29)** and **European American (N = 18)** *completed responses only*. Participants with missing data were removed from the ANOVA. In a test of between-subjects effects, race/ethnicity was *not* found to be significant.

higher than SAAE and Proper on "Geechee" and "Ghetto," and SAAE was rated higher than Proper, yielding a distinct Gullah > SAAE > Proper hierarchy for "Geechee" and "Ghetto." For "Proper," there was a mirror-image effect, displaying a distinct Proper > SAAE > Gullah hierarchy. The opposing continua for "Geechee" and "Ghetto" versus "Proper" are marked by circles in Figure 6.9.

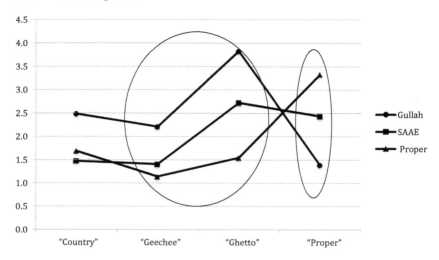

Figure 6.9 Estimated marginal means of label*voice ratings for responses to (sucking teeth) "Whatever!"

Note that "Country" patterned closer to "Geechee" and "Ghetto" here, but with no significant difference between the SAAE and Proper voices.

The label*voice*gender results showed that Gullah was rated as significantly more "Country" and "Geechee" than both the SAAE and Proper female and male voices. For "Ghetto" there was a clear Gullah > SAAE > Proper hierarchy for both the female and male voices. And "Proper" displayed the mirror-image Proper > SAAE > Gullah hierarchy for both female and male voices. In this case, "Country" and "Geechee" patterned closer to "Ghetto," though no significant difference between SAAE and Proper emerged when the data were divided by gender. These results are displayed in Figure 6.10, again with mirror-image hierarchies circled.

Mary Had a Little Lamb

The final utterance that participants heard was the first stanza of "Mary had a little lamb," illustrated by Sound Files 6.3a–f.[11] For this stimulus, listeners

---

[11] In an *ABC World News Tonight* episode on linguistic profiling that aired February 7, 2002, John Baugh used recitations of "Mary had a little lamb" to demonstrate listeners' ability to identify the racial or ethnic background of speakers based strictly on their voices. Baugh coined the term "linguistic profiling" to refer to the practice of discriminating against someone based on the sound of their voice – a phenomenon that he observed while conducting research on housing discrimination (Baugh 1996, 2000b; Purnell et al. 1999).

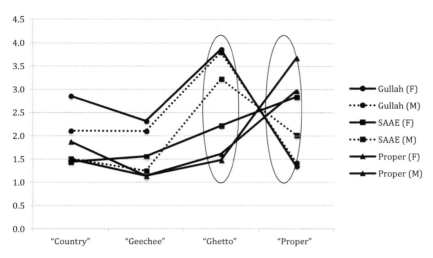

Figure 6.10 Estimated marginal means of label*voice*gender ratings for
responses to (sucking teeth) "Whatever!"

were asked to rate the voices that they heard on nine social characteristics,
distributed over four dimensions, as shown in Table 6.5. These characteristics
were chosen based on my own observations about the kinds of commentary
that the voices in question tend to invoke. The order of presentation for this
stimulus alternated between female and male voices, as shown at the bottom of
Table 6.6.

As with the other stimuli, my primary goal in conducting the statistical
analysis was to look for significant interactions between "voice" and "social
characteristics" (cf. label). A test of between-subjects effects revealed no significant differences by race/ethnicity. The main effects and interactions that were
found to be significant are displayed in Table 6.7. The discussion of these results
is divided into four sections, according to the dimensions outlined above.

Solidarity The only solidarity characteristic that received ratings over
"3" in Table 6.6 was "friendly," which AA participants associated with both
SAAE voices and the Proper female voice. EA participants rated all of the
voices except that of the SAAE male speaker above "3" on friendliness. The
association of the SAAE and Proper voices with "friendliness" is somewhat
surprising, given findings reported in other matched guise studies that high-
status voices tend to be rated lower on solidarity (see, e.g., Lambert et al.,
1960; Preston 1996, 2004). However, these results are similar to those reported
in studies such as Buck (1968) and Tucker and Lambert (1975), where college

a. Gullah Female	b. Gullah Male
c. SAAE Female	d. SAAE Male
e. Proper Female	f. Proper Male

Sound Files 6.3a-f "Mary had a little lamb"

Table 6.5 *Social characteristics on which voices were rated in response to the "Mary had a little lamb" stimulus*

Dimensions	Social Characteristics
Solidarity	*Cool, Friendly, Snooty*
Status	*Educated, Nerdy*
Gender/Sexuality	*Sexy, Feminine, Masculine*
Racial Identity	*Strong Black Identity*

Table 6.6 *Mean ratings of overall responses to "Mary had a little lamb"*
(N = 96)

		African American Responses (N = 54)					
	Social	Female Voices			Male Voices		
Dimensions	Characteristics	Gullah	SAAE	Proper	Gullah	SAAE	Proper
Solidarity	Cool	2.61	2.76	1.95	2.88	2.95	2.08
	Friendly	2.9	3.54	3.82	2.8	3	2.9
	Snooty	1.55	1.4	2.26	1.18	1.21	2.6
Status	Educated	3.02	4.05	4.19	3.08	3.65	3.98
	Nerdy	1.46	1.38	2.03	1.63	1.79	3.49
Gender/	Sexy	1.53	1.59	1.35	1.85	1.95	1.45
Sexuality	Feminine	4.12	4.51	4.57	1.31	1.33	2
	Masculine	1.44	1.13	1.08	4.44	4.79	3.17
Racial Identity	Strong Black Identity	4.23	4.03	1.26	4.19	4.24	1.38

		European American Responses (N = 42)					
	Social	Female Voices			Male Voices		
Dimensions	Characteristics	Gullah	SAAE	Proper	Gullah	SAAE	Proper
Solidarity	Cool	2.35	2.82	2	2.97	2.95	1.72
	Friendly	3.03	3.31	3.63	3.27	2.91	3.03
	Snooty	1.31	1.94	2.61	1.31	1.75	2.71
Status	Educated	2.59	3.67	4.08	3.24	3.35	3.85
	Nerdy	1.36	1.47	1.92	1.28	1.43	3.63
Gender/	Sexy	1.36	1.67	1.53	1.78	1.78	1.17
Sexuality	Feminine	3.92	4.05	4.54	1.26	1.11	2.22
	Masculine	1.55	1.31	1.22	4.36	4.53	3.08
Racial Identity	Strong Black Identity	4.23	3.41	1.11	4.41	3.83	1.25

Note: Order of presentation: PF→GM→SF→SM→GF→PM.

students rated standard voices favorably not only on status dimensions, but also on solidarity dimensions. Thus, the friendliness results in this study might be tied, at least in part, to the observation made earlier about participants perceiving their own voices as "Standard" or "Proper" and perhaps viewing the SAAE and Proper voices favorably because they found them to be relatable to their own.

Table 6.7 *ANOVA results of significant main effects and interactions for "Mary had a little lamb"*

social characteristics: f (8,49) = 45.575, p = 0.000

voice: f (2,55) = 12.664, p = 0.000

social characteristics*gender: f (8,49) = 61.058, p = 0.000

social characteristics*voice: f (16,41) = 25.969,   **social char.*voice*gender**: f (16,41)
  p = 0.000   = 10.695, p = 0.000

Solidarity		
Cool	**Gullah** > Proper (0.000) **SAAE** > Proper (0.000)	**Female**: **Gullah** > Proper (p = 0.004) **SAAE** > Proper (p = 0.000) **Male**: **Gullah** > Proper (p = 0.000) **SAAE** > Proper (p = 0.000)
Friendly	*no significant differences*	**Female**: **Proper** > Gullah (p = 0.005)
Snooty	**Proper** > Gullah (p = 0.000), SAAE (p = 0.000) **SAAE** > Gullah (p = 0.027)	**Female**: **Proper** > Gullah (p = 0.000), SAAE (p = 0.000) **Male**: **Proper** > Gullah (p = 0.000), SAAE (p = 0.000)

Status		
Educated	**Proper** > Gullah (p = 0.000), SAAE (p = 0.020) **SAAE** > Gullah (p = 0.000)	**Female**: **Proper** > Gullah (p = 0.000) **SAAE** > Gullah (p = 0.000) **Male**: **Proper** > Gullah (p = 0.000), SAAE (p = 0.016) **SAAE** > Gullah (p = 0.030)
Nerdy	**Proper** > Gullah (p = 0.000), SAAE (p = 0.000)	**Female**: **Proper** > Gullah (p = 0.003), SAAE (p = 0.002) **Male**: **Proper** > Gullah (p = 0.000), SAAE (p = 0.000)

Gender/Sexuality		
Sexy	**SAAE** > Proper (p = 0.003)	**Male**: **Gullah** > Proper (p = 0.004) **SAAE** > Proper (p = 0.003)
Feminine	**Proper** > Gullah (p = 0.000), SAAE (p = 0.000)	**Female**: **Proper** > Gullah (p = 0.006) **Male**: **Proper** > Gullah (p = 0.000), SAAE (p = 0.000)

Table 6.7 *(cont.)*

Masculine	Gullah > Proper (p = 0.000) SAAE > Proper (p = 0.000)	**Female:** Gullah > SAAE (p = 0.031), Proper (p = 0.009) **Male:** Gullah > Proper (p = 0.000) SAAE > Proper (p = 0.000)
Racial Identity		
Strong Black Identity	Gullah > SAAE (p = 0.010), Proper (p = 0.000) SAAE > Proper (p = 0.000)	**Female:** Gullah > Proper (p = 0.000), SAAE (p = 0.035) SAAE > Proper (p = 0.000) **Male:** Gullah > Proper (p = 0.000) SAAE > Proper (p = 0.000)

Note: These results are based on **African American (N = 29)** and **European American (N = 29)**
completed responses only. Participants with missing data were removed from the ANOVA. In a
test of between-subjects effects, race/ethnicity was *not* found to be significant.

The ANOVA results in Table 6.7 revealed no significant differences
between the voices on friendliness, except in the case of the Proper female,
who was rated as significantly more friendly than the Gullah female. In the
case of "coolness," however, the Gullah and SAAE voices were rated significantly higher than the Proper voices in both two-way (social characteristics*
voice) and three-way (social characteristics*voice*gender) interactions. By
contrast, the Proper voices were rated as significantly more "snooty" than the
Gullah and SAAE voices across both two-way and three-way interactions. The
two-way interaction also indicated a significant difference between the SAAE
and Gullah voices on this dimension, revealing a clear Proper > SAAE >
Gullah hierarchy for "snooty" that was practically the mirror image of "cool,"
as illustrated in Figures 6.11 and 6.12.

While the relative patterning of the Proper and Gullah voices is perhaps
unsurprising as it relates to "snootiness" and "coolness," it is noteworthy here
that the SAAE voices patterned closer to Gullah than to Proper on these
characteristics, thus capturing the "positive valences" of the solidarity dimension (i.e., more "cool" and less "snooty" than the Proper voices, though
slightly more "snooty" than the Gullah voices).

Status On the status dimension, AA respondents rated all of the voices
above "3" for sounding educated. And EA respondents rated all of the voices,
except that of the Gullah female, above "3" on this characteristic, as shown in
Table 6.6. The only voice rated above "3" for "nerdy" was that of the Proper

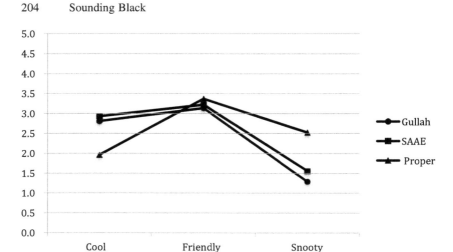

Figure 6.11 Estimated marginal means of label*voice ratings for responses to "Mary had a little lamb" on the solidarity dimension

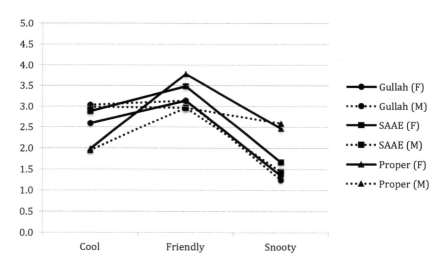

Figure 6.12 Estimated marginal means of label*voice*gender ratings for responses to "Mary had a little lamb" on the solidarity dimension

male, who received high ratings for this characteristic by both AA and EA participants. The two-way interaction results in Table 6.7 point to a clear Proper > SAAE > Gullah hierarchy for "educated." For "nerdy" the Proper voice was rated significantly higher than Gullah and SAAE. But there was no

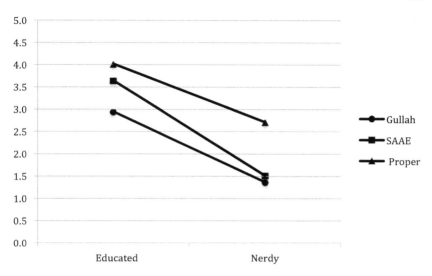

Figure 6.13 Estimated marginal means of label*voice ratings for responses to "Mary had a little lamb" on the status dimension

significant difference between Gullah and SAAE, as illustrated in Figure 6.13. As with the solidarity results discussed above, the relative patterning of the Proper and SAAE voices along the status dimension seem consistent with expectations, given their relative positioning along the standard-vernacular continuum. SAAE again appears to find an intermediate niche, where it is perceived as more "educated" than Gullah, but less "nerdy" than Proper. There is, however, an interesting gender dynamic with regard to the Gullah female and the Proper male that emerges more clearly in the three-way interaction results.

Among the female voices, both Proper and SAAE were rated as significantly more "educated" than Gullah, but there was no significant difference between Proper and SAAE. The male voices exhibited a distinct Proper > SAAE > Gullah hierarchy for "educated." But for "nerdy," the Proper voices, and especially the Proper male voice, stood out as significantly different from the other two sets of voices, as illustrated in Figure 6.14. Thus, while all of the voices were rated relatively high for sounding "educated" and relatively low for "sounding" nerdy, the Gullah female was perceived as least educated and the Proper male as most nerdy at rates that were statistically significant.

Gender/Sexuality With regard to gender/sexuality, the female speakers were rated above "3" on femininity and the male speakers were rated above "3"

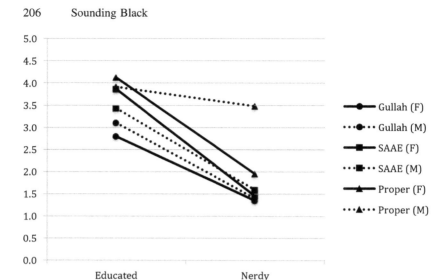

Figure 6.14 Estimated marginal means of label*voice*gender ratings for responses to "Mary had a little lamb" on the status dimension

on masculinity. However, none of the voices were rated above "3" on sexiness by either the AA or EA respondents. Admittedly, the nature of the stimulus likely played a role in these results, as a children's poem does not lend itself readily to demonstrations of sexiness. However, the results from the statistical analysis did point to a significant difference between the SAAE and Proper voices on sexiness (Figure 6.15). And a breakdown by gender showed that both the Gullah and SAAE male voices were perceived as more sexy than the Proper male voice (Figure 6.16).

Listeners rated the Proper voices as more feminine, overall, than the Gullah and SAAE voices. However, a breakdown by gender showed the Proper female was only perceived as sounding more feminine than the Gullah female, whereas the Proper male was perceived as sounding more feminine than both the Gullah and SAAE males. Conversely, the Gullah and SAAE voices were rated, overall, as sounding more masculine than the Proper voices. Among females, the Gullah female was rated as more masculine sounding than both the SAAE and Proper female voices. And the Gullah and SAAE male voices were rated as more masculine than the Proper male voice. These results support trends in the literature suggesting that vernacular voices tend to be associated more with masculinity and standard voices with femininity (see, e.g., Trudgill 1972), which once again places the Proper male and Gullah female speakers at the extreme ends of the respective hierarchies for these characteristics.

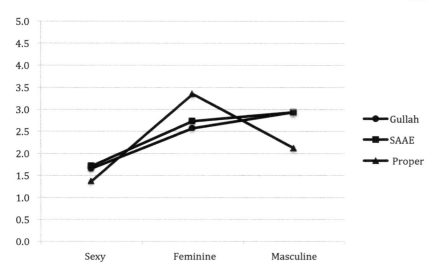

Figure 6.15 Estimated marginal means of label*voice ratings for responses to "Mary had a little lamb" on the gender/sexuality dimension

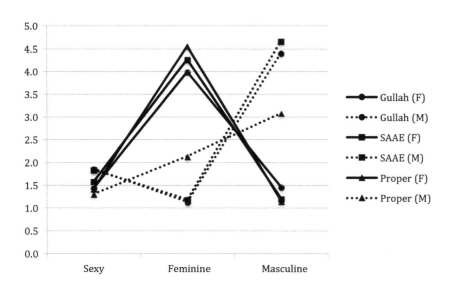

Figure 6.16 Estimated marginal means of label*voice*gender ratings for responses to "Mary had a little lamb" on the gender/sexuality dimension

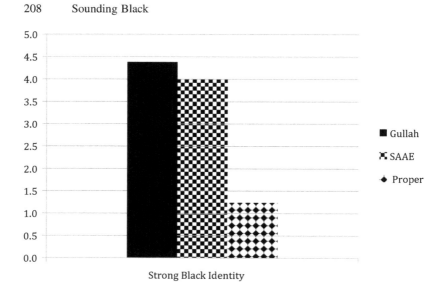

Figure 6.17 Estimated marginal means of label*voice ratings for responses to "Mary had a little lamb" on the racial identity dimension

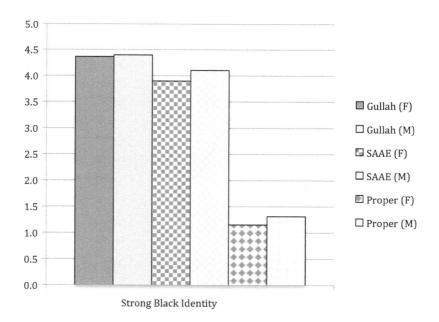

Figure 6.18 Estimated marginal means of label*voice*gender ratings for responses to "Mary had a little lamb" on the racial identity dimension

Racial Identity Finally, both AA and EA participants rated the Gullah and SAAE voices above "3" for having a "strong Black identity," while the "Proper" voices received low ratings on this characteristic. The ANOVA results in Table 6.7 point to a distinct Gullah > SAAE > Proper hierarchy, illustrated in Figure 6.17. This same hierarchy is displayed among the female speakers, as shown in Figure 6.18. Among the male speakers, the Gullah and SAAE voices received significantly higher ratings in comparison to the Proper speaker, but no statistically significant differences relative to one another. These results are consistent with lay perceptions of "Proper" voices as a rejection of African American culture and values and also point to a clear association of both Gullah and SAAE voices with a strong African American identity.

Conclusion

The results of this study show that "sounding Black" is a rich and complex phenomenon. While the findings reported here more or less confirmed my predictions regarding the association of Gullah voices with the label "Geechee" and Proper and SAAE voices with the label "Proper," there were some surprising trends across racial groups, and to some extent by gender, that should provide fodder for future investigations. While the statistical analyses failed to show any significant differences in how AA and EA listeners rated the Gullah, SAAE, and Proper voices relative to one another, the fact that so many EA participants were unfamiliar with the Geechee label is, itself, indicative of a racial divide, at least in the regional context where this study was conducted. While perceptions of voices as having a strong Black identity appear to pattern with notions of "coolness" and a general lack of "nerdiness" or "snootiness," they seem to do so at some cost, particularly in the context of more ethnically loaded expressions, which, for the Gullah speakers, seem to lend themselves more readily to perceptions of sounding "Ghetto" (and to some extent "Country"). There also appears to be some challenge for female Gullah speakers who desire to be perceived as sounding educated or feminine.

At the other end of the spectrum, Proper speakers are closely associated with sounding "educated," and female speakers with sounding "feminine" and to some extent "friendly." However, such associations appear to come at the expense of sounding like they have a strong Black identity, and are, instead, associated with perceptions of "snootiness" and a lack of "coolness." Furthermore, Proper voices are more likely to be perceived as sounding "nerdy," and especially Proper males, who also appear to be perceived as less masculine and more feminine than their Gullah and SAAE counterparts.

Relative to these more extreme associations indexed by Gullah and Proper voices, the SAAE voices appear to find a "happy medium." In instances where distinct hierarchies emerged, for example, in perceptions of sounding "Ghetto" or "Proper," they managed to fill the intermediate spaces between the two extremes. And yet, they trended closer to Gullah in being perceived as sounding "cool" but not "snooty" or "nerdy." And they trended closer to Proper in being perceived as sounding "educated." The SAAE female speaker rated high on femininity and the SAAE male speaker rated high on masculinity. And, like the Gullah speakers, they were perceived by both AA and EA listeners as having a strong Black identity.

Of course, the findings reported here do raise questions about the generalizability of the observed patterns beyond this study. For example, to what extent are female Gullah speakers judged more harshly than male Gullah speakers on intellect? To what extent are male Proper speakers rated lower on masculinity and higher on nerdiness than other male speakers?[12] Some results are likely to be specific to the region, like the perception of Gullah as a regionally and ethnically marked variety with a complex assortment of identities – for example, "Country," "Ghetto," "Geechee." Other findings are likely to be reflective of middle-class speech communities, such as the rating of SAAE and Proper (i.e., high status) voices as "friendly" – a finding that challenges conventional wisdom about the compatibility of "high status" voices with high solidarity ratings. And, of course, the perception of Proper voices as *not* "sounding Black" and SAAE voices as "sounding Black" but without many of the negative connotations associated with more saliently marked varieties, is one that may be generalizable well beyond the South and perhaps applicable to African American, and especially, middle-class African American speech communities in general. In sum, the nuanced meanings and associations highlighted here not only speak to the many and varied ways in which African American speakers "sound Black," they also demonstrate that listeners are attuned to the differences and well equipped to assess them.

---

[12] None of the speakers was asked about their own gender identities or sexual orientation, which could have had a significant impact on the ways in which their voices were perceived and rated by the participants.

7   Looking Ahead

"Funny how I've never heard you speak Ebonics before," she told Blaine, the first time she heard him talking to Mr. White. His syntax was different, his cadences more rhythmic. "I guess I've become too used to my White People Are Watching Us voice," he said. "And you know, younger black folk don't really do code switching anymore. The middle-class kids can't speak Ebonics and the inner-city kids speak only Ebonics and they don't have the fluidity that my generation has."
—Chimamanda Ngozi Adichie (2013)
Excerpt from *Americanah*

While drawn from fiction, the epigraph at the start of this chapter describes a world in which class differences among African Americans have created a linguistic fissure, with middle-class speakers melding into the American mainstream, as working-class speakers become further alienated from it. Ironically, this is, largely, the reality that sociolinguists have imagined for decades, as we have focused our interests almost exclusively on the vernacular varieties of working-class speech communities. However, in so doing, we have missed an opportunity to explore the ways in which many middle-class African Americans also draw on the African American repertoire, including the use of vernacular features once thought to have been eschewed by speakers higher on the socioeconomic spectrum. And we have largely ignored the more standard end of the continuum, where vernacular feature usage gets minimized, but racial and ethnic identities get performed through the strategic use of more nuanced linguistic features. Admittedly, gaining entrée into the linguistic practices of the African American middle class can be challenging, as many middle-class African American speakers have been socialized to mask their more vernacular linguistic tendencies behind the veil of their "White people are watching us" voices (cf. Adichie 2013). But, as the current study demonstrates, there are ways to tap into the linguistic practices and perspectives of this community that can illuminate aspects of the AAE continuum that extend far beyond the current reaches of our research. In this chapter, I reflect on the future of middle-class AAE and future directions of research that might prove fruitful in our efforts to incorporate middle-class speakers into expanded definitions of the African American speech community.

The Future of Middle-Class AAE

In many ways, the future of middle-class AAE is contingent upon the future of the American middle class and African Americans' place in it. Those who study the economy have expressed concern about the stability of the American middle class, which remains in a fragile state of recovery over a decade after the Great Recession of 2008. Stagnant wages, declining job prospects for "middle-skill" workers (Lowrey 2017), and the rising costs of housing, healthcare, childcare, and college have put tremendous pressure on middle-income families across the board (Krause and Sawhill 2018). And for African Americans, the economic impact has been even greater, as losses in home equity, predatory lending practices, racist mortgage policies, higher levels of unemployment, and lower incomes have exacerbated the already significant racial wealth gap (White 2015). According to a Pew Research study, "The wealth of white households was 13 times the median wealth of black households in 2013, compared with eight times the wealth in 2010," marking the widest gap between Blacks and Whites since 1989 (Kochhar and Fry 2014). And predictions are all the more dire for middle-class African American males, who tend to experience higher rates of downward mobility as they move into adulthood (Krause and Sawhill 2018). Thus, in spite of increases in the number of racial and ethnic minorities in the USA and predictions that "[m]inorities will compose the majority of the middle class by 2042" (Reeves and Busette 2018), the promise of a thriving African American middle class remains tenuous at best.[1]

As described in Rickford (1987 [1999]), the linguistic impact of such a state of affairs can be considered from both ecological and ethological perspectives. Despite the *Brown* v. *Board of Education* decision in 1954 and the Civil Rights Act of 1964, outlawing racial segregation in schools and communities, Blacks and Whites in the USA have remained largely segregated in many aspects of their daily lives. In a 2018 article in *The Atlantic*, Will Stancil provides compelling evidence that racially divided schools are a "major and intensifying problem" in the USA that might even be reaching crisis-level proportions. He writes:

---

[1] According to a 2018 Brookings Institute study, in which "middle class" is defined as "prime-age adults between the 20th and 60th percentiles of household income, measured by the household head in the CPS [Current Population Survey]" the percentage of Whites in the middle class dropped from 78% in 1980 to 55% in 2017, and is predicted to drop to 49% by 2042. The percentage of middle-class Blacks went from 11% in 1980 to 14% in 2017 and is only expected to increase to 15% by 2042. The greatest predicted increases are among Hispanics, who made up 6% of the middle class in 1980, 22% in 2017, and are predicted to comprise 26% of the middle class by 2042 (Reeves and Busette 2018). Source: www.brookings.edu/blog/social-mobility-memos/2018/02/27/the-middle-class-is-becoming-race-plural-just-like-the-rest-of-america/.

According to my analysis of data from the National Center on Education Statistics, the number of segregated schools (defined in this analysis as those schools where less than 40 percent of students are white) has approximately doubled between 1996 and 2016. In that same span, the percentage of children of color attending such a school rose from 59 to 66 percent. For black students, the percentage in segregated schools rose even faster, from 59 to 71 percent. (Stancil 2018)

While some have attributed these trends to the growing diversity of the US population, Stancil argues that these patterns reflect more intentional efforts to resegregate our public schools (e.g., through strategic school openings and closings, restructuring of school districts along racial lines, and the practice of "racial sorting" through the charter school system). Furthermore, there are economic implications to these patterns, as the poorest schools tend to be racially segregated, and the poorest students tend to be disproportionately non-White (Stancil 2018).[2]

Housing patterns have exhibited similarly persistent patterns of racial segregation. In 1968, the Fair Housing Act (Title VIII of the Civil Rights Act) was enacted to prevent housing discrimination and "dismantle the lingering legacy of Jim Crow laws" (Williams and Emamdjomeh 2018). And yet, according to a *Washington Post* analysis of census data collected since 1990, the country remains largely segregated by race, even as it has become more racially diverse (Williams and Emamdjomeh 2018). According to this study, the suburbs have experienced the greatest increases in racial and ethnic diversity, in large part because many of these communities were established following the implementation of the Fair Housing Act of 1968. However, in cities with large African American populations, like Chicago, the legacy of "deep segregation" remains largely intact. Citing the observations of American University sociology professor, Michael Bader, the authors explain,

Persistent and deep segregation is somewhat unique to African Americans, Bader said, for several reasons: the legacy of segregated neighborhoods created during the era of Reconstruction and Jim Crow; enduring racial preferences among whites who choose to live near other white people; and significant Latino and Asian immigration after fair housing laws were in place. (Williams and Emamdjomeh 2018)

And wealthier neighborhoods have not been immune to these trends. For example, Prince George's County, Maryland, which is home to some of the wealthiest Black neighborhoods in the country, was predominately White in the 1970s and 1980s. However, according to Bader, "[a]s the black middle class moved in, the white middle class stopped moving in" (Williams and Emamdjomeh 2018).

---

[2] For more on school (re)segregation patterns in the USA, see Hannah-Jones (2014).

In addition to the geographic barriers reflected in these patterns of Black-White interaction, there has been an observable spike in racial tensions in recent years that speaks to the ethological side of this issue. According to a 2017 Pew Research Center survey[3] of 1,503 adults, conducted between November 29 and December 4, 56% of participants said that race relations in the USA were "generally bad," 44% said that they were "getting worse" (a statistic that was up from 38% in 2016), and 65% said that conflicts between Blacks and Whites in the USA were "strong" or "very strong." Furthermore, these perceptions differed by race, as Blacks who felt that race relations were getting worse rose from 37% in May 2016 to 51% in December 2017, compared to Whites, who only displayed a two percentage point increase in the same time period, from 39% to 41%. In a 2017 Gallup poll[4] of 1,018 adults, conducted between March 1 and 5, a record high 42% of participants said that they "worried a great deal" about race relations in the USA.[5]

While some might presume that more affluent African Americans, given their material success in the mainstream economy, would be more optimistic about the state of US race relations compared to those lower on the socio-economic spectrum, a 1998 article published by the Brookings Institute found just the opposite to be true. Based on conventional measures of income, education, and occupation, Jennifer Hochschild estimated that, at the time that the article was written, roughly one-third of African Americans and one-half of whites were middle class.[6] She described this level of Black middle-class success as a "historically unprecedented" change from the early 1960s, "when blacks enjoyed the 'perverse equality' of almost uniform poverty in which even the best-off blacks could seldom pass on their status to their children" (Hochschild 1998). And yet, when asked about the state of race relations in the USA and opportunities for upward mobility, poor and working-class Blacks expressed far more optimism than did middle-class Blacks. Citing a 1995 *Washington Post* survey that asked whether discrimination was the major cause for the "economic and social ills blacks face," Hochschild noted that 84 percent of middle-class Blacks answered affirmatively, compared to just 66 percent of poor and working class-Blacks. Hochschild explained,

An observer from Mars might suppose that the black middle class would be highly gratified by its recent and dramatic rise in status and that persistently poor blacks would be frustrated and embittered by their unchanging or even worsening fate. But today's

---

[3] Source: www.people-press.org/2017/12/19/most-americans-say-trumps-election-has-led-to-worse-race-relations-in-the-u-s/.
[4] Source: https://news.gallup.com/poll/206057/americans-worry-race-relations-record-high.aspx.
[5] This rate represented a record high in Gallup's seventeen-year trend.
[6] Source: www.brookings.edu/articles/american-racial-and-ethnic-politics-in-the-21st-century-a-cautious-look-ahead/.

middle-class African Americans express a "rage," to quote one popular writer, that has, paradoxically, grown along with their material holdings. (Hochschild 1998)

If, as Hochschild claims, the African American middle class was reluctant to embrace the promises of the "American Dream" in 1998, at a time when economic opportunities appeared to be at an all-time high, what might their stance be today, with Affirmative Action and voting rights under attack, news feeds filled with stories of police brutality and the killing of unarmed Black people, patterns of de facto segregation holding steady, racial and political tensions rising, and growing concerns about the security of the American middle class? And what predictions might be made in such a context about the future of middle-class AAE?

To the extent that distinctive linguistic norms are built around physical, psychological, and emotional barriers, it seems likely that language *will* remain an important symbolic tool through which many middle-class African American speakers can continue to carve out distinctive racial and socio-economic identities for themselves. The "Black Lives Matter" (BLM) movement, which arose in protest to the systemic violence and racist practices that have been leveled against Black people in the USA, could play a pivotal role in directing this linguistic trajectory, as its approach to civil rights has marked a considerable departure from the "respectability politics" of earlier generations. In a 2015 *Washington Post* article, veteran civil rights activist, Barbara Reynolds, lamented the generational divide that seems to be forming between members of the BLM movement and more seasoned activists:

The baby boomers who drove the success of the civil rights movement want to get behind Black Lives Matter, but the group's confrontational and divisive tactics make it difficult. In the 1960s, activists confronted white mobs and police with dignity and decorum, sometimes dressing in church clothes and kneeling in prayer during protests to make a clear distinction between who was evil and who was good.

But at protests today, it is difficult to distinguish legitimate activists from the mob actors who burn and loot. The demonstrations are peppered with hate speech, profanity, and guys with sagging pants that show their underwear. Even if the BLM activists aren't the ones participating in the boorish language and dress, neither are they condemning it. (Reynolds 2015)

Her lament was countered by BLM supporter, Shannon M. Houston, in a Salon.com article that roundly rejected the "dignity and decorum" mandate of Reynolds' generation:

Respectability will not save us. And even if it could – even if we had proof that dressing up in our Sunday best and never using profanity and always wearing belts to keep our pants up and never throwing a rock at a police officer guaranteed us safety or equality – it would not be intelligent for us to accept or embrace the notion of respectability. (Houston 2015)

If the nonconformist views of the BLM generation are in any way indicative of linguistic trends, we might find that younger speakers will be less inclined to codeswitch in compliance with mainstream linguistic norms or to otherwise adhere to the linguistic expectations imposed on them by "respectability politics." Like the BLM movement itself, however, such linguistic distinctiveness is not likely to be guided solely by "rage," fear, or the rejection of mainstream norms (cf. Ransby 2015). Racial pride, social consciousness, and the celebration of Black language and culture will also likely continue to motivate many middle-class African American speakers to align themselves with the African American speech community. A key consideration in this regard may be the more inclusive approach taken by members of the BLM movement (Ransby 2015), which was founded by three Black women[7] in an effort to give voice and dignity to more marginalized and disenfranchised members of the Black community, including women, members of the LGBTQIA+ community, the poor, and the incarcerated. This approach also represents a departure from the Civil Rights movement of the 1960s, which was a decidedly male-dominated, hetero-normative, Christian movement (Houston 2015). Thus, to the extent that the BLM movement is able to maintain its momentum and extend its reach within the African American community, and the ideologies that it embraces find correlates in the linguistic trends of its generation, we are likely to witness a linguistic trajectory that encapsulates the intersectionality (Crenshaw 1989) and diversity of the Black lived experience.

Future Directions of Research on Middle-Class AAE

So how might we, as linguists, position ourselves to bear witness to this linguistic trajectory? And what are some of the more promising research opportunities that lie ahead for Middle-Class AAE? While far from exhaustive, the following areas seem ripe for exploration.

Standard African American English (SAAE)

As described in Chapter 1, references to the more standard end of the AAE continuum date back to some of the earliest research on the variety, though the labels to describe it, including Black Standard English (BSE), Standard Black English (SBE), African American Standard English (AASE),[8] and Standard

---

[7] Three professional organizers, Alicia Garza, Opal Tometi, and Patrisse Cullors, are credited for starting the #BlackLivesMatter movement in 2013 (https://blacklivesmatter.com/about/herstory/).
[8] As noted in Chapter 1 and elaborated on more fully later in this chapter, Spears 2015 makes a distinction between Standard African American English and African American Standard English, the latter of which he defines as an endangered variety, marked by the presence of Distinctively Black Grammatical Features (DBGFs).

African American English (SAAE), have varied over the years (see, e.g., Taylor 1975, 1983; Hoover 1978; Spears 1988, 1998, 2015; Mufwene 2001; Rahman 2008). Among those who have referenced it, there is a general agreement that the structure of SAAE consists primarily of racially or ethnically marked phonological, prosodic, lexical and rhetorical features (as well as DBGFs such as remote past BEEN), but with few to no overtly stigmatized grammatical features. Despite the general consensus regarding its structure, research on SAAE has remained woefully underexplored, in part because of the "strategic essentialism" (Bucholtz 2003) that has kept us laser focused on the vernacular, but also because of the "erasure" (Irvine 2001) of middle-class African Americans (i.e., arguably, the speakers for whom SAAE is most accessible), from our conceptualizations of the African American speech community. Additional research into standard varieties of AAE is, therefore, needed to correct the false dichotomy between AAE and SAE that has gone unchecked for so many decades. As observed by Spears (2015): "It is essential to draw attention to the existence of African American Standard English (AASE) since many linguists, other scholars, and laypersons typically make a distinction between African American English (AAE) and Standard American English (SAE), erroneously implying that all AAE is vernacular (i.e., nonstandard). Taylor (1983) made this point, and it still holds" (Spears 2015: 786).

SAAE serves an essential function for many middle-class African Americans who wish to carve out both class-based and race-based identities for themselves (cf. Lacy 2007), through the strategic manipulation of linguistic features that minimize stigma while maximizing perceptions of in-group affiliation and racial/ethnic marking. Drawing inspiration from Hoover's 1978 Language Levels Grid, presented in Chapter 1, Table 7.1 illustrates the ways in which SAAE seems to accomplish this task.

Performative contexts aside, nonstandard grammatical features, which are high in salience and stigma, tend to mark speakers as less educated or of a lower socioeconomic status. Thus, regardless of race, a key element in the construction of middle-class identities in the USA is the *avoidance* of nonstandard grammatical constructions (see, e.g., Wolfram and Schilling-Estes 1998). And given the high racial/ethnic marking associated with many nonstandard grammatical forms (e.g., copula absence, negative concord, subject-verb nonagreement, the use of *ain't*), the avoidance of nonstandard grammatical features is perhaps even more important for African American speakers trying to construct middle-class identities for themselves. Thus, in order to construct race-based identities that do not compete with their class-based identities, many middle-class African American speakers turn to racially/ethnically marked phonological and prosodic features, some of which may be perceived by mainstream listeners as carrying moderate levels of

Table 7.1 *The construction of class/race-based identities through SAAE*

Features	Salience	Stigma	Racial/Ethnic Marking	SAAE	Community Perceptions
Class-based identities					
Nonstandard Grammatical	High	High	High	–	Middle class
Race-based identities					
Nonstandard Phonological	Moderate	Moderate	High	+	"Sounding Black"
Prosodic	Moderate	Moderate	High	+	"Sounding Black"
Lexical	High	Low	High	+	"Talking Black"
Discourse/Rhetorical	High	Low	High	+	"Talking Black"
Camouflaged Features (cf. DBGFs)	Low	Low (*)	Moderate	+	"Talking Black" or N/A

Note: *Perceptions could vary across racial groups
+ = Features appear in SAAE
– = Features do not appear in SAAE

stigma, but which are balanced by their capacity to leverage community perceptions of "sounding Black." Similarly, the use of racially/ethnically marked lexical, rhetorical, and discourse features, which tend to be more salient to casual observers, contribute to community perceptions of "talking Black," but often incur lower levels of overt stigma and, in fact, often get perceived positively by mainstream listeners. Camouflaged features, as the label suggests, seem to carry less salience and stigma, because they get used below the level of conscious awareness, though little is known about how such features get perceived along the standardness continuum and whether such perceptions differ across racial lines. However, to the extent that the racial/ethnic distinctiveness of these features gets "noticed" by listeners (cf. Squires 2016), they may also contribute to perceptions of "talking Black."

As discussed earlier, camouflaged features are also a key component of what Spears (2015) calls African American Standard English (AASE), in other words "a variety of AAE (and also SAE) that has no grammatical features usually considered nonstandard and no stigmatized ones but, nevertheless, has DBGFs" (792), such as remote past *BEEN* and semi-auxiliary *come*. In Spears' view, it is the presence of these DBGFs that distinguishes AASE from SAAE. The former, Spears argues, emerged during the era of segregation, in all-black, multiclass neighborhoods, "in a zone where capital accumulation was systematically repressed by community-external forces," and language served as a proxy for social status (2015: 797). Today, Spears views AASE as an endangered dialect, spoken primarily by those aged 60 and above, and SAAE as a variety spoken by those under the age of 60, from "solidly middle-class backgrounds" (2015: 791). Such a distinction seems to presume that DBGFs are themselves in danger of extinction among middle-class speakers and that the socioeconomic and racial conditions that provided the "social locus" for the emergence of AASE have no correlate in contemporary society. However, as the evidence presented in Chapter 5 of this book and the sociopolitical context described at the start of this chapter suggest, more research on standard varieties of AAE is needed to determine the direction of these trajectories.

Sounding Black

Another promising area of research on Middle-Class AAE is the concept of "sounding Black." In a 2017 documentary on "Talking Black in America," Sonja Lanehart described the ways in which prosodic information informs our perceptions of racial identity and affiliation: "When I talk to people and I ask them about that, ask them about what Blackness is, what Black language is to them, what does sounding Black mean to them, more often than not, it's about a sound and a rhythm, this sort of movement and fluidity."

While the terms "sounding Black" and "talking Black" can be used to refer to different levels of language, as alluded to in Table 7.1, these terms are often used interchangeably within the African American speech community, with primary emphasis on a speaker's phonology and prosody. (See also Mufwene 2001.) Excerpt 7.1 from "Talking Black in America" illustrates the importance of "sounding Black" to the overall concept of "talking Black." In this exchange, Speaker 1 defends his accent (*Because I choose to pronounce my words, I'm not talking Black?*), while also asserting his membership in the African American community (*I'm totally Black. I'm Black.*).[9] Notable in this exchange is his repeated pronunciation of *talking* with an engma [ŋ] rather than an [n], his pronunciation of *defines* and *I'm* with a full diphthong [ay] rather than a monophthong [a:], and his pronunciation of *you're* with [r] constriction, rather than deletion or vocalization (see bolded text in

---

[9] In this exchange, Speaker 1's reference to "pronouncing his words" seems to invoke the label "articulate," which is often used in lay terms to describe speakers who use more formal, careful, or standard speech. Many take offense to the use of this label to describe African American speakers who use more standard varieties, as it reinforces the stereotype that the typical African American speaker is a nonstandard (or "nonarticulate") speaker. It was this phenomenon that was the inspiration for the title of Alim and Smitherman's 2012 book on President Barack Obama, *Articulate while Black*.

Excerpt 7.1 "Talking Black in America"[10]

SPEAKER 1:   What defines[ay] "talk**ing[iŋ]** Black"? That's my like, that's the real
             question to me. Because "talking Black," "talking Black" to me is an
             insult, when you say "you**'re[r]** talk**ing[iŋ]** Black" or "you**'re[r]**
             talk**ing[iŋ]** White." Because I choose to pronounce my words, I'm
             not talking Black? I'm totally Black. I'm Black.
SPEAKER 2:   Yeah.
SPEAKER 1:   So, every word that comes out of my mouth is me talk**ing[iŋ]**.
SPEAKER 2:   Yeah, but you don't–
SPEAKER 1:   So, **I'**m[ay] talk**ing[iŋ]** Black.
SPEAKER 2:   Yeah, but you don't– you're not talking Black 'cause you don't
             sound Black while you talking.

Excerpt 7.1). Because the variables (ing), (ay), and (r) function as shibboleths
in the African American speech community, signaling racial affinity and
community membership, his use of the more formal variants here serves to
reinforce Speaker 2's retort (*Yeah, but you don't– you're not talking Black
'cause you don't sound Black while you talking*).

Among middle-class speakers, the concept of sounding Black is a particularly important element in the construction of African American identity,
because it is at the level of phonology and prosody that speakers are often
able to align themselves with the African American speech community without
running the risk of being perceived as "uneducated" or "lower status." As
demonstrated in Chapter 6, listeners are able to use minimal acoustic cues to
identify the more nuanced distinctions indexed by various African American
voices in much the same way that they can identify a speaker's racial/ethnic
background (cf. Buck 1968; Abrams 1973; Lass et al. 1979; Baugh 1996;
Purnell et al. 1999; Foreman 2000; Wolfram 2001a; Thomas and Reaser
2004). While the study of AAE prosody dates back to as early as Tarone
(1973), it is only in recent years that we have been able to apply more
sophisticated instrumental analysis to the study of pitch, tone, intonation,
stress, and tempo, and the ways in which they inform what it means to "sound
Black" (see, e.g., Thomas and Carter 2006; Rahman 2008; Thomas 2015;
Holliday 2016). There is still much to be learned about the extent to which
listeners' "sociolinguistic monitors" (Labov et al. 2011) are attuned to the
variable frequencies of community shibboleths such as those described above.
For example, *How many formal variants must occur in a given stretch of
speech before a speaker gets perceived as "sounding White/Proper"? How*

---

[10] Source: https://languageandlife.org/documentaries/talking-black-in-america/.

many informal variants must occur in a given stretch of speech before a speaker gets perceived as "sounding Black"? There is also much to be learned about how various contextual cues (i.e., social, stylistic, linguistic) impact the perceptions of these variable frequencies and how much awareness and control speakers have over the production of such forms (cf. Babel 2016). Thus, it is here as well, that we find an area ripe for investigation in the study of middle-class AAE.

Media Representations

Another promising area of investigation is the representation of middle-class AAE in the media. Because media representations play an important role in shaping popular opinion about linguistic varieties and their communities of speakers, it is important for linguists to observe what messages are being presented to the public and the extent to which they both reflect and mold linguistic perceptions. As Fought (2006) explains, "[T]here are people in less diverse communities who may be getting their ideas about other ethnic groups (African-Americans and others) partly or primarily from media representations ... Therefore, it is important for us to know how accurate these representations are and what sorts of ideologies about language and ethnicity they are presenting" (67–68).

One strategy that has been observed in the study of media representations of AAE is what Fine and Anderson (1980) call "black, but not too black." In an analysis of the dialect usage in three popular television sitcoms from the 1970s and 1980s – *Good Times* (1974–79), *The Jeffersons* (1975–85), and *What's Happening* (1976–79)[11] – Fine and Anderson observed a "whitewashing" effect by which the characters used vernacular features shared by other varieties of English, but few that were unique to or even particularly characteristic of AAVE. "By rarely introducing the variants of BEV [Black English Vernacular], which almost exclusively are used by blacks, television presents BEV not as a dialect with linguistic integrity, but merely as the high density of otherwise widely occurring, and usually stigmatized forms" (Fine and Anderson 1980: 405).

At the other extreme are media portrayals reflecting a sort of minstrel-like performance, in which African American characters use language bearing little to no basis in reality. Green (2002) observed such usage in films like *Imitation of Life* (1934), *Bulworth* (1998), and *Bamboozled* (2000) and presented sentences 1–4, from the speech of the Aunt Delilah character in *Imitation of Life*, as illustrative of this phenomenon (Green 2002: 203).

[11] The years during which these shows aired were found at www.imdb.com.

1. Why, she am an angel, Miss Bea.
2. Is somebody died?
3. Is somebody been left you money?
4. What is this business of hisn?

In an analysis of the style-shifting strategies employed by four African American actors[12] starring in major Hollywood films, Harper (2006, 2008) observed the use of AAVE to index low socioeconomic status, low levels of education, and high levels of crime and aggression, thereby reinforcing a variety of circulating tropes about African Americans in popular culture. (See also Fought and Harper 2004; Lopez 2009, 2014; Bucholtz and Lopez 2011.) Such imagery has also permeated other types of media, including the negative stereotyping and mock representations of the vernacular that flooded the Internet in the wake of the 1996–97 Oakland Ebonics controversy (see, e.g., Ronkin and Karn 1999; Rickford and Rickford 2000) and the social media responses to Rachel Jeantel's witness testimony in the trial of George Zimmerman for the 2012 shooting of Trayvon Martin (see, e.g., Rickford and King 2016). Such representations have undoubtedly played a role in both reflecting and perpetuating some of the negative perceptions of African American (Vernacular) English that are held by the public-at-large.

In 1915, the release of *Birth of a Nation* spearheaded the production of a genre of films aimed at degrading the Black middle class that had emerged during the period of post–Civil War Reconstruction (Landry 1987). Images of the "lustful, unstable mulatto" extended the tradition of blackface minstrelsy[13] that had become so popular in the early 1800s (Robinson 2005). Since this time, negative depictions of African Americans have saturated popular media, while portrayals of successful, upwardly mobile African American characters have struggled to compete for airtime. Perhaps the most iconic modern-day representation of middle-class African American life remains *The Cosby Show*, a hugely successful television sitcom that ran from 1984 to 1992. As described in Kendall (2005), while earlier sitcoms like *Julia* and *Good Times* "relied on characters and interactions that were comfortable to white viewers," *The Cosby Show* altered this narrative with its portrait of an intact African American family that reflected middle-class morals and values. Despite its huge

---

[12] Based on a survey that asked college students to identify the top male and top female African American actors at the time and in consultation with Bogle's seminal (2001) text on the history of Blacks in American film, Harper selected for analysis four contemporary actors – Halle Berry, Whoopi Goldberg, Eddie Murphy, and Denzel Washington. Five films from each actor were subsequently chosen for review.

[13] The minstrel show was a nineteenth-century slapstick comedy tradition in US theater in which White (and later Black) actors applied burnt cork or other darkening agents to their skin to perform stereotypically negative portrayals of Blacks as lazy, subservient, and buffoonish (see, e.g., Toll 1974; Mahar 1999).

crossover appeal, however, *The Cosby Show* did little to alter popular perceptions of African American Vernacular English. While the show undoubtedly infused some African American linguistic and cultural practices into the American mainstream, vernacular feature usage was not portrayed as a central component of middle-class African American life.

However, the late 1990s/early 2000s saw the emergence of a group of films portraying predominately middle-class African American characters using a range of linguistic forms, which served as a powerful counternarrative to the kinds of portrayals described above, which had previously saturated the mainstream media. Table 7.2 is illustrative of some of the films in this group (cf. Harper 2006, 2008). To the extent that films such as these represented more "authentic" portrayals of African American language, a number of factors seemed to be at work. With the exception of *Waiting to Exhale* and *How Stella Got Her Groove Back*, which were co-written by European American screenwriter Ronald Bass, in collaboration with African American author Terry McMillan, on whose books the films were based, all of the films listed in Table 7.2 were written and directed by African Americans. And all of the films featured predominately African American casts. It is, therefore, likely that the filmic representations of AAE portrayed in these films reflected at least some familiarity with the rules and norms governing use of the language (whether consciously or not). (See also Wilkerson 2000; Harper 2008.) Secondly, because most of the films were low to moderately grossing productions, catering primarily to African American audiences, there was little incentive to engage in the kind of "whitewashing" often observed in higher-grossing productions aimed at more mainstream audiences. Thirdly, all of the films in Table 7.2 represented "blended genres" of comedy and drama or romance and drama. None fell squarely under the categories of straight comedy or straight drama, where one might be more likely to find exaggerated depictions of characters such as those observed in comedies such as *B*A*P*S* or dramas such as *Monster's Ball* (see Harper 2008). Thus, what emerged was a group of films depicting a more nuanced representation of African American language than many of the films that preceded it.

For example, in an analysis of the language depicted in *The Best Man*, a film that might be described as an iconic representation of this group of films, Green (2002) observed the nuance with which habitual *be* was used by Quentin and Lance – two of the male leading characters: "The use of aspectual *be* cannot be accidental; it is used by the two male characters who seem to be the more 'worldly' and thus who may be expected to have a broader language repertoire. But worldly here does not mean of 'the street'" (Green 2002: 210). Sentences 5–11 illustrate the use of habitual *be* by these two characters.

Table 7.2 *Contemporary African American films featuring middle-class characters*[a]

Film	Year	Screenwriter	Director	Rating	Genre	Gross
Waiting to Exhale	1995	Ronald Bass (EA) Terry McMillan (AA)	Forest Whitaker (AA)	R	Comedy/Drama	$67M
Love Jones	1997	Theodore Witcher (AA)	Theodore Witcher (AA)	R	Romance/Drama	$12M
Soul Food	1997	George Tillman, Jr. (AA)	George Tillman, Jr. (AA)	R	Comedy/Drama	$43M
How Stella Got Her Groove Back	1998	Ronald Bass (EA) Terry McMillan (AA)	Kevin Rodney Sullivan (AA)	R	Romance/Drama	$37M
The Best Man	1999	Malcolm D. Lee (AA)	Malcolm D. Lee (AA)	R	Comedy/Drama	$34M
The Wood	1999	Rick Famuyiwa (AA) Todd Boyd (AA)	Rick Famuyiwa (AA)	R	Comedy/Drama	$25M
Love and Basketball	2000	Gina Prince-Bythewood (AA)	Gina Prince-Bythewood (AA)	PG-13	Romance/Drama	$27M
The Brothers	2001	Gary Hardwick (AA)	Gary Hardwick (AA)	R	Comedy/Drama	$27M
Brown Sugar	2002	Michael Elliott (AA)	Rick Famuyiwa (AA)	PG-13	Romance/Drama	$27M
This Christmas	2007	Preston A. Whitmore II (AA)	Preston A. Whitmore II (AA)	PG-13	Comedy/Drama	$49M
Why Did I Get Married	2007	Tyler Perry (AA)	Tyler Perry (AA)	PG-13	Comedy/Drama	$55M

Notes: AA = African American; EA = European American.
[a] Sources: http://boxofficemojo.com/about/boxoffice.htm;
www.imdb.com/.

224

Quentin

5. Don't sweat none o' that shit, joe. Seriously, though. That book is like dat. I still think you might have exaggerated a brother's character a li'l' bit. I mean, my mama not bein' around ain't got shit to do wit' how I **be** treatin' these bitches.
6. That's what I **be** puttin' on my ladies when I do my thang.
7. Nigga, you **be** havin' these girlfriends. No, better yet, these jive-ass public relationships, talkin' about, "Oh, this is my queen" and shit.
8. You know how many single honeys **be** at weddin's? It's about to be a hoasis in that baby, honey.
9. You know you don't like the way she **be** carryin' you. None of us like it. It's time for you to just stand up an' you know, grow some balls an' be a man or somethin'.

Lance

10. They **be** makin' breakfast for this fool, buyin' him jewelry, and den dey try to figure out why they do dis shit 'cause dey really hate his yellow ass.
11. Yeah, you know how Harp **be** kissin' the babes on the forehead, man. Panties drop with the quicks.

As noted by Green (2002), the use of AAE, particularly among the male characters in *The Best Man*, spanned a continuum of usage, that was reflective of individual characters/personalities. For example, Quentin was characterized as a street-savvy, multifaceted playboy who had not yet committed to a single career path, in spite of the fact that his father, who owned a hotel, was trying to groom him for the hotel management business. His consistent use of AAE throughout the film seemed to reflect, in part, his rejection of this corporate world, in contrast to Harper, an aspiring novelist, whose complex and, at times, conflicting set of identities included, but was not limited to, an adherence to such norms. The tension between Quentin and Harper was exhibited throughout the movie by heated exchanges that often involved verbal dueling (cf. Chapter 3). In one such example, illustrated by Excerpt 7.2, Quentin used the vernacular to urge Harper to reveal his "authentic self."

Excerpt 7.2 Quentin and Harper (*The Best Man*)

HARPER: It's cool. It's cool. Is your pop still trying to groom you for the, uh, hotel management business?

QUENTIN: Yeah, for like the last twenty years. I ain't, no, I'm just not tryin' to hear none o' that stuff, you know? Dealin' with complainin'-ass guests, and unions, and payrolls, and all that.

(cont.)

HARPER:	Too much like a real job, huh?
QUENTIN:	You know, nigga, fuck you, a'ight? You're my judge, right? That's your job. You judge me.
HARPER:	I'm only playin', man.
QUENTIN:	No, nigga. You– it's just amazin' how you, you've always analyzed everybody else's shit and then you don't do the same thing for your ownself.
HARPER:	Will you chill?
QUENTIN:	No, 'cause you've done dirt too, motherfuckah. And you doin' more dirt. That's right. You fuckin' Jordan tonight. Remember? Jordan. See, you ain't no better than the rest of us, (got it)? Your shit just ain't caught you yet.

Quentin's fluency in the vernacular was also positioned in stark contrast to that of Murch, who used no vernacular features at all. Murch's use of "Proper" language (cf. Chapter 6) and lack of fluency in the vernacular was used to characterize him as the uncool, emasculated member of the group, as illustrated in Excerpt 7.3, where Quentin berated Murch for allowing his girlfriend, Shelby, to boss him around.

Excerpt 7.3 Quentin and Murch (*The Best Man*)

MURCH:	Hey, Quentin, uh, can I use your phone?
QUENTIN:	Who you callin'?
MURCH:	Shelby.
QUENTIN:	Oh, hell, no.
MURCH:	Excuse me?
QUENTIN:	I said no, man. You can't be lettin' her know your every move. That's– that's played.
MURCH:	Sometimes you are such an a-hole.
QUENTIN:	Yeah, well, she's a–
MURCH:	Hey! Don't you dare!
QUENTIN:	Oh, come on. You know you don't like the way she be carryin' you. None of us like it. It's time for you to just stand up, and you know, grow some balls and be a man or somethin'.

Quentin's use of the vernacular was not always used to challenge or threaten, however. In Excerpt 7.4, for example, Quentin used the vernacular to assuage Lance, a star professional football player, who was threatening to throw Harper over the balcony after suspecting that Harper had cheated with Lance's fiancée, Mia.

Excerpt 7.4 Quentin, Lance and Harper (*The Best Man*)

QUENTIN: Yo, L-baby.
HARPER: You– tell him.
LANCE: What you want, man?
HARPER: Please.
QUENTIN: You really gonna do this?
LANCE: Hell, yeah, I'm gonna do this shit.
QUENTIN: No, you ain't. You gonna marry you a beautiful woman tomorrow.
           A girl that loves you and that's only loved you.
HARPER: Oh, my God!
QUENTIN: You ain't throwin' all that away.
HARPER: Listen, you know he's right. Listen, listen to Q, Lance.
LANCE: Shut the fuck up!
HARPER: OK, OK, OK. It's best to drop it.
QUENTIN: Listen to me. Now we know that Harper's a bitch-ass. But this cat is
           your man a hundred grand. He wouldn't do that to you, man. Karma
           don't come back that strong, L-baby.

As noted above, Lance was a professional football player, who graduated Summa Cum Laude from college. He had swarms of female admirers but was putting his womanizing past behind him as he prepared to wed his college sweetheart. He was also a devout Christian with conservative ideas about women and relationships. Unlike Quentin who used the vernacular regularly and Murch who never used it, Lance's complex identity in the film was indexed through the use of topical codeswitching, as illustrated by the contrasting tone of sentences 12 and 13.

      Lance

12. No, I do understand. Let me tell you somethin', man, I am not afraid. You see, I made God a promise, right, that if He ever gave me another chance with Mia, I would do right by her. She has forgiven me for all my indiscretions, man. That's amazing. So, if she ever slept with somebody else . . .

13. Oh, hell, yeah. I'm tellin' you– once he does Oprah, man, it's gon be on. Harp ain't gon never have to work for the quality ass again. Panties gon drop without coercion, cuddlin', caressin', or, uh, ha ha ha . . .

While the proliferation of films such as these has tapered off in recent years, there are still many opportunities to explore such representations in contemporary media. In 2013, *The Best Man Holiday*, the sequel to *The Best Man*, grossed a commendable $71 million worldwide, an indication of the continuing interest in these types of films among African American audiences.[14] In 2018, two films,

---

[14] Source: https://en.wikipedia.org/wiki/The_Best_Man_Holiday.

Sorry to Bother You and *Black KKKlansman*, probed the concept of "the White voice" as a symbol of African American double consciousness. Television networks catering to predominately African American audiences, such as Oprah Winfrey's OWN network, have also found success with dramas such as *Greenleaf* and *The Haves and the Have Nots*, which feature predominately middle-class African American casts. And sitcoms such as *Black-ish* and *Empire* have enjoyed considerable success with some crossover appeal. Even reality television shows such as *The Real Housewives of Atlanta* and *Married to Medicine*, though complicit in perpetuating a certain stereotypical image of African American women, have brought the language of upwardly mobile, career-oriented, college-educated African American speakers into the homes of mainstream America.

Community-Based Studies

Finally, as we broaden our definitions of the African American speech community to include middle-class speakers, it will be important to return to community-based studies, such as those conducted in Michigan (Wolfram 1969; Nguyen 2006; Jones and Preston 2011), where we can observe the perspectives and experiences of everyday speakers and the use of AAE in its local and regional contexts. Beyond the studies conducted in Michigan, there remains a need for more research in African American communities throughout the country, comparing the stratification of linguistic variables across social classes. We need to hear the perspectives of middle-class parents and teachers of middle-class students on African American English and its role in schools and communities (cf. Hoover 1975, 1978). And we need to hear more from African American professionals about the role that African American English plays in various aspects of their daily lives (cf. Grieser 2014). As the country becomes more racially diverse and the middle class struggles to maintain an economic foothold, it will be important to consider the impact of these changing dynamics from a community perspective – rural versus urban versus suburban, racially integrated versus racially segregated, etc. And it will be important to consider the generational changes that are taking place both socially and politically, as they find parallels in linguistic variation and change.

As I reflect on my own experience growing up in a racially segregated neighborhood where AAE was the norm and codeswitching was the expectation, and I compare it to that of my children, who are growing up in a racially integrated neighborhood quite different from my own upbringing, I wonder (and sometimes worry) about what their linguistic trajectories will be.[15] I find

---

[15] This struggle is one that likely resonates with many middle-class African American parents, and perhaps especially those raising children in suburban American neighborhoods. Those familiar with the documentary "American Tongues" (Kolker et al. 1987) will recall the segment in which an African American father admits to being questioned by relatives about the way his sons talk, an observation about which he feigns ignorance in the moment, but in a tone that betrays concern not only about his sons not "sounding black" enough to be accepted by the community, but about his own language.

myself making intentional efforts to model AAE in the home and to surround them with African American peers and role models that challenge the negative stereotypes about African American language and identity that too often surround them. The choices that my husband and I have to make are not always easy, as the invisible barriers of race and class often require us to choose between "White spaces" (e.g., schools, programs, activities) that are celebrated and sought after, but where my children are often singled out as the only African American or one of only a few, or immersing them in "Black spaces" that are too often cast aside and disparaged, but where they can be surrounded by African American peers and role models who can help socialize them into African American cultural practices and ways of speaking. Their path to AAE will not be the same as mine. And their use of the language will differ as well. But as they learn to navigate the rocky linguistic terrain ahead of them, it is my hope that they will come to appreciate the value of AAE as a marker of racial solidarity and pride. As a mother, I hope that they and others of their generation will come to define their voices in ways that allow them to embrace their racial and cultural identities and not feel compelled to mask them. And as a linguist, I hope that we will correct the erasures of the past by giving visibility and credence to their experiences and to the contributions of middle-class speakers to the strength and vitality of the African American speech community.

References

Abrams, Albert S. (1973). "Minimal auditory cues for distinguishing Black from White talkers," PhD Dissertation, City University of New York.

Adams, Tony E., Stacy Holman Jones, and Carolyn Ellis. (2014). *Autoethnography: Understanding Qualitative Research*, Oxford and Malden, MA: Oxford University Press.

Adichie, Chimamanda Ngozi. (2013). *Americanah*, New York and Toronto: Alfred A. Knopf.

Alim, Samy. (2004). *You Know My Steez: An Ethnographic and Sociolinguistic Study of Styleshifting in a Black American Speech Community* (Publication of the American Dialect Society 89), Durham, NC: Duke University Press.

Alim, Samy and Geneva Smitherman. (2012). *Articulate while Black: Barack Obama, Language, and Race in the U.S.*, Oxford and New York: Oxford University Press.

Alleyne, Mervyn C. (1971). Acculturation and the cultural matrix of creolization. In Dell Hymes, ed., *Pidginization and Creolization of Languages*, Cambridge: Cambridge University Press, 169–86.

   (1980). *Comparative Afro-American: An Historical-Comparative Study of English-Based Afro-American Dialects of the New World*, Ann Arbor, MI: Karoma.

Anderson, Bridget. L. (2002). Dialect leveling and /ai/ monophthongization among African American Detroiters. *Journal of Sociolinguistics*, 6(1), 86–98.

   (2003). "An acoustic study of southeastern Michigan Appalachian and African American southern migrant vowel systems," PhD Dissertation, University of Michigan.

Ash, Sharon. (2004). Social class. In J. K. Chambers, Peter Trudgill, and Natalie Schilling-Estes, eds., *The Handbook of Language Variation and Change*, Malden, MA: Blackwell, 402–22.

Audacity 1.3.13-beta (Unicode) Digital Audio Editor. Developed by Richard Ash, Michael Chinen, James Crook, and Roger Dannenberg.

Babel, Anna. (2016). *Awareness and Control in Sociolinguistic Research*, Cambridge: Cambridge University Press.

Bailey, Beryl L. (1965). Toward a new perspective in Negro English dialectology. *American Speech*, 40(3), 171–77.

Bailey, Guy and Erik Thomas. (1998). Some aspects of African American vernacular English phonology. In Salikoko Mufwene, John R. Rickford, Guy Bailey, and John Baugh, eds., *African American English: Structure, History, and Use*, London and New York: Routledge, 85–109.

Bailey, Guy and Natalie Maynor. (1987). Decreolization?. *Language in Society*, 16(4), 449–73.

Bailey, Guy, Natalie Maynor, and Patricia Cukor-Avila, eds. (1991). *The Emergence of Black English: Texts and Commentary*, Amsterdam: Benjamins.

Baldwin, James. (1979). If Black English isn't a language, then tell me, what is? *The New York Times*, July 29, 1979. https://archive.nytimes.com/www.nytimes.com/books/98/03/29/specials/baldwin-english.html?mcubz=3

Baugh, John. (1980). A reexamination of the Black English copula. In William Labov, ed., *Locating Language in Time and Space*, New York: Academic Press, 83–106.

(1983). *Black Street Speech: Its History, Structure, and Survival*, Austin: University of Texas Press.

(1984). Steady: Progressive aspect in Black Vernacular English. *American Speech*, 59(1), 3–12.

(1996). Perceptions within a variable paradigm: Black and White racial detection and identification based on speech. In Edgar W. Schneider, ed., *Focus on the USA*, Amsterdam: Benjamins, 169–82.

(2000a). *Beyond Ebonics: Linguistic Pride and Racial Prejudice*, Oxford and New York: Oxford University Press.

(2000b). Racial identification by speech. *American Speech*, 75(4), 362–64.

(2003). Linguistic profiling. In Sinfree Makoni, Geneva Smitherman, Arnetha F. Ball, and Arthur K. Spears, eds., *Black Linguistics: Language, Society, and Politics in Africa and the Americas*, New York: Routledge, 155–63.

Bell, Allan. (1984). Language style as audience design. *Language in Society*, 13(2), 145–204.

Bennett, John. (1908). Gullah: A Negro patois. *South Atlantic Quarterly*, 7, 332–47.

Benor, Sarah Bunim. (2010). Ethnolinguistic repertoire: Shifting the analytic focus in language and ethnicity. *Journal of Sociolinguistics*, 14(2), 159–83.

Berdan, Robert. (1977). Polylectal comprehension and the polylectal grammar. In Ralph Fasold and Roger Shuy, eds., *Studies in Language Variation: Semantics, Syntax, Phonology, Pragmatics, Social Situations, Ethnographic Approaches*, Washington, DC: Georgetown University Press, 12–29.

Bereiter, Carl and Siegfried Englemann. (1966). *Teaching Disadvantaged Children in the Pre-School*, Englewood Cliffs, NJ: Prentice-Hall.

Bernstein, Cynthia. (1993). Measuring social causes of phonological variables in Texas. *American Speech*, 68(3), 227–40.

(2006). Drawing out the /ai/: Dialect boundaries and /ai/ variation. In Thomas E. Murray and Beth Lee Simon, eds., *Language Variation and Change in the American Midland: A New Look at "Heartland" English*, Philadelphia, PA: Benjamins, 209–32.

Bickerton, Derek. (1981). *Roots of Language*, Ann Arbor, MI: Karoma.

Blackshire-Belay, Carole. (1996). The location of Ebonics within the framework of the Africological Paradigm. *Journal of Black Studies*, 27, 5–23.

Blake, Renee. (1997). Defining the envelope of linguistic variation: The case of "don't count" forms in the copula analysis of African American Vernacular English. *Language Variation and Change*, 9(1), 57–79.

Blake, Renee and Isabelle Buchstaller, eds. (2019). *The Routledge Companion to the Work of John R. Rickford*, New York: Routledge.

Blom, Jan-Petter and John J. Gumperz. (1972). Social meaning in linguistic structures: Code-switching in Norway. In John J. Gumperz and Dell Hymes, eds., *Directions in Sociolinguistics: The Ethnography of Communication*, Oxford: Basil Blackwell, 407–34.

Bogle, Donald. (2001). *Toms, Coons, Mulattoes, Mammies, and Bucks: An Interpretive History of Blacks in American Films*, New York: Continuum.

Bourdieu, Pierre. (1986). The forms of capital. In John Richardson, ed., *Handbook of Theory and Research for the Sociology of Education*, New York: Greenwood, 241–58.

    (1991). *Language and Symbolic Power*, Cambridge: Polity Press.

Bowser, Benjamin P. (2007). *The Black Middle Class: Social Mobility and Vulnerability*, Boulder, CO: Lynne Rienner.

Britt, Erica. (2011a). "Can the church say amen": Strategic uses of African American preaching style at the State of the Black Union. *Language in Society*, 40(2), 211–33.

    (2011b). "Talking Black in public spaces: An investigation of the identity and the use of preaching style in Black public speech," PhD Dissertation, University of Illinois at Urbana-Champaign.

Britt, Erica and Tracey Weldon. (2015). African American English in the middle class. In Sonja Lanehart, ed., *The Oxford Handbook of African American Language*, Oxford and New York: Oxford University Press, 800–16.

Brown, Claude. (1968). The language of soul. *Esquire*, April 1968, 88, 160–61.

Bucholtz, Mary. (2003). Sociolinguistic nostalgia and the authentication of identity. *Journal of Sociolinguistics*, 7(3), 398–416.

Bucholtz, Mary and Quiana Lopez. (2011). Performing blackness, forming whiteness: Linguistic minstrelsy in Hollywood film. *Journal of Sociolinguistics*, 15(5), 680–706.

Buck, Joyce. (1968). The effects of Negro and White dialectal variations upon attitudes of college students. *Speech Monographs*, 35(2), 181–86.

Butters, Ronald. (1989). *The Death of Black English: Divergence and Convergence in Black and White Vernaculars*, Frankfurt am Main: Peter Lang.

Canagarajah, A. Suresh. (2006). The place of world Englishes in composition: Pluralization continued. *College Composition and Communication*, 57(4), 586–619.

Choi, Julie. (2016). *Creating a Multivocal Self: Autoethnography as Method*, New York: Routledge.

Clifton, James. (1981). The rice driver: His role in slave management. *South Carolina Historical Magazine*, 82(4), 331–53.

Coates, Ta-Nehisi. (2004). Ebonics! Weird names! $500 shoes! Shrill Bill Cosby and the speech that shocked black America. *Village Voice*, May 26–June 1, 2004.

Collins, Chris, Simanique Moody, and Paul Postal. (2008). An AAE camouflage construction. *Language*, 84(1), 29–68.

Cosby, Bill. (2004). Dr. Bill Cosby speaks: 50th anniversary commemoration of the *Brown* vs. *Topeka Board of Education* Supreme Court Decision. *The Black Scholar*, 34(4), 2–5. DOI: https://doi.org/10.1080/00064246.2004.11413278

Coupland, Nikolas. (1980). Style-shifting in a Cardiff work-setting. *Language in Society*, 9(1), 1–12.

Craig, Holly K. and Julie A. Washington. (2006). *Malik Goes to School: Examining the Language Skills of African American Students from Preschool–5th Grade*. Mahwah, NJ: Lawrence Erlbaum Associates, Inc.

Crenshaw, Kimberle. (1989). Demarginalizing the intersection of race and sex: A Black feminist critique of antidiscrimination doctrine, feminist theory and antiracist politics. *University of Chicago Legal Forum*, 1(8), 139–67.

Crum, Mason. (1940). *Gullah: Negro Life in the Carolina Sea Islands*, Durham, NC: Duke University Press.

Cutler, Cecilia A. (1999). Yorkville Crossing: White teens, hip hop and African American English. *Journal of Sociolinguistics*, 3(4), 428–42.

D'Eloia, Sarah. (1973). Issues in the analysis of nonstandard Negro English: A review of J.L. Dillard's *Black English: Its History and Usage in the United States*. *Journal of English Linguistics*, 7(1), 87–106.

Dalby, David. (1971). Communication in Africa and the New World. In Walt Wolfram and Nona H. Clark, eds., *Black-White Speech Relations*, Arlington, VA: Center for Applied Linguistics, 99–138.

Daniels, John. (1914). *In Freedom's Birthplace: A Study of the Boston Negroes*, New York: Houghton Mifflin.

Dayton, Elizabeth. (1996). "Grammatical categories of the verb in African-American Vernacular English," PhD Dissertation, University of Pennsylvania.

Debose, Charles. (1992). Codeswitching: Black English and Standard English in the African-American linguistic repertoire. *Journal of Multilingual and Multicultural Development*, 13(1), 157–67.

Debose, Charles and Nicholas Faraclas. (1993). An Africanist approach to the linguistic study of Black English: Getting to the roots of the tense-modality-aspect and copula systems in Afro-American. In Salikoko Mufwene and Nancy Condon, eds., *Africanisms in Afro-American Language Varieties*. Athens: University of Georgia Press, 364–87.

Denning, Keith. (1989). Convergence with divergence: A sound change in Vernacular Black English. *Language Variation and Change*, 1(2), 145–67.

Dillard, Joe L. (1972). *Black English: Its History and Usage in the United States*, New York: Random House.

Dodsworth, Robin. (2009). Modeling socioeconomic class in variationist sociolinguistics. *Language and Linguistics Compass*, 3(5), 1314–27.

Doss, Richard C. and Alan M. Gross. (1994). The effects of Black English and code-switching on intraracial perceptions. *Journal of Black Psychology*, 20(3), 282–93.

Drake, St. Clair and Horace R. Cayton. (1945). *Black Metropolis*, New York: Harcourt, Brace and Company.

Du Bois, W. E. B. (1903). *The Souls of Black Folk*, New York: Bantam Classic.

(1967). *The Philadelphia Negro*, New York: Schocken Books.

Dunn, Ernest F. (1976). The Black-Southern white dialect controversy: Who did what to whom?. In Deborah S. Harrison and Tom Trabasso, eds., *Black English: A Seminar*, Hillsdale, NJ: Erlbaum, 105–22.

Dyson, Michael Eric. (2005). *Is Bill Cosby Right? Or Has the Black Middle Class Lost Its Mind?*, New York: Basic Civitas Books.

Eckert, Penelope. (1989). *Jocks and Burnouts: Social Identity in the High School*, New York: Teachers College Press.

(2001). Style and social meaning. In Penelope Eckert and John R. Rickford, eds., *Style and Sociolinguistic Variation*, Cambridge: Cambridge University Press, 119–26.

(2008). Variation and the indexical field. *Journal of Sociolinguistics*, 12(4), 453–76.

(2001). Style and social meaning. In Penelope Eckert and John R. Rickford, eds., *Style and Sociolinguistic Variation*, Cambridge: Cambridge University Press, 119–26.

(2012). Three waves of variation study: The emergence of meaning in the study of variation. *Annual Review of Anthropology*, 41(1), 87–100.

Eckert, Penelope and John R. Rickford. (2001). *Style and Sociolinguistic Variation*, Cambridge: Cambridge University Press.

Edwards, Walter. (1992). Sociolinguistic behavior in a Detroit inner-city black neighborhood. *Language in Society*, 21(1), 93–115.

Ervin-Tripp, Susan. (2001). Variety, style-shifting, and ideology. In Penelope Eckert and John R. Rickford, eds., *Style and Sociolinguistic Variation*, Cambridge: Cambridge University Press, 44–56.

Fasold, Ralph. (1976). One hundred years from syntax to phonology. In Sanford Steever, Carol Walker, and Salikoko Mufwene, eds., *Papers from the Parasession on Diachronic Syntax*, Chicago, IL: Chicago Linguistic Society, 79–87.

(1981). The relationship between Black and White speech in the South. *American Speech*, 56(3), 163–89.

Fasold, Ralph and Walt Wolfram. (1970). Some linguistic features of Negro dialect. In Ralph Fasold and Roger Shuy, eds., *Teaching Standard English in the Inner City*, Washington, DC: Center for Applied Linguistics, 41–86.

Fasold, Ralph W., William Labov, Fay Boy Vaughn-Cooke, Guy Bailey, Walt Wolfram, Arthur K. Spears, and John R. Rickford. (1987). Are black and white vernaculars diverging? Papers from the NWAVE-XVI panel discussion. *American Speech*, 62(1), 3–80.

Feagin, Crawford. (1979). *Variation and Change in Alabama English: A Sociolinguistic Study of the White Community*, Washington, DC: Georgetown University Press.

Fine, Marlene G. and Carolyn Anderson. (1980). Dialectal features of black characters in situation comedies on television. *Phylon*, 41(4), 396–409.

Fix, Sonya. (2011). "Dark-skinned White girls: Linguistic and ideological variation among White women with African American ties in the urban Midwest," PhD Dissertation, New York University.

Fordham, Signithia and John U. Ogbu. (1986). Black students' school success: Coping with the "burden of 'Acting White'." *The Urban Review*, 18(3), 176–206.

Foreman, Christina. (2000). Identification of African American English from prosodic cues. *Texas Linguistic Forum*, 43, 57–66.

Fought, Carmen. (2006). *Language and Ethnicity*, Cambridge: Cambridge University Press.

Fought, Carmen and Lea Harper. (2004). "African Americans and language in the media: An overview." *Paper Presented at New Ways of Analyzing Variation (NWAV) 33 conference*, Ann Arbor, MI.

Frazier, E. Franklin. (1957). *African American Bourgeoisie: The Rise of the New Middle Class in the United States*, London: Collier Books.

Garner, Thurmon and Donald L. Rubin. (1986). Middle class African Americans' perceptions of dialect and style shifting: The case of Southern attorneys. *Journal of Language and Social Psychology*, 5(1), 33–48.

Giles, Howard, ed. (1984). *The Dynamics of Speech Accommodation*, Amsterdam: Mouton.

Giles, Howard, Justine Coupland, and Nikolas Coupland. (1991). *Contexts of Accommodation: Developments in Applied Sociolinguistics*, Cambridge: Cambridge University Press.

Gilyard, Keith. (1991). *Voices of the Self: A Study of Language Competence*, Detroit, MI: Wayne State University Press.

Gonzales, Ambrose. (1922). *The Black Border: Gullah Stories of the Carolina Coast*, Columbia, SC: The State Company.

Goodman, Leo A. (1961). Snowball sampling. *Annals of Mathematical Statistics*, 32(1), 148–70.

Gordon, Matthew J. (2000). Phonological correlates of ethnic identity: Evidence of divergence?. *American Speech*, 75(2), 115–36.

Graham, Lawrence Otis. (1999). *Our Kind of People: Inside America's Black Upper Class*, New York: Harper Collins.

Green, Lisa. (2002). *African American English: A Linguistic Introduction*, Cambridge and New York: Cambridge University Press.

Greene, Rebecca. (2010). "Language, ideology, and identity in rural Eastern Kentucky," PhD Dissertation, Stanford University.

Grieser, Jessica. (2014). "The language of professional blackness: African American English at the intersection of race, place, and class in Southeast, Washington, D.C.," PhD Dissertation, Georgetown University.

Gumperz, John J. (1964). Linguistic and social interaction in two communities. *American Anthropologist*, 66(6), 137–54.

Hannah, Dawn. (1997). Copula absence in Samaná English: Implications for research on the linguistic history of African-American Vernacular English. *American Speech*, 72(4), 339–72.

Hannah-Jones, Nikole. (2014). School segregation, the continuing tragedy of Ferguson. *ProPublica*, December 18, 2014. www.propublica.org/article/ferguson-school-segregation

Harper, Lea. (2006). "The representation of African American Vernacular English in the media," MA Thesis, University of California, Santa Barbara.
   (2008). Style shifting by African American actors in Hollywood films. Unpublished manuscript. University of California, Santa Barbara.

Hay, Jennifer, Stefanie Jannedy, and Norma Mendoza-Denton. (1999). Oprah and /ay/: Lexical frequency, referee design and style. In *Proceedings of the 14th International Congress of Phonetic Sciences*, San Francisco, CA, CD-ROM.

Hazen, Kirk and Ellen Fluharty. (2004). Defining Appalachian English. In Margaret Bender, ed., *Linguistic Diversity in the South: Changing Codes, Practices, and Ideology*, Athens: University of Georgia Press, 50–65.

Herskovits, Melville J. ([1941] 1970). *The Myth of the Negro Past*, Gloucester, MA: Peter Smith.

Higginbotham, Evelyn Brooks. (1993). *Righteous Discontent: The Women's Movement in the Black Baptist Church 1880–1920*, Cambridge, MA and London: Harvard University Press.

Hochschild, Jennifer. (1998). American racial and ethnic politics in the 21st century: A cautious look ahead. *The Brookings Institute*, 16(2), 43–46. DOI: https://doi.org/10.1080/00064246.2004.11413278

Holliday, Nicole R. (2016). "Intonational variation, linguistic style and the Black/biracial experience," PhD Dissertation, New York University.

Holm, John. ([1976] 1984). Variability of the copula in Black English and its Creole kin. *American Speech*, 59(4), 291–309.

Hoover, Mary Rhodes. (1975). "Appropriate use of Black English by Black children as rated by their parents," PhD Dissertation, Stanford University.

   (1978). Community attitudes toward Black English. *Language in Society*, 7(1), 65–87.

Houston, Shannon. M. (2015). Respectability will not save us: Black Lives Matter is right to reject the "dignity and decorum" mandate handed down to us from slavery. *Salon.com*, August 25, 2015. www.salon.com/2015/08/25/respectability_will_not_save_us_black_lives_matter_is_right_to_reject_the_dignity_and_decorum_mandate_handed_down_to_us_from_slavery/

Hunter, Margaret. (2007). The persistent problem of colorism: Skin tone, status, and inequality. *Sociology Compass*, 2(1), 237–54. DOI: https://doi.org/10.1111/j.1751-9020.2007.00078.x

Hymes, Dell. (1967). Models of the interaction of language and social setting. *Journal of Social Issues*, 23(2), 8–28.

Irons, Terry. (2007). On the southern shift in Appalachia. *University of Pennsylvania Working Papers in Linguistics*, 13(2), 121–34.

Irvine, Judith T. (2001). "Style" as distinctiveness: The culture and ideology of linguistic differentiation. In Penelope Eckert and John Rickford, eds., *Style and Sociolinguistic Variation*, Cambridge and New York: Cambridge University Press.

Jacobs-Huey, Lanita. (2006). *From the Kitchen to the Parlor: Language and Becoming in African American Women's Hair Care*, New York: Oxford University Press.

Jensen, Arthur. (1969). How much can we boost IQ?. *Harvard Educational Review*, 39(1), 1–123.

Johnstone, Barbara. (1996). *The Linguistic Individual: Self-Expression in Language and Linguistics*, New York and Oxford: Oxford University Press.

Jones, Jamila and Dennis R. Preston. (2011). AAE & identity: Constructing & deploying linguistic resources. In David Dwyer, ed., *The Joy of Language: Proceedings of a Symposium Honoring the Colleagues of David Dwyer on the Occasion of his Retirement*. www.msu.edu/%7Edwyer/JOLIndex.htm

Kautzsch, Alexander and Edgar W. Schneider. (2000). Differential creolization: Some evidence from Earlier African American Vernacular English in South Carolina. In Ingrid Neumann-Holzschuh and Edgar W. Schneider, eds., *Degrees of Restructuring in Creole Languages*, Amsterdam: Benjamins, 247–74.

Kearse, Randy. (2006). *Street Talk: Da Official Guide to Hip-Hop and Urban Slanguage*. Fort Lee, NJ: Barricade Books.

Kendall, Diana. (2005). *Framing Class: Media Representations of Wealth and Poverty in America*, Oxford: Rowman & Littlefield.

Kendall, Tyler and Walt Wolfram. (2009). Local and external language standards in African American English. *Journal of English Linguistics*, 37(4), 5–30.

Knowles-Borishade, Adetokunbo F. (1991). Paradigm for classical African orature: Instrument for scientific revolution?. *The Journal of Black Studies*, 21(4), 488–500.

Koch, Lisa, Alan Gross, and Russell Kolts. (2001). Attitudes toward African American English code switching. *Journal of African American Psychology*, 27(1), 29–42.

Kochhar, Rakesh and Richard Fry. (2014). "Wealth inequality has widened along racial, ethnic lines since end of Great Recession," *Pew Research Center*, December 12, 2014. www.pewresearch.org/fact-tank/2014/12/12/racial-wealth-gaps-great-recession/

Kochman, Thomas. (1981). *Black and White Styles in Conflict*, Chicago, IL: University of Chicago Press.

Kohn, Mary. (2015). (De)Segregation: The impact of de-facto and de-jure segregation on African American English in the New South. *LAVIS IV: Language Variation in the South*, Raleigh, NC. April.

Kolker, Andrew, Louis Alvarez, Trey Wilson, Susan Milano, and Lora Myers. (1987). "American Tongues." New York: Center for New American Media. CNAM Film Library.

Krapp, George Philip. (1924). The English of the Negro. *American Mercury*, 2, 190–95.

Krause, Eleanor and Isabel V. Sawhill. (2018). Seven reasons to worry about the American Middle Class. *Brookings Institute: Social Mobility Memos*, June 5, 2018. www.brookings.edu/blog/social-mobility-memos/2018/06/05/seven-reasons-to-worry-about-the-american-middle-class/.

Kurath, Hans. (1928). The origin of dialectal differences in spoken American English. *Modern Philology*, 25(4), 285–95.

(1949). *A Word Geography of the Eastern United States*, Ann Arbor: University of Michigan Press.

Kurath, Hans and Raven McDavid, Jr. (1961). *The Pronunciation of English in the Atlantic States*, Ann Arbor: University of Michigan Press.

Labov, William. (1966). *The Social Stratification of English in New York City*, Washington, DC: Center for Applied Linguistics.

(1969). Contraction, deletion, and inherent variability of the English copula. *Language*, 45(4), 715–62.

(1972a). *Language in the Inner City: Studies in the Black English Vernacular*, Philadelphia: The University of Pennsylvania Press.

(1972b). Some principles of linguistic methodology. *Language in Society*, 1(1), 97–120.

(1972c). *Sociolinguistic Patterns*, Philadelphia: University of Pennsylvania Press.

(1982). Objectivity and commitment in linguistic science: The case of the Black English trial in Ann Arbor. *Language in Society*, 11(2), 165–201.

(1998). Coexistent systems in African-American Vernacular English. In Salikoko Mufwene, John R. Rickford, Guy Bailey, and John Baugh, eds., *African American English: Structure, History, and Use*, London and New York: Routledge, 110–53.

(2010). Unendangered dialect, endangered people: The case of African American Vernacular English. *Transforming Anthropology*, 18(1), 15–27.

Labov, William, Malcah Yaeger, and Richard Steiner. (1972). *A Quantitative Study of Sound Change in Progress*, Philadelphia, PA: US Regional Survey.

Labov, William, Paul Cohen, and Clarence Robbins. (1965). *A Preliminary Study of the Structure of English Used by Negro and Puerto Rican Speakers in New York City.* Co-operative Research Project No. 3091. Washington, DC: Educational Resources Information Center.

Labov, William, Paul Cohen, Clarence Robbins, and John Lewis. (1968). *A Study of the Non-standard English of Negro and Puerto-Rican Speakers in New York City.* Final Report, Cooperative Research Project 3228. Vols. I and II. Philadelphia, PA: US Regional Survey.

Labov, William, Sharon Ash, and Charles Boberg. (2006). *The Atlas of North American English: Phonetics, Phonology and Sound Change – A Multimedia Reference Tool,* Berlin and New York: Mouton de Gruyter.

Labov, William, Sharon Ash, Maya Ravindranath, Tracey Weldon, Maciej Baranowski, and Naomi Nagy. (2011). Properties of the sociolinguistic monitor. *Journal of Sociolinguistics,* 15(4), 431–63.

Labov, William and Wendell A. Harris. (1986). De facto segregation of Black and White vernaculars. In David Sankoff, ed., *Diversity and Diachrony,* Amsterdam: Benjamins, 1–24.

Lacy, Karyn R. (2007). *Blue-Chip Black: Race, Class, and Status in the New Black Middle Class,* Berkeley and Los Angeles: University of California Press.

Lambert, Wallace E., Richard C. Hodgson, Robert C. Gardner, and Stanley Fillenbaum. (1960). Evaluational reactions to spoken languages. *Journal of Abnormal and Social Psychology,* 60(1), 44–51.

Landry, Bart. (1987). *The New Black Middle Class,* Los Angeles: University of California Press.

Lanehart, Sonja, ed. (2015). *The Oxford Handbook of African American Language,* Oxford and New York: Oxford University Press.

Lanehart, Sonja and Ayehsa Malik. (2015). Language use in African American communities: An introduction. In Sonja Lanehart, ed., *The Oxford Handbook of African American Language,* Oxford and New York: Oxford University Press, 1–19.

Lass, Norman J., John E. Tecca, Robert A. Mancuso, and Wanda I. Black. (1979). The effect of phonetic complexity on speaker race and sex identifications. *Journal of Phonetics,* 7(2), 105–18.

LeClair, Thomas. (1981). The language must not sweat: A conversation with Toni Morrison. *New Republic,* March 21, 1981. https://newrepublic.com/article/95923/the-language-must-not-sweat

LePage, Robert. (1960). An historical introduction to Jamaican Creole. In Robert B. LePage and David DeCamp, eds., *Jamaican Creole: Creole Language Studies 1,* London: Macmillan, 1–124.

  (1977). *Processes of Pidginization and Creolization: Pidgin and Creole Linguistics,* Bloomington: Indiana University Press.

LePage, Robert B., and Andrée Tabouret-Keller. (1985). *Acts of Identity: Creole-Based Approaches to Language and Ethnicity,* Cambridge: Cambridge University Press.

Lewis, Catherine M. and J. Richard Lewis. (2009). *Jim Crow America: A Documentary History,* Fayetteville: The University of Arkansas Press.

Linnes, Kathleen. (1998). Middle-class AAVE versus middle-class bilingualism: Contrasting speech communities. *American Speech,* 73(4), 339–67.

Lippi-Green, Rosina. (1997). *English with an Accent: Language, Ideology, and Discrimination in the United States,* New York: Routledge.

(2012). *English with an Accent: Language, Ideology, and Discrimination in the United States*, 2nd edn, New York: Routledge.

Lopez, Qiuana. (2009). Imitation or influence: White actors and Black language in film. *Texas Linguistic Forum 53: Proceedings of the Seventeenth Annual Symposium About Language and Society*. Austin, Texas, 110–20.

(2014). Aggressively feminine: The linguistic appropriation of sexualized blackness by white female characters in film. *Gender and Language*, 8(3), 289–310.

Lowrey, Annie. (2017). The Great Recession is still with us. *The Atlantic*, December 1, 2017. www.theatlantic.com/business/archive/2017/12/great-recession-still-with-us/547268/

Mahar, William J. (1999). *Behind the Burnt Cork Mask: Blackface Minstrelsy and Antebellum American Popular Culture*, Urbana: University of Illinois Press.

Major, Clarence. (1994). *Juba to Jive: A Dictionary of African American Slang*, New York: Penguin.

Mallinson, Christine. (2007). Social class, social status and stratification: Revisiting familiar concepts in sociolinguistics. *University of Pennsylvania Working Papers in Linguistics*, 13(2), 149–63.

Martin, Stefan and Walt Wolfram. (1998). The sentence in African American Vernacular English. In Salikoko Mufwene, John R. Rickford, Guy Bailey, and John Baugh, eds., *African American English: Structure, History, and Use*, London and New York: Routledge, 11–36.

Milroy, James and Leslie Milroy. (1991). *Authority in Language: Investigating Language Prescription and Standardization*, London and New York: Routledge.

Milroy, Leslie. (1980). *Language and Social Networks*, Oxford: Blackwell.

Mishel, Lawrence, Josh Bivens, Elise Gould, and Heidi Shierholz. (2012). *The State of Working America: Wealth*, 12th edn, Economic Policy Institute Digital Edition.

Mitchell-Kernan, Claudia. (1971). *Language Behavior in a Black Urban Community*, Berkeley, CA: Language Behavior Research Laboratory.

Moody, Simanique. (2011). "Language contact and regional variation in African American English: A study of southeast Georgia," PhD Dissertation, New York University.

Morgan, Marcyliena (1994). The African American speech community: Reality and sociolinguistics. In Marcyliena Morgan, ed., *Language and the Social Construction of Identity in Creole Situations*, Los Angeles, CA: Center for African American Studies, 121–48.

(2002). *Language, Discourse, and Power in African American Culture (Studies in the Social and Cultural Foundations of Language)*, Cambridge and New York: Cambridge University Press.

Morse, J. Mitchell. (1973). The shuffling speech of slavery: Black English. *College English*, 34(6), 834–43.

Mufwene, Salikoko. (1992). Ideology and facts on African American English. *Pragmatics*, 2(2), 141–68.

(1997). Gullah's development: Myths and sociohistorical evidence. In Cynthia Bernstein, Thomas Nunnally, and Robin Sabino, eds., *Language Variety in the South Revisited*, Tuscaloosa and London: University of Alabama Press, 113–23.

(1998). The structure of the noun phrase in African American Vernacular English. In Salikoko Mufwene, John R. Rickford, Guy Bailey, and John Baugh, eds., *African*

American English: Structure, History, and Use, London and New York: Routledge, 69–81.

(2001). What is African American English? In Sonja Lanehart, ed., *Sociocultural and Historical Contexts of African American English*, Amsterdam: Benjamins, 21–51.

Mufwene, Salikoko, John R. Rickford, Guy Bailey, and John Baugh, eds. (1998). *African American English: Structure, History, and Use*, London and New York: Routledge.

Myers-Scotton, Carol. (1998). A theoretical introduction to the markedness model. In Carol Myers-Scotton, ed., *Codes and Consequences: Choosing Linguistic Varieties*, New York: Oxford University Press, 18–38.

Myhill, John. (1995). The use of features of present-day AAVE in the ex-slave recordings. *American Speech*, 70(2), 115–47.

Newton, James E. (1977). Slave artisans and craftsmen: The roots of Afro-American art. *The Black Scholar*, 9(3), 35–42.

Nguyen, Jennifer. (2006). "The changing social and linguistic orientation of the African American middle class," PhD Dissertation, University of Michigan.

Nichols, Patricia. (1983). Linguistics options and choices for Black women in the Rural South. In Barrie Thorne, Cheris Kramrae, and Nancy Henley, eds., *Language, Gender, and Society*, New York: Newbury House, 54–68.

Nicolis, Marco. (2008). The null subject parameter and correlating properties: The case of Creole languages. In Theresa Biberauer, ed., *The Limits of Syntactic Variation*, Amsterdam: Benjamins, 271–94.

Norwood, Kimberly J., ed. (2014). *Color Matters: Skin Tone Bias and the Myth of a Postracial America*, New York: Routledge.

Pattillo-McCoy, Mary. (1999). *African American Picket Fences: Privilege and Peril among the African American Middle Class*, Chicago: University of Illinois Press.

Pederson, Lee. (1983). *East Tennessee Folk Speech*. Frankfurt am Main and New York: Peter Lang.

Poplack, Shana, ed. (2000). *The English History of African American English*, Oxford and Malden, MA: Blackwell.

Poplack, Shana and David Sankoff. (1987). The Philadelphia story in the Spanish Caribbean. *American Speech*, 62(4), 291–314.

Poplack, Shana and Sali Tagliamonte. (1991). African American English in the diaspora: Evidence from old-line Nova Scotians. *Language Variation and Change*, 3(3), 301–39.

Praat: Doing phonetics by computer. Version 5.3.80. Developed by Paul Boersma and David Weenink.

Preston, Dennis R. (1992). Talking Black and talking White: A study in variety imitation. In Joan H. Hall, Nick Doane, and Dick Ringler, eds., *Old English and New: Papers in Honor of Frederic G. Cassidy on the Occasion of His 85th Birthday*, New York: Garland, 327–55.

(1996). Where the worst English is spoken. In Edgar Schneider, ed., *Focus on the USA*, Amsterdam and Philadelphia: Benjamins, 297–360.

(2004). Language attitudes to speech. In Edward Finegan and John R. Rickford, eds., *Language in the USA*, Cambridge: Cambridge University Press, 480–92.

Pullum, Geoffrey. (1999). African American Vernacular English is not Standard English with mistakes. In Rebecca Wheeler, ed., *The Workings of Language: From Prescriptions to Perspectives*, Westport, CT: Praeger, 39–58.

Purnell, Thomas, William Idsardi, and John Baugh. (1999). Perceptual and phonetic experiments on American English dialect identification. *Journal of Language and Social Psychology*, 18(1), 10–30.

Rahman, Jacqueline. (2004). "It's a serious business: The linguistic construction of middle-class White characters by African American narrative comedians," PhD Dissertation, Stanford University.

  (2007). An ay for an ah: Language of survival in African American narrative comedy. *American Speech*, 82(1), 65–96.

  (2008). Middle-class African Americans: Reactions and attitudes toward African American English. *American Speech*, 83(2), 141–76.

Ransby, Barbara. (2015). The class politics of Black Lives Matter. *Dissent. University of Pennsylvania Press*, 62(4), 31–34. DOI: https://doi.org/10.1353/dss.2015.0071

Reaser, Jeffrey, Eric Wilbanks, Karissa Wojcik, and Walt Wolfram, eds. (2018). *Language Variety in the New South: Contemporary Perspectives on Change and Variation*, Chapel Hill: University of North Carolina Press, 175–202.

Reed, Paul. (2016). "Sounding Appalachian: Monophthongization, rising pitch accents, and rootedness," PhD Dissertation, The University of South Carolina.

Reeves, Richard and Camille Busette. (2018). The middle class is becoming race-plural, just like the rest of America. *Brookings Institute: Social Mobility Memos*, February 27, 2018. www.brookings.edu/blog/social-mobility-memos/2018/02/27/the-middle-class-is-becoming-race-plural-just-like-the-rest-of-america/

Renn, Jennifer. (2007). "Measuring style shift: A quantitative analysis of African American English," MA Thesis, University of North Carolina at Chapel Hill.

  (2010). "Acquiring style: The development of dialect shifting among African American children," PhD Dissertation, University of North Carolina at Chapel Hill.

Reynolds, Barbara. (2015). I was a civil rights activist in the 1960s. But it's hard for me to get behind Black Lives Matter. *The Washington Post*, August 24, 2015. www .washingtonpost.com/posteverything/wp/2015/08/24/i-was-a-civil-rights-activist-in-the-1960s-but-its-hard-for-me-to-get-behind-black-lives-matter/?postshare= 5221440433170944&utm_term=.591bd8830a67/

Rickford, John R. (1975 [1999]). Carrying the new wave into syntax: The case of Black English BÍN. In Ralph Fasold and Roger Shuy, eds., *Analyzing Variation and Language*, Washington, DC: Georgetown University Press, 162–83. Reprinted in *African American Vernacular English: Features, Evolution, Educational Implication*, Oxford and Malden, MA: Blackwell, 15–33.

  (1977). The Question of Prior Creolization in Black English. In Albert Valdman, ed., *Pidgin-Creole Linguistics*, Bloomington: University of Indiana Press, 199–221.

  (1986). The need for new approaches to social class analysis in sociolinguistics. *Language and Communication*, 6(3), 215–21.

  (1987 [1999]). Are Black and White vernaculars diverging? *American Speech*, 62(1), 55–62. Reprinted in *African American Vernacular English: Features, Evolution, Educational Implications*, Malden, MA and Oxford: Blackwell, 252–60.

  (1992). Grammatical variation and divergence in Vernacular Black English. In Marinel Gerritsen and Dieter Stein, eds., *Internal and External Factors in Syntactic Change*, Berlin: Mouton de Gruyter, 175–200.

  (1996). Copula variability in Jamaican Creole and African American Vernacular English: A reanalysis of DeCamp's texts. In Gregory Guy, John Baugh, Deborah

Schiffrin, and Crawford Feagin, eds., *Towards a Social Science of Language: A Festschrift for William Labov*, Philadelphia, PA and Amsterdam: Benjamins, 357–72.

(1998). The Creole origins of African American Vernacular English: Evidence from copula absence. In *African American English: Structure, History, and Use*, London and New York: Routledge, 154–200.

(1999a). *African American Vernacular English: Features, Evolution, Educational Implications*, Oxford and Malden, MA: Blackwell.

(1999b). Phonological and grammatical features of African American Vernacular English. In John R. Rickford, *African American Vernacular English: Features, Evolution, Educational Implications*, Oxford and Malden, MA: Blackwell, 3–14.

(1999c). Prior creolization of African American Vernacular English? Sociohistorical and textual evidence from the seventeenth and eighteenth centuries. In John R. Rickford, *African American Vernacular English: Features, Evolution, Educational Implications*, Oxford and Malden, MA: Blackwell, 232–51.

(2001). Style and stylizing from the perspective of a non-autonomous sociolinguistics. In Penelope Eckert and John R. Rickford, eds., *Style and Sociolinguistic Variation*, Cambridge: Cambridge University Press, 220–31.

(2006). Down for the count? The Creole Origins Hypothesis of AAVE at the hands of the Ottawa Circle, and their supporters. A review article on *The English History of African American English*. Shana Poplack, ed. *Journal of Pidgin and Creole Languages*, 21(1), 98–155.

(2010). Geographical diversity, residential segregation, and the vitality of African American Vernacular English and its speakers. *Transforming Anthropology*, 18(1), 28–34.

(2019). The continuing need for new approaches to social class analysis in sociolinguistics. In John R. Rickford, *Variation and Versatility in Sociolinguistics and Creole Studies*, Cambridge: Cambridge University Press, 301–27.

Rickford, John R. and Angela Rickford. (1976 [1999]). Cut-eye and suck-teeth: African words and gestures in New World guise. *Journal of American Folklore*, 89(353), 294–309. Reprinted in *African American Vernacular English: Features, Evolution, Educational Implications*, Oxford and Malden, MA: Blackwell, 157–73.

Rickford, John R., Arnetha Ball, Renee Blake, Raina Jackson, and Nomi Martin. (1991). Rappin on the copula coffin: Theoretical and methodological issues in the analysis of copula variation in African American Vernacular English. *Language Variation and Change*, 3(1), 103–32.

Rickford, John R. and Faye McNair-Knox. (1994). Addressee- and topic-influenced style shift: A quantitative sociolinguistic study. In Douglas Biber and Edward Finegan, eds., *Perspectives on Register: Situating Register Variation within Sociolinguistics*, Oxford: Oxford University Press, 235–76.

Rickford, John R. and Mackenzie Price. (2013). Girlz II women: Age-grading, language change and stylistic variation. *Journal of Sociolinguistics*, 17, 143–79. DOI: 10.1111/josl.12017

Rickford, John R. and Renee Blake. (1990). Copula contraction and absence in Barbadian English, Samaná English and Vernacular Black English. In Kira Hall, Jean-Pierre Koenig, Michael Meacham, Sondra Reinman, and Laurel Sutton, eds.,

BLS *16: Proceedings of the Sixteenth Annual Meeting of the Berkeley Linguistics Society*, Berkeley, CA: Berkeley Linguistics Society, 257–68.

Rickford, John R. and Russell J. Rickford. (2000). *Spoken Soul: The Story of Black English*, New York: John Wiley & Sons, Inc.

Rickford, John R. and Sharese King. (2016). Language and linguistics on trial: Hearing Rachel Jeantel (and other vernacular speakers) in the courtroom and beyond. *Language*, 92(4), 948–88.

Robinson, Cedric J. (2005). The Black middle class and the Mulatto motion picture. *Race & Class*, 47(1), 14–34.

Robinson, Eugene. (2010). *Disintegration: The Splintering of Black America*, New York: Doubleday.

Ronkin, Maggie and Helen E. Karn. (1999). Mock Ebonics: Linguistic racism in parodies of Ebonics on the internet. *Journal of Sociolinguistics*, 3(3), 360–80.

Rosiek, Jerry and Kathy Kinslow. (2016). *Resegregation as Curriculum: The Meaning of the New Racial Segregation in U.S. Public Schools*, New York and London: Routledge.

Russell, Kathy, Midge Wilson, and Ronald Hall. (1993). *The Color Complex: The Politics of Skin Color among African Americans*, New York: Anchor Books/Doubleday.

Sankoff, David and Suzanne Laberge. (1978). The linguistic market and the statistical explanation of variability. In David Sankoff, ed., *Linguistic Variation: Models and Methods*, New York: Academic Press, 239–50.

Scanlon, Michael and Alicia Beckford Wassink. (2010). African American English in urban Seattle: Accommodation and intraspeaker variation in the Pacific Northwest. *American Speech*, 85(2), 205–24.

Schilling-Estes, Natalie. (1998). Investigating "self-conscious" speech: The performance register in Ocracoke English. *Language in Society*, 27(1), 53–83.

Schneider, Edgar W. (1989). *American Earlier Black English: Morphological and Syntactic Variables*, Tuscaloosa: University of Alabama Press.

Schneider, Edgar W., ed. (1996). *Focus on the USA*, Philadelphia and Amsterdam: John Benjamins.

Sells, Peter, John Rickford, and Thomas Wasow. (1996). Negative inversion in African American Vernacular English. *Natural Language and Linguistic Theory*, 14(3), 591–627.

Sharma, Devyani. (2018). Style dominance: Attention, audience, and the "real me." *Language in Society*, 47(1), 1–31.

Silverstein, Michael. (2003). Indexical order and the dialectics of sociolinguistic life. *Language & Communication*, 23(3–4), 193–229.

Simpkins, Gary C., Grace Holt, and Charlesetta Simpkins (1977). *Bridge: A Cross-Cultural Reading Program*, Boston, MA: Houghton Mifflin.

Singler, John Victor. (1991). Copula variation in Liberian Settler English and American Black English. In Walter Edwards and Donald Winford, eds., *Verb Phrase Patterns in Black English and Creole*, Detroit, MI: Wayne State University Press, 129–64.

(1998). What's not new in AAVE. *American Speech*, 73(3), 227–56.

Smitherman, Geneva. (1977). *Talkin and Testifyin: The Language of Black America*, Boston, MA: Houghton Mifflin.

(1994). *Black Talk: Words and Phrases from the Hood to the Amen Corner*, Boston, MA: Houghton Mifflin.

(1998). Word from the hood: The lexicon of African-American Vernacular English. In Salikoko Mufwene, John R. Rickford, Guy Bailey, and John Baugh, eds., *African American English: Structure, History, and Use*, New York and London: Routledge, 203–25.

(2000). *Black Talk: Words and Phrases from the Hood to the Amen Corner*, revised edn, Boston, MA: Houghton Mifflin.

(2006). *Word from the Mother: Language and African Americans*, New York and London: Routledge.

Spears, Arthur K. (1982). The Black English semi-auxiliary "come." *Language*, 58(4), 850–72.

(1988). Black American English. In Johnetta B. Cole, ed., *Anthropology for the Nineties*, New York: The Free Press, 96–113.

(1998). African-American Language use: Ideology and so-called obscenity. In Salikoko Mufwene, John R. Rickford, Guy Bailey, and John Baugh, eds., *African-American English: Structure, History, and Use*, London and New York: Routledge, 226–50.

(2000). Stressed stay: A new African-American English aspect marker. Paper presented at the annual meeting of the American Dialect Society, Chicago, IL.

(2004). The question of tone in African American English. Paper presented at the joint conference of the Society for Caribbean Linguistics, Society for Pidgin and Creole Linguistics, and Asociасión de Criollos de Base Lexical Portuguesa e Española, Curaçao, Netherlands Antilles, August 10–16.

(2006). Disapproval markers – A creolism: Re-examining the African American English/Creole relationship. Papers from the Society for Caribbean Linguistics, Sixteenth Biennial Conference, Roseau, Dominica [on CD, 27 pp.].

(2008). Pidgins/creoles and African American English. In Silvia Kouwenberg and John Victor Singler, eds., *The Handbook of Pidgin and Creole Studies*, Oxford and Malden, MA: Blackwell, 512–42.

(2009). On shallow grammar: African American English and the critique of exceptionalism. In Jo Anne Kleifgen and George C. Bond, eds., *The Languages of Africa and the Diaspora: Educating for Language Awareness*, Bristol: Multilingual Matters, 231–48.

(2015). African American Standard English. In Sonja Lanehart, ed., *The Oxford Handbook of African American Language*, Oxford and New York: Oxford University Press, 786–99.

(2017). Unstressed *BEEN*: Past and present in African American English. *American Speech*, 92(2), 151–75.

Squires, Lauren. (2016). Processing grammatical differences: Perceiving versus noticing. In Anna M. Babel, ed., *Awareness and Control in Sociolinguistic Research*, Cambridge: Cambridge University Press, 80–103.

Stanback, Marsha Houston. (1984). "Code-switching in Black women's speech," MA Thesis, University of Massachusetts.

Stancil, Will. (2018). School segregation is not a myth. *The Atlantic*, March 14, 2018. www .theatlantic.com/education/archive/2018/03/school-segregation-is-not-a-myth/555614/

Stevens, William K. (1985). Study finds Blacks' English increasingly different. *The New York Times*, March 15, 1985. www.nytimes.com/1985/03/15/us/study-finds-blacks-english-increasingly-different.html

Stewart, William. (1967). Sociolinguistic factors in the history of American Negro dialects. *The Florida FL Reporter*, 5(2), 11, 22, 24, 26, 28.

(1968). Continuity and change in American Negro dialects. *The Florida FL Reporter*, 6(1), 3–4, 14–16, 18.

(1975). Teaching Blacks to read against their will. In Philip Luelsdorff, ed., *Linguistic Perspectives on Black English*, Regensburg: Verlag Hans Carl, 107–32.

Tarone, Elaine. (1973). Aspects of intonation in Black English. *American Speech*, 48(1/2), 29–36.

Tatum, Beverly Daniel. (2017). *Why Are All the Black Kids Sitting Together in the Cafeteria?: And Other Conversations about Race*, New York: Basic Books.

Taylor, Orlando. (1975). Black language and what to do about it: Some Black community perspectives. In Robert L. Williams, ed., *Ebonics: The True Language of Black Folks*, St. Louis, MO: Institute of Black Studies, 29–39.

(1983). Black English: An agenda for the 1980's. In John Chambers, Jr., ed., *Black English: Educational Equity and the Law*, Ann Arbor, MI: Karoma, 133–43.

Thomas, Erik R. (2001). *An Acoustic Analysis of Vowel Variation in New World English (Publication of the American Dialect Society 85)*, Durham, NC: Duke University Press.

(2007). Phonological and phonetic characteristics of African American Vernacular English. *Language and Linguistics Compass*, 1(5), 450–75.

(2015). Prosodic features of African American English. In Sonja Lanehart, ed., *The Oxford Handbook of African American Language*, Oxford and Malden, MA: Oxford University Press, 420–35.

Thomas, Erik R. and Jeffrey Reaser. (2004). Delimiting perceptual cues used for the ethnic labeling of African American and European American voices. *Journal of Sociolinguistics*, 8(1), 54–87.

Thomas, Erik R. and Phillip M. Carter. (2006). Prosodic rhythm and African American English. *English World-Wide*, 27(3), 331–55.

Toll, Robert C. (1974). *Blacking Up: The Minstrel Show in Nineteenth-Century America*, New York: Oxford University Press.

Trudgill, Peter. (1972). Sex, covert prestige and linguistic change in the urban British English of Norwich. *Language in Society*, 1(2), 179–95.

(1983). *On Dialect*, Oxford: Blackwell.

(1986). *Dialects in Contact*, Oxford: Blackwell.

Tucker, Richard G. and Wallace E. Lambert. (1975). Listeners' reactions to various American-English dialects. In Joey Dillard, ed., *Perspectives on Black English*, The Hague and the Netherlands: Mouton, 369–77.

Turner, Lorenzo Dow. (1949). *Africanisms in the Gullah Dialect*, New York: Arno Press.

Vanhofwegen, Janneke and Walt Wolfram. (2010). Coming of age in African American English: A longitudinal study. *Journal of Sociolinguistics*, 14(4), 427–55.

Van Sertima, Ivan. (1976). My Gullah brother and I: Exploration into a community's language and myth through its oral tradition. In Deborah S. Harrison and Tom Trabasso, eds., *Black English: A Seminar*, Mahwah, NJ: Lawrence Erlbaum Associates, Inc., 123–46.

Vaughn-Cooke, Fay Boyd. (1986). Lexical diffusion: Evidence from a decreolizing variety of Black English. In Michael B. Montgomery and Guy Bailey, eds.,

Language Variety in the South: Perspectives in Black and White, Tuscaloosa: University of Alabama Press, 111–30.

Veblen, Thorstein. (1899 [1994]). *Theory of the Leisure Class: An Economic Study in the Evolution of Institutions*, New York: MacMillan. Reprinted in 1994 Dover Paperback Edition, ISBN 0-486-28062-4, 1994 Penguin Classics Edition, ISBN 0-14-018795-2.

Walker, James. (2000). Rephrasing the copula: Contraction and zero in early African American English. In Shana Poplack, ed., *The English History of African American English*, Malden, MA and Oxford: Blackwell, 35–72.

Walker, Sheila. (1971). Black English: Expression of the Afro-American experience. *Black World*, 20(8), 4–16.

Warner, W. Lloyd and Paul S. Lunt. (1941). *The Social Life of a Modern Community*, New Haven, CT: Yale University Press.

Weber, Max. ([1920] 1968). *Economy and Society*, Guenther Roth and Claus Wittich, eds. Berkeley: University of California Press.

Weinreich, Uriel. (1953). *Languages in Contact*, The Hague: Mouton.

Weldon, Tracey. (1994). Variability in negation in African-American Vernacular English. *Language Variation and Change*, 6(3), 359–97.

(1998). "Exploring the AAVE-Gullah connection: A comparative study of copula variability," PhD Dissertation, The Ohio State University.

(2003a). Copula variability in Gullah. *Language Variation and Change*, 15(1), 37–72.

(2003b). Revisiting the Creolist Hypothesis: Copula variability in Gullah and southern rural AAVE. *American Speech*, 78(2), 171–91.

(2004). African American English in the middle classes: Exploring the other end of the continuum. Paper presented at New Ways of Analyzing Variation (NWAV) 33 Conference, Ann Arbor, MI.

(2018). Sounding Black: Labeling and perceptions of African American voices on Southern college campuses. In Jeffrey Reaser, Eric Wilbanks, Karissa Wojcik, and Walt Wolfram, eds., *Language Variety in the New South: Contemporary Perspectives on Change and Variation*, Chapel Hill: University of North Carolina Press, 175–202.

Weldon, Tracey and Simanique Moody. (2015). The place of Gullah in the African American linguistic continuum. In Sonja Lanehart, ed., *The Oxford Handbook of African American Language*, Oxford and New York: Oxford, 163–80.

Whinnom, Keith. (1971). Linguistic hybridization and the "special case" of pidgins and creoles. In Dell Hymes, ed., *Pidginization and Creolization of Languages*, Cambridge: Cambridge University Press, 91–115.

White, Gillian B. (2015). The recession's racial slant. *The Atlantic*, June 24, 2015. www .theatlantic.com/business/archive/2015/06/black-recession-housing-race/396725/

Widawski, Maciej. (2015). *African American Slang: A Linguistic Description*, Cambridge: Cambridge University Press.

Wilkerson, Rose. (2000). African-American English in film: "Be" variability. In Julie Auger and Andrea Word-Allbritton, eds., *IUWPL 2: The CVC of Sociolinguistics: Contact, Variation, and Culture*, Bloomington, IN: IULC Publications, 139–56.

Williams, Aaron and Armand Emamdjomeh. (2018). America is more diverse than ever – but still segregated. *The Washington Post*, May 10, 2018.

Williams, Robert. (1975). *Ebonics: The True Language of Black Folks*, St. Louis, MO: Robert Williams and Associates.

www.washingtonpost.com/graphics/2018/national/segregation-us-cities/?utm_term=.826634c6a817

Williamson, Juanita. (1968). A phonological and morphological study of the speech of the Negro in Memphis, Tennessee. *American Dialect Society*, 50, 1–54.

Winford, Donald. (1992a). Another look at the copula in Black English and Caribbean creoles. *American Speech*, 67(1), 21–60.

  (1992b). Back to the past: The BEV/creole connection revisited. *Language Variation and Change*, 4(3), 311–57.

  (1997). On the origins of African American Vernacular English – A creolist perspective. Part I: The sociohistorical background. *Diachronica*, 14(2), 305–44.

  (1998). On the origins of African American Vernacular English – A creolist perspective. Part II: Linguistic features. *Diachronica*, 15(1), 99–154.

Woldoff, Rachael A. (2011). *White Flight/Black Flight: The Dynamics of Racial Change in an American Neighborhood*, Ithaca, NY: Cornell University Press.

Wolfram, Walt. (1969). *A Sociolinguistic Description of Detroit Negro Speech*, Washington, DC: Center for Applied Linguistics.

  (1971). Black-White speech differences revisited. In Walt Wolfram, ed., *Black-White Speech Relationships*, Washington, DC: Center for Applied Linguistics, 139–61.

  (1973). *Sociolinguistic Aspects of Assimilation: Puerto Rican English in New York City*, Washington, DC: Center for Applied Linguistics.

  (1974). The relationship of White Southern speech to Vernacular Black English. *Language*, 50(3), 498–527.

  (1994). On the sociolinguistic significance of obscure dialect structures: The [NPi Call NPi, V-ing] construction in African-American Vernacular English. *American Speech*, 69(4), 339–60.

  (1998). Black children are verbally deprived. In Laurie Bauer and Peter Trudgill, eds., *Language Myths*, London: Penguin Books, 103–12.

  (2001a). On constructing vernacular dialect norms. In Arika Okrent and John Boyle, eds., *Chicago Linguistic Society 36: The Panels*, Chicago, IL: University of Chicago Press, 335–58.

  (2001b). Reconsidering the Sociolinguistic agenda for African American English: The next generation of research and application. In Sonja Lanehart, ed., *Sociocultural and Historical Contexts of African American English*, Amsterdam: Benjamins, 331–62.

Wolfram, Walt, Caroline Myrick, Michael J. Fox, and Jon Forrest. (2016). The significance of linguistic variation in the speeches of Dr. Martin Luther King Jr. *American Speech*, 91(3), 269–300.

Wolfram, Walt and Erik Thomas. (2002). *The Development of African American English*, Oxford and Malden, MA: Blackwell.

Wolfram, Walt and Natalie Schilling. (2016). *American English: Dialects and Variation*, 3rd edn, Oxford and Malden, MA: Blackwell.

Wolfram, Walt and Natalie Schilling-Estes. (1998). *American English: Dialects and Variation*, Oxford and Malden, MA: Blackwell.

Wolfram, Walt and Ralph Fasold. (1974). *The Study of Social Dialects in the United States*, Englewood Cliffs, NJ: Prentice Hall.

Young, Vershawn. (2007). *Your Average Nigga: Performing Race, Literacy, and Masculinity*, Detroit, MI: Wayne State University Press.

(2009). "Nah, we straight": An argument against code-switching. *Journal of Advanced Composition*, 29(1/2), 1–2, 49–76.

Young, Vershawn Ashanti and Aja Y. Martinez, eds. (2011). *Code-Meshing as World English: Pedagogy, Policy, Performance*, Urbana, IL: National Council of Teachers of English.

Index

Ingram Content Group UK Ltd.
Milton Keynes UK
UKHW020152100723
424827UK00024B/406